Capital, Profits, and Prices

Capital, Profits, and Prices

An Essay in the Philosophy of Economics

DANIEL M. HAUSMAN

New York   Columbia University Press   *1981*

As a dissertation, this book was awarded the
Bancroft Dissertation Award by a committee of the faculty of
the Graduate School of Arts and Sciences of Columbia University

Library of Congress Cataloging in Publication Data

Hausman, Daniel M., 1947–
Capital, profits, and prices.

Revision of thesis (Ph. D.)—Columbia
University, 1978.
Bibliography: p.
Includes index.
1. Capital. 2. Profit. 3. Prices.
4. Interest and usury. 5. Value. 6. Economics.
I. Title.
HB501.H384   1981   330.1   81-9968
ISBN 0-231-05090-9   AACR2

Columbia University Press
New York   Guildford, Surrey

Copyright © 1981 by Columbia University Press
All Rights Reserved
Printed in the United States of America

Clothbound Columbia University Press Books are
Smyth-sewn and printed on permanent and durable acid-free paper.

Contents

Preface

A teacher of mine once commented that capital theory is mostly metaphysics. This book takes his jocular comment more seriously than he intended. It investigates what contemporary philosophy of science can contribute to understanding and solving the puzzles that capital and interest present. It also considers what understanding capital and interest theory can contribute to philosophy of science and philosophy of social science. Although my inquiry into capital theory borrows heavily from well known work in the philosophy of science, I was neither able, nor content, to apply ready-made philosophical wisdom to the mysteries of capital. New philosophical tools needed fashioning. Old philosophical questions demanded new and more detailed answers. In the course of clarifying the problems in capital theory, I hope to contribute to the philosophy of science—particularly to the understanding of the role and legitimacy in the sciences of rough generalizations and simplifications. I offer an original construal of the structure of equilibrium economics and a critical appraisal of our knowledge concerning capital and interest. This book is addressed to those who have an interest in philosophy of science or in the theoretical foundations of economics. It does not presuppose extensive knowledge either of philosophy or of economics, although most of the material will be more familiar to economists.

So many people have helped me directly or indirectly in writing this book, that at times I have felt as if I were merely a compiler of their wisdom. For help with the first draft of this book, I am deeply indebted to Sidney Morgenbesser. He helped by providing not only criticisms and suggestions, but also a model of uncompromising intellectual integrity and decency. Ronald Findlay and Isaac Levi, were indispensable. Without having drawn heavily on their fund of knowledge and good sense, I could never have written the first draft of this book. I am indebted to Columbia University for conferring on me the Bancroft Award, which provided the incentive to revise this work and publish it. J. Richard Fehler and Subiah Mani read the whole of the manuscript and made numerous suggestions. Others who helped with the early draft are Ernest Alleva, Elizabeth Blackmar, Brian Butters, Steven Cardin, Ellen Farrell, Catherine Kautsky, Kelvin Lancaster, Howard Stein, Carol Tatge, Bob Tashman, and Barbara Hohol. During the past two years I have learned a great deal from my colleagues at the University of Maryland, particularly from Margaret Atherton, Lindley Darden, Philip Ehrlich, Conrad Johnson, Eva Kittay, Jerry Levinson, Robert Schwartz, Dudley Shapere, Allen Stairs, Stephen Stich, Frederick Suppe, and Lars Svenonius, all of whom read parts of this manuscript. Materials from this book were delivered to audiences at the City University of New York, the University of Maryland, Michigan State University, the 1980 meetings of the Philosophy of Science Association, the University of Pittsburgh, the State University of New York at Stony Brook, and at Virginia Polytechnic Institute and State University. I am indebted to members of all those audiences. The postscript is an adaptation of my "How to Do Philosophy of Economics" (1980), while materials from my "Are General Equilibrium Theories Explanatory?" (1981) are incorporated into chapters 6 and 7. Lindley Darden, Alexander Rosenberg, and Paul Thagard read the whole of this manuscript and offered detailed and useful criticisms and suggestions. The General Research Board of the University of Maryland provided support for my investigation in chapter 7 of *ceteris paribus* clauses in economics. The National Science Foundation (Grant # SES 8007385) is supporting work on the questions raised in chapter 9 concerning causal judgments in economics. I would like to thank Leslie Bialler for his expert editorial assistance. The errors which have withstood all this help are, of course, mine.

Now, in whatever science there are systematic differences of opinion—which is as much to say, in all the moral or mental sciences, and in Political Economy among the rest; in whatever science there exist, among those who have attended to the subject, what are commonly called differences of principle, as distinguished from differences of matter-of-fact or detail,—the cause will be found to be, a difference in their conceptions of the philosophic method of the science. The parties who differ are guided, either knowingly or unconsciously, by different views concerning the nature of the evidence appropriate to the subject. They differ not solely in what they believe themselves to see, but in the quarter whence they obtained the light by which they think they see it. (*Mill 1836:141*)

Capital, Profits, and Prices

Introduction

The social sciences raise perplexing methodological and epistemological questions. Economics, as the most developed social science, deserves particular philosophical scrutiny. To what extent does its methodology resemble that of the natural sciences? What is the structure of economic theory? What is the subject matter of economics? What is the relationship of its subject matter to that of other disciplines? What special difficulties do economists face? To what extent does economics provide knowledge of its subject matter? In answering these questions, one may hope to understand better the prospects, problems and limitations of the social sciences in general.

Unfortunately, these questions concerning economics are not clearly posed and are not easy to answer. In this book I shall consider only one esoteric area within economics, the theory of capital and interest and of their relations to exchange values. Examining this area in detail helps with these general philosophical questions.

I am focusing on capital and interest theory because I believe that it is essential to concentrate on a limited area of economics. As this book illustrates, answers to general philosophical questions concerning economic theory require detailed examination of economic theory. No single work can examine more than a small part of economic theory in the required detail. The philosophical issues addressed in this essay do, however, arise in much of economics and my conclusions apply to more than just the theory of capital and interest.

My method demands that in conducting a philosophical inquiry into economics one consider some specific aspect in detail. The reasons for choosing the theory of capital and interest instead of some other topic are twofold. First, that theory is of considerable theoretical importance. As I shall explain in chapter 1, one's views concerning capital and interest are intimately tied to one's general perspective on economics. Second, the issues in capital and interest theory are emotionally charged. People have passionate views, for example, on why the rate of interest or profit is normally positive. Capital and interest theory is thus especially suitable for studying how descriptive and normative issues interact in economics and how ideology matters to economic theory.

The idea of conducting a philosophical inquiry into capital theory was suggested by a course of lectures given by John Eatwell on Value Theory in the Fall of 1977 at Barnard College (see Eatwell 1975c). In thinking about the so-called Cambridge Controversy in capital theory of the 1960s, I came to the conclusion that philosophical disagreements lay behind the economic controversy and constituted an important part of it. I thus saw capital and interest theory not simply as an interesting subject for philosophical scrutiny, but as one to which the philosopher could hope to contribute directly. Mill's comments quoted above apply well to the controversies in capital theory.

Capital theory deals with many different questions. One would like to know what capital goods are. What contribution do they make to an economy's wealth and possibilities for growth? What factors influence the size and composition of the economy's stock of capital goods? How are the prices and rentals of capital goods determined? These questions are difficult and important, but not nearly as mysterious as the questions concerning *capital*, with which I shall be concerned. In an economy in which one can freely make investments and receive returns on them, one can normally expect one's money to be fruitful and to multiply. How does ownership of a certain quantity of money permit one to receive income? What determines the distribution of income between those who possess "capital" and those who don't? How is capital related to capital goods? Capital not only earns interest or profits,[1] but, after one allows for various complications, competition among owners of capital leads (given freedom to redirect one's capital) to a rough equality of returns on investments. Those whose earnings are low will shift their investments. Although some theorists now believe that it is senseless to speak of a resultant uniform rate of return (rate of profit or interest), a traditional problem of the theory of capital and interest has been to explain what determines this rate of return.

The answers given to the many questions concerning capital are at least as diverse as the questions themselves. I shall be particularly interested in theories of the relations between capital, interest, and

---

[1] There are many differences between the interest a pensioner earns at a savings bank, the dividends General Motors pays its stockholders, the profits real estate speculators garner and the corporate profits oil companies can barely count. Yet at the level of theoretical abstraction at which I shall proceed, it is not even necessary to distinguish between interest and profits. In chapter 1 I explain why.

prices. It is difficult to explain briefly in an introduction what these theories are about, since their subject matter is theoretical and controversial. Speaking loosely, we may say that capital goods are reproducible commodities which can be used to make other commodities. We may or may not want to include goods workers consume (which are, in a sense, needed for production) as capital goods. Although an individual regards his or her money as capital, the capital that a whole economy possesses is certainly not just a quantity of money. The quantity of capital a society possesses should measure the quantity and the quality of the capital goods it has. Heavily industrialized nations possess more capital than do hunters and gatherers. Destructive wars decrease the amount of capital a nation possesses. To speak of the quantity of capital goods poses difficult problems. In what units can one add together tractors and microprocessors to get a single sum? After one corrects for inflation, economists generally suppose one can get some indication of this quantity by considering the total *value* of all capital goods.

Given this sketchy notion of what capital is, we can see that the relations between capital, interest, and prices are puzzling. An individual's capital (which may be in the form of money or of commodities) enables that individual to earn interest. If the capital is invested in a machine, the sum of the rentals the machine earns over its lifetime is thus greater than the machine's cost. Why? How does the price system adjust itself so that owners of capital can earn interest? This is perhaps the central question: Why are there normally profits? For Ricardo (1817) and Marx (1967), profit or interest is part of the surplus of goods (or of the value of goods) produced after all inputs, including labor, are replaced. Capitalists are able to appropriate a portion of the surplus because of their ownership of the means of production. According to Ricardo and Marx, profits are thus not a payment for a commodity or service.

From the neoclassical revolution in economic theory of the 1870s until the development of intertemporal general equilibrium theories after World War II, most economists regarded capital as either itself a scarce input needed for production or as a proxy for some other scarce input. The rate of interest was in their view the price of this input. This input was, however, a rather mysterious entity. For J. B. Clark (1902), it was a permanent "fund of productive wealth." Böhm-Bawerk and the Austrian school of economists were critical of attempts to regard capital as itself some entity which contributes to production. Instead they stressed the connections between interest and time or "waiting." Böhm-Bawerk (1888) suggested that people can produce more if they produce in a more roundabout way. If they pick berries, they get food right away. If people instead make plows, domesticate animals, and tend their crops, they must employ a much longer period of production, but they get a much larger output. Currently available stocks of commodities give people the power to use more efficient roundabout methods of production. People are thus willing and able to repay the owners of these commodities with interest, if the owners will advance these stocks. Present goods are, according to Böhm-Bawerk, also more valuable than future goods for subjective reasons. Capital is not some entity that contributes to production. "Waiting," that is, deferring consumption to permit a lengthening of the period of production, contributes to production. Interest is the price of this "waiting." In everyday life, capital appears to earn interest. According to the Austrian theorists appearances are misleading. Capital appears to earn interest only because its value roughly indicates the quantity of waiting or the degree of roundaboutness.

Since World War II, general equilibrium theorists have shown how in principle to derive interest from productive contributions and subjective valuations of capital goods without taking capital itself to be an input into production or an indicator of some other single input like "waiting." In empirical research economists nevertheless make use of more traditional theories, like Clark's, since the general equilibrium approach is difficult or impossible to apply. Other contemporary economists have resurrected Ricardo and regard interest as part of the surplus of output over input. Controversy concerning all these positions (and many others) has been incessant. The greater part of this book is devoted to clarifying and assessing the positions sketched in the last few paragraphs.

In considering theories of the relations between capital, interest, and prices I shall be discussing a good deal of economics. In chapters 1 and 2 I shall, in a roughly historical manner, explain why theories of the relations between capital, interest, and prices are important and what problems they face. In chapter 3 I shall develop the Austrian theory, which I regard as the most intelligible of traditional neoclassical theories of these relations. In chapter 4 I shall argue that while the Cambridge Controversy does not *refute* the Austrian theory or demonstrate any logical error in it, the critics have shown that traditional neoclassical theories, including the Austrian theory, are *unfounded*. Chapters 5 through 7 develop and criticize general equilibrium approaches to the relations between capital, interest, and prices. Chapter 8 sets forth Sraffa's neo-Ricardian contribution and criticizes some extravagant claims which have been made on its behalf. Chapter 9 will argue that the differences between general equilibrium theories of the relations between capital, interest, and prices and neo-Ricardian theories are conceptual and methodological. In chapters 6, 7 and 9, I explore these conceptual and methodological issues. In chapter 10 I reach generally negative conclusions: (1) Economists know little about the relations between capital, interest, and prices. The problem is not a lack of interesting theorems, but a lack of confirmation for these theorems. (2) Many economists adhere so tenaciously to what I shall call "equilibrium theory" that they restrict their methodological options unreasonably. (3) More resources should be devoted to exploring the as yet unproven possibilities of piecemeal theorizing like that exemplified by Sraffa's work.

In carrying out my philosophical inquiry into the theory of capital and interest, I deal with a number of general questions. Some of the most important of these are:

(1) What is the subject matter of economic theory?
(2) What is the logical structure of an economic model? How are models and theories related to one another? Do economic theories explain anything? If so, what structure do such explanations have? What other than explanatory worth might they have?
(3) Does economics have any laws? If the fundamental generalizations of economics are not laws, how are they to be analyzed? In what ways are they general? What sort of evidence can one have for them?
(4) How are the many simplifications upon which economists rely to be analyzed? Under what conditions are they legitimate?
(5) What kinds of theoretical strategies are employed in economics? How are we to assess such strategies?
(6) What is the role of ideology in economic theory?

What I shall say about these questions applies to more than just theorizing concerning capital and interest.

These six questions cross the boundaries between economics and philosophy. My attempts to answer them should be of interest to philosophers as well as to economists, since the answers have important implications for epistemology and the philosophy of science. In order to make my argument accessible to both philosophers and economists, I have presupposed very little knowledge of either field. Except for a few details, everything I have to say should be comprehensible to readers with no training in either discipline. Those who would like to consider my philosophical contributions without studying any more economic theory than is absolutely necessary can work backwards from the summary in §3 of chapter 10. I urge economists to think seriously about the more philosophical sections in this book, because I believe that the philosophy I present is indispensable to understanding and evaluating theories of the relations between capital, interest and prices. The conclusions I reach concerning the merits of the theories discussed and concerning the structure and program of neoclassical economics cannot be reached without philosophical analysis. Besides, despite the low regard economists sometimes profess for philosophizing, economic theorists continue to write a great deal on methodology. I hope in this book to make a sober contribution to this extensive and uneven literature.

Yet this is not a traditional essay on the methodology of economics. Some philosophers and some economists may, indeed, find my intentions puzzling. In what sense does economics deserve "philosophical scrutiny"? What is a philosopher doing writing a book on theories of the relations between capital, interest, and prices? In what sense of the word "philosophical" are questions like "what is the subject matter of economics?" philosophical ones? What sort of enterprise am I undertaking? Philosophers have questions to answer concerning the methodology of the sciences and the manner in which the sciences provide us with knowledge. Economists have important questions to answer concerning their subject matter and discipline. Historians have questions to answer concerning past economic work. Yet these questions appear distinct. Why are they joined together in this book?

Although questions of academic taxonomy are of little intrinsic interest, I owe the reader an explanation of why I undertook this inquiry and how I pursued it. There is, after all, the traditional philosophical task of reflecting on what one is doing. A serious question for the philosophy of science is "What is the philosophy of science and how is it related to the sciences?" How distinct are the concerns of economists, historians of economics, and philosophers of economics? What sort of scholar is a philosopher of economics?

The reader impatient to know my general answers to these questions should turn to the postscript. I hope, however, that my inquiry itself answers these questions. Unfamiliar approaches are clearer in practice than in precept.

It is artificial to separate philosophical work from reflections on that work, to write about how to do philosophy of economics separately from doing philosophy of economics. It is particularly misleading to begin with methodological discussion and present the work which follows as the application of that methodology. Philosophy of science develops along with the sciences. Its methods develop with its conclusions. It is less misleading to begin with an actual investigation and to present the methodological discussion as a summing up and reflection on that investigation. Let us follow this order and proceed directly to examine theories of the relations between capital, interest, and prices.

CHAPTER ONE
Capital Theory and Classical Value Theory

I suggested in the introduction that capital theory is of considerable theoretical significance. In this chapter and the next I shall describe the domain of capital theory, the principal problems capital theory is supposed to solve, and the relations between capital theory and the theory of equilibrium prices. In showing how the phenomena of capital and interest complicate the tasks of other economic theories, I shall explain why capital theory is important.

1. What Is Economics About?

To place capital theory within economics, something must be said concerning what economics is. Economists and philosophers of economics have offered many different definitions. Most of these have been variations on two basic ones. Lionel Robbins defines economics as "the science which studies human behavior as a relationship between ends and scarce means which have alternative uses" (1932:15). According to this definition, economics is concerned with one aspect of much of human behavior. Robbins' definition has been called a "formal" definition of economics. The other basic definition, which is implicit in Plato's *Republic* and which was generally accepted until the twentieth century, takes economics to be the science of the production, exchange, distribution, and consumption of those goods and services that contribute to our material well-being. This second definition has been called "substantive."

The formal definition of economics has been criticized as both too narrow and too broad. It seems to exclude much of Keynes's work. It seems to include Abraham's decision to sacrifice Isaac. The substantive definition of economics has also been criticized as both too broad and too narrow. Purely technological questions concern our material well-being but are not a part of economics. The behavior of a concert pianist has an economic aspect, even though it does not perhaps, contribute to our material well-being. Although I shall not deal with detailed efforts that have been made to deal with the implausible implications of either definition, I shall in chapter 10 give reasons to prefer a substantive definition of economics.

It is senseless to enter into this dispute about how to define economics now. First, we should examine the phenomena economists study and the sort of things they say about those phenomena. One might begin by accepting tentatively one of these definitions, subject to later review and assessment. I prefer, however, to approach the subject in a more neutral way.

Related to the controversies concerning the definition of economics have been disagreements about whether economics can or should provide general laws. As thus stated, the issue is far from clear. What is a "general law"? I am not sure that any good answer can be given in the abstract. Even if one were available, I do not think it would be helpful in considering whether economics can or should provide general laws. Marx and Veblen have substantive objections to economists' claims to have discovered such general laws. Marx alleges that purported general laws in economics are either trivial or illegitimate generalizations of regularities which are peculiar to capitalism. (1973:86–88). Veblen criticizes the presuppositions of the "laws" espoused by the orthodox economists of his day (Lerner 1948:244f). The question "should or can economics provide general laws?" is distinct from the problem of defining economics, although related to it. Later I shall consider carefully the scope and status of the "laws" concerning capital and interest and employ my conclusions in arguing for a definition of economics. Once again, I would prefer to begin without either entering or prejudging the controversy.

But something must be said concerning what economics is. I think it is best to begin by considering what the subject matter or domain of economics has been. Economists, of course, do not always agree about whether a given phenomenon is an economic phenomenon or whether a given analysis is an economic analysis. Yet the overlap is large. Almost all economists agree that the subject matter of economics includes the principal features of production, exchange, and distribution that have been studied by well-known economists of the past two centuries. Let us focus on this portion of the domain of economics.

I thus think it is useful and fair as a first approximation to regard economic theories as accounts of how capitalist economies function.

Although economists do study other sorts of economies as well as institutions which are usually not regarded as part of any economy, I shall nevertheless assume that in examining theories of production, exchange, distribution, and consumption in modern competitive economies, one is studying the core of economic theory. To understand what economics is, let us thus consider the dominant object in the domain of economics, the capitalist economy.

2. What Is a Capitalist Economy?

If we are to consider economic theories as accounts of the functioning of a capitalist economy, we must first determine what a capitalist economy is. Capitalist economies come in many varieties, and they differ considerably in economically relevant respects. Adam Smith's society was not even industrial, while today we find huge firms dominating economies. Can any single kind of economy have such vastly different instances? Furthermore, even if there is a sense in which England had a capitalist economy in both 1776 and 1976, not every feature of England's economy in either year, or in any year in between, was capitalist. There are no instances of a purely capitalist economy. Actual economies are always mixed and messy. It is impossible to discover what a capitalist economy is merely by describing exhaustively any existing economy.

To talk of "a capitalist economy" is, therefore, to employ a theoretical term. Economists have developed *models* whose assumptions define this term. For now we can think of such models as a description of a kind of theoretical system. Different schools of economists employ different models of capitalism. Sometimes these differences are large. Orthodox neoclassical economists and Marxian economists, for example scarcely seem to be talking about the same economic system. Theorists in the mainstream of economics, both classical and neoclassical, are in closer agreement. Their models overlap sufficiently for us to take the shared assumptions as roughly specifying what the principal object of economic theory, the capitalist economy, is. Proceeding within the confines of these basic assumptions, we shall be able to see why capital theory is of great importance to the foundations of mainstream economic theory and why certain methodological positions are especially attractive to mainstream theorists.

What follows is in effect the mainstream definition of the capitalist economic system. The notion of *system* here is important. Perhaps the central insight that distinguishes mainstream economic theorizing of the past two centuries from earlier comments on economics is to conceive of production, distribution, and exchange as interconnected in a self-regulating system. Within a certain legal, moral, and political environment, the economy as a whole is supposed to function without regulation. The following definition or sketch is not implicit in *all* economic work of the past two centuries. Marx accepts a different sketch (see chapter 9). Keynes's work is also largely independent. Empirical work that involves few theoretical presuppositions is also possible. This section provides an account of the foundations of mainstream classical and neoclassical theory, not a survey of approaches to economic theory.

Since the following sketch is fleshed out in many different ways and not explicitly stated, there can be no canonical formulation. Yet there is a recognizable core to the many economic models developed by classical and neoclassical economists. The following three claims characterize the object of mainstream economic theory:

(1) Individuals are well-informed, rational, and self-interested (mutually disinterested).
(2) In the production of goods, and especially in the distribution of goods and services, individuals only interact through voluntary exchange.
(3) The result of voluntary exchanges among rational and self-interested individuals is an efficient and mutually beneficial systematic organization of production and distribution.
Corollary: The distribution of income and other advantages is determined principally by the assets with which individuals begin and the amount of effort they exert.

The above sketch of a capitalist economy may be interpreted in several ways. At first glance it seems a rough description of capitalist economies that economic theorists endeavor to refine. More cautiously, (1) and (2) might be regarded merely as presuppositions of laws and auxiliary assumptions economic theorists employ. They are basic components of standard models. One can leave open the question of whether theorists believe these presuppositions to be true, yet still recognize that (1) and (2) provide the core of refined theoretical models of capitalism. (3) raises a crucial theoretical problem. One may also regard the above sketch either as a methodological directive concerning how to develop economic theory or simply as a set of claims about capitalist economies. I formulated (1)–(3) as assertions, but I might just as well have stated them as rules for theorizing.

One might plausibly think of the statements above as characterizing market societies in general and add a proviso like "For the economy to be capitalist, . . . money profit must be the sole objective of the units engaged in production" (Lange 1945–46:27). I think most mainstream economists would have regarded Lange's proviso as an implication of (1)–(3). The characterization provided by (1)–(3) only attempts to capture what has generally been taken to be the principal object of economic theory. (See for example Friedman 1962:13).

Obviously almost everybody knows that people are not invariably well-informed, rational or self-interested. (1) merely tells the economist that the deviations are not relevant to understanding basic economic phenomena and can be omitted from the most fundamental theories. In explaining specific happenings, economists may investigate particular limitations on rationality, information, or self-interest.

(2) is concerned with institutions. It is a strongly (methodological) individualist thesis. It tells the economist what are the atoms out of which the economic system is constructed and what are the principles of construction. Notice that competition may be (and usually has been) considered to involve no actual interactions between people except voluntary exchanges. Competition is reflected in the properties of those exchanges. After a poor harvest, grain sellers will find their stocks declining and will try to raise the price of grain. They will succeed because individual buyers who are short of grain will offer more and more until they withdraw from the market or find a willing seller. Actual struggle between people, with its concomitant dissimulation, victories, and defeats, has no role in traditional treatments of competition.

(2) is a strong claim. It excludes, for example, the internal structure of a firm from the subject matter of economics—which, in fact, until recently was the case. Other social practices and interactions—family size and structure, moral precepts, political demands, etc.—will, of course, influence the operation of any economy. (2) tells economists to abstract from these in developing their most general theoretical account. In less general work, economists can investigate the influence on voluntary exchanges of background constraints like taxes or tariffs and of aberrations like monopolies.

Given (1) and (2), an economist can take it for granted that the basic elements of economic life are voluntary exchanges between informed rational and mutually disinterested individuals. (1) and (2) are presupposed by mainstream classical and neoclassical theory. To show that (3) then follows from (1) and (2) is perhaps the central problem. The corollary is mentioned because of its normative significance and because of its importance to the specific controversies I discuss below.

3. The Theory of Exchange Value

A fundamental problem for mainstream economics has thus been to explain how exchanges between individuals systematically organize production and distribution. The sketch above tells theorists that, given certain background constraints, the significant features of a pure capitalist economy result from the exchanges between individuals.

How do these voluntary exchanges, in the environment provided by law and custom (which is usually taken for granted), lead to order in production and distribution? To answer, one needs to discover and analyze basic regularities in capitalist economies. In exchanging commodities or performing services in exchange for commodities, people unintentionally establish orderly exchange ratios between commodities or between services and commodities. Money can be used as a generalized means of exchange and as a store of wealth because of this order. Individuals generally know the prevailing prices, and they make their decisions on the basis of this knowledge. Although individuals may by bargaining affect the ratio in some particular exchange, the range for bargaining is limited. People must generally take exchange ratios or prices as given.

Economists take a further step. Assume that the data upon which economic agents act, except for relatively fixed information concerning technological possibilities and their own wants, consist only of prices of available commodities. Economic theorists should thus look to prices to discover how the actions of self-interested agents on the market are coordinated. One then shows that individual actions are efficiently coordinated by showing the prices are so determined that they make advantageous to rational self-interested individuals those activities which efficiently satisfy the needs of people. If theorists can demonstrate this, they have explained how the exchanges of rational and self-interested individuals lead (given background institutional arrangements) to economic order. The theory of prices is thus central to mainstream explanations of the functioning of capitalist economic systems.

Yet exchange ratios or prices are not absolutely stable. Fluctuations are frequent, and sometimes large. Relatively permanent changes also occur. Consider these fluctuations first. Observation and reflection show that price fluctuations often direct self-interested individuals to act in a way which leads to economic order. If incomes rise and people seek to consume more meat, the price of meat will rise. The price increase will ration the given meat supplies, so that those individuals who are willing and able to sacrifice a considerable quantity of commodities in exchange for meat will be able to acquire it. Meat sellers will receive more commodities (or their money equivalent) for the meat they have on hand. Those individuals who have a choice between selling corn or using it to fatten cattle and hogs will discover that it is to their advantage to produce more meat. A shortage will give rise to an increase in price which will motivate people to increase the supplies. Fluctuations in prices serve as signals that direct individuals toward activities that provide for unsatisfied needs.

Much more than a theory of price fluctuations is needed. I have explained roughly how price changes enable competitive economies respond to changes in demand, but nothing I have so far said demonstrates that, at the more or less stable prices around which fluctuations occur, the proper amount of resources is devoted to producing meat. Indeed, I have not yet discussed criteria for what that proper amount is. All I have argued is that, with an increase in demand for meat, the price system will lead to an increase in supply. How does one know that meat production is not already inefficiently large? Knowing the dynamic forces that enable the system to respond to change does not tell one how the system functions after such response is complete. The above account of price fluctuations shows how prices signal needs (and changes in supply conditions), but not how individual actions in response to these signals lead to a systematic organization of the economy. Do these fluctuations tend toward some sort of order? Economists need a theory of *long-run equilibrium prices* or of *exchange values* in order to understand how capitalist economies can operate systematically (and efficiently) without centralized control. The exchange value of a commodity or service is its equilibrium price, the price around which market price fluctuates and toward which market price tends. In distinguishing market price and exchange value (or long-run equilibrium price), mainstream economists are, as it were, identifying the two separate components which together determine actual (market) prices—short-run supply and demand relations and factors influencing "long-run" equilibrium.

4. Do Exchange Values Reflect Physical Costs?

The most primitive theory of exchange value might be called a "physical cost" theory. Provided that one does not have any accidental disproportions between supply and demand which lead market price to differ from exchange value, exchange ratios reflect the physical costs or sacrifices involved in supplying the respective commodities

(Eatwell 1975c). Thus Adam Smith writes, "The real price of everything, what everything really costs to the man who wants to acquire it, is the toil and trouble of acquiring it. . . . What is bought with money or with goods is purchased by labor as much as what we acquire by the toil of our own body" (1776:26). If prices reflect physical costs, the economy will be organized efficiently. For each commodity, individuals will have to pay exactly what it costs in resources and exertion. Just that amount of labor and resources will be directed into each activity as is required by the demand. Not all needs or wants, of course, are reflected in market demand. Some people have little or nothing to offer in exchange for what they need or want. Such ineffective needs or wants are largely ignored in traditional discussions of the efficiency of forms of economic organization.

How can exchange ratios equal physical cost ratios? In Adam Smith's deer and beaver fable (1776:41f), one beaver will exchange for two deer if it requires twice the effort to trap a beaver as it does to kill a deer. Physical cost here is quantity of unassisted labor. If hunting and trapping require the same effort per unit time, the quantity of labor can be measured by labor time. With sufficient simplifying assumptions, Smith has a precise and unambiguous measure of physical cost.

In any real economy, one has no simple way of measuring physical cost. Yet one might nevertheless argue that exchange value *must* equal physical cost. If two commodities did not exchange in proportion to their physical costs, some exchanges must be involuntary or some exchangers must be irrational or misinformed. How else in equilibrium could unequal physical costs exchange for one another? Obviously people make many mistakes, but economists may reasonably inquire about how the economy would operate in the absence of irrationality, compulsion, altruism, or misinformation.

Simple physical cost theories of exchange value run into several problems. If one adds up the money cost of the physical inputs needed to produce anything, the total is less than the price of the commodity produced. Otherwise there could be no profit or interest. Depending on the precise interpretation of physical inputs, there might be some difficulties about rent, too. I shall not discuss the complications that rent and various grades of skilled labor introduce. Profits and interest are not the same thing, neither in ordinary language nor in the technical language of economists. Economists usually distinguish interest (which is equal to the return on a secure loan) from profit (the return from an investment which is over and above the return on a secure loan). Most contemporary economists regard interest as a cost, while profits may be a surplus. Classical economists usually called the whole of the return of an investment, "profits." For my purposes there is no reason to distinguish profits and interest or to distinguish between the rate of profit and the rate of interest. In the models I shall be discussing there is no excess or "pure" profits and thus no important difference between what Marx and the classical political economists called "the rate of profits" and what neoclassical economists since the 1870s have more often called "the rate of interest." Physical cost theories of exchange value do not appear to allow for profits or interest. They thus seem doomed right from the start.

Furthermore, one might object that a physical cost theory of exchange value requires impossible comparisons between commodities. How is an individual to compare the physical cost of his or her beef with that of a neighbor's broom? Each requires for its production many inputs, and each of these inputs in turn requires many inputs. It seems that we need to know all of the physical costs before we can discover any. If physical costs are not easily discoverable, it is hard to see how they can determine exchange values. Physical cost theories of exchange value thus seem unpromising.

5. The Labor Theory of Value

The labor theory of exchange value or equilibrium price provides a way around the above two objections to simple physical cost theories of value. The price of commodities is more than the sum of the costs of the physical inputs because some of the exertions of the laborer are unpaid. There is a surplus out of which profits may be apportioned. The value of a commodity is equal to the amount of labor needed to produce it, plus the labor needed to produce all of the inputs. As in the deer and beaver example, labor is measured in terms of time, and we assume that the different kinds of labor can be reduced to multiples of a single kind. Labor must be efficiently applied. The existence of profit does not undermine the labor theory of value, because the value of the labor power (the wage), which is equal to the labor needed to produce and reproduce the worker's ability to work, is less than the labor which must be exerted by the worker in making commodities.

The labor theory of value remains a physical cost theory of value, where labor time is used as the unit to measure physical cost. In building an automobile, one uses up some fraction of a large stamping machine and thereby incurs a physical cost. The idea of the labor theory of value is that this physical cost can be represented as a fraction of the amount of labor time needed to build the stamping machine (and all its inputs). The labor theory of value enables us to reduce a vector (a heterogenous list) of physical costs to a scalar (a single magnitude).

The labor theory of value thus makes plausible the thesis that exchange values are proportional to physical costs. Labor times can be estimated, particularly in primitive economies. No one will ordinarily exchange a given quantity of labor for a lesser. The labor theory of value faces, however, serious difficulties which demonstrate that physical cost theories of exchange value are impossible.[1] The most crucial difficulty leads us directly to the problems with capital and interest. In order to present this refutation of the labor theory of exchange value or of any other physical cost theory of exchange value, we must note one further critical feature of a capitalist economy. Individuals may exchange either money or commodities for the services of laborers. If these laborers are supplied with machinery and raw materials, they produce new commodities. The sum of the exchange values of the raw materials, machinery, and wage is less than the exchange value of the commodities produced. The difference is the interest or profit that a capitalist earns. Capitalists will invest so as to make the largest profit they can. If we assume that capitalists are rational and well-informed, there will be a tendency for the rate of profit to become equal on all employments of capital. Apart from a risk premium, the rate of profit should equal the rate of interest if capitalists can freely shift from making loans to making investments.

Actually, as Ricardo points out, the rate of profit should not be *precisely* equal in all employments. "He [a capitalist] may therefore be willing to forgo a part of his money profit, in consideration of the security, cleanliness, ease, or any other real or fancied advantage which

---

[1] Paul Samuelson (1959:21f) argues that the phenomenon of rent itself refutes the labor theory of value. In Ricardo's view (which has been very generally accepted), when the size of the labor force increases and demand for grain increases, farmers begin to cultivate inferior land or to cultivate the same land more intensively. Unless there is technological progress, they get a smaller return for their efforts. The value of the grain must increase or else the profits on such marginal agricultural ventures would be lower than average and capitalists would refuse to grow the extra grain. The extra profits on more fertile lands and on less intensive cultivation are absorbed as rent. Demand thus influences exchange value. If the labor theory of value denies this, it must be wrong. But the labor theory of value only asserts that the exchange value of a commodity is proportional to the amount of labor socially necessary to produce the commodity. It can concede that the amount of labor socially necessary to produce a commodity depends on demand. From the perspective of neoclassical theory, this last construal of the labor theory of value seems trivial and empty. Yet I am not convinced that the dependence of exchange values on demand shows that the labor theory of value is false or trivial. It may be sensible to deal with economic phenomena in a piecemeal fashion. Samuelson's argument raises basic questions (see ch. 9).

one employment may possess over another" (1817:90; see also Smith 1776:99).

The equalizing of the rate of profit conflicts with any physical cost theory of exchange value. Consider two commodities x and y which require the same inputs and the same amount of direct labor. Suppose x takes two years to make while y takes one year; x and y are different kinds of chairs; they take the same amount of labor time to make, but the glue in x takes a year to dry while y is made with screws. The exchange values of x and y cannot be equal, because interest must be paid twice on the investment in making x, but only once on the investment in making y. If x and y were to exchange one for one on the market, no capitalist would invest in making x, because the profit or interest per year would be smaller (Ricardo 1817:30–38).

Another way of putting essentially the same difficulty is as follows. Suppose that q and r, say chairs and tables, are both produced by labor and the same wood-working machine, M. If the production of one chair or one table requires the same total money investment, their equilibrium prices on the market must be equal. Suppose, however, that out of the total investment in producing chairs very little is spent on wages and a great deal on M, while the bulk of the investment in producing tables is devoted to wages. The labor value and physical cost of tables must be larger than that of chairs, because the exertions, the actual laboring, of workers are a cost (a quantity of labor time) larger than that needed to purchase their wages, while the physical costs or labor values of inputs contribute no more than their own cost to the value of the output (Marx 1967, 3, ch. 9). A simple arithmetical example may help here. Suppose that $p_M = \$10$ and the labor socially necessary to make M is 5 hours. Suppose that wages are \$1 per hour and that nine machines and 10 hours of labor are used to produce a chair, while one machine and 90 hours of labor are used to produce a table. Let the rate of profit be 100%. The price of a table is the same as that of a chair (\$200). The labor needed to produce chairs, however, is only 55 hours, while that needed to produce tables is 95 hours. As the rate of profit tends toward zero, prices tend toward labor values.

Consider more carefully what happens with a change in distribution of income between wages and profits. In the first example, if the rate of interest or profit is very high, the value of x will be far higher than the value of y. As the rate of interest declines toward zero, the value of x declines toward the value of y. In the second example, the equilibrium price of tables relative to that of chairs increases as profits decrease and wages increase. Since the physical inputs are by hypothesis in both cases absolutely unchanged, exchange values cannot possibly be measures of physical cost alone. Ricardo sought an "invariable standard of value" as a way out of this difficulty (1823:361–412; 1817:43–47). But there is no way out. Exchange values are not determined by physical costs alone.

6. Capital, Distribution, and Exchange Values

Since a physical cost theory of exchange values *cannot* be correct, the fundamental problem of mainstream economic theory, the explanation of the systematic functioning of a capitalist economy, remains unsolved. Most economists believe that the physical cost theory of exchange value the classical political economists pursued is a dead end. The divergence of exchange values and physical costs shows that costs are not exclusively physical costs. Since it is interest, in particular, which makes exchange values and physical costs (as socially necessary labor time) differ, they argue that we must regard interest as a cost. But what is interest the cost of? "Capital" is the apparent answer. Neoclassical economists have attempted to make sense of this answer. In doing so and in attempting to explain how capitalism functions, they have offered a new theory of value.

One might, however, draw a different conclusion from the failure of physical cost theories of value. Perhaps exchange values are not proportional to costs. Those economists who have sought to revive classical political economy recognize that exchange values are sensitive to the distribution of income. Yet they deny that interest is another kind of cost and that the classical conception of costs was a mistake. Instead, following Sraffa (1960) they explain exchange values in terms of both physical costs and the distribution of income.

To suggest that values are determined by costs *and* distribution is to conceive of capitalist economies in quite a different way than have mainstream classical and neoclassical theorists. It is to abandon the strategy of relying on the theory of exchange value to explain all fundamental economic phenomena. Since in Sraffa's work exchange values depend on the distribution of income (which is not itself a "cost"), Sraffa cannot employ the theory of exchange value to explain the distribution of income. Moreover, denying that exchange values are proportional to costs leads one to question the theoretical sketch of a capitalist economy presupposed by both classical and neoclassical economists. Once one denies that distribution of income can be explained by the theory of exchange values, can one continue to regard economic agents as interacting only through voluntary exchange? Once one regards interest as requiring that exchange values differ from physical costs, can one continue to regard capitalist economic organization as efficient and mutually beneficial? Can one continue to regard the distribution of income as determined by individual assets and efforts? Theories of the relations between capital, interest, and prices are thus fundamental to how one conceives of capitalist economies.

Mainstream economists have worked with models of capitalist economies in which the individual agents were rational and self-interested, their interactions were voluntary exchanges and the results of their interactions were efficient and mutually beneficial. In working with such models, the theory of prices or exchange ratios has been fundamental. Price fluctuations are relatively easy to understand but relatively superficial. Theories of equilibrium prices or of exchange *values* are much more important and much more difficult to provide. Classical physical cost theories of exchange values are irremedial failures. They give no account of the relations between interest and exchange values. They thus fail to articulate the basic sketch of a capitalist economy as a vast system of efficient voluntary cooperation through exchange. Let us turn now to another way to develop that sketch and to the subtle and elaborate attempts of mainstream neoclassical theorists to understand the relations between capital, interest, and exchange values.

CHAPTER TWO
Capital Theory, Utility Theory, and Economic Equilibrium

In the 1870s a new attempt was made to explain how economic order results from individual exchanges. Out of the refinements, changes, and additions of this neoclassical revolution arose a systematic vision of economics, which is still dominant today. In writing about neoclassical economic theory, I am writing about the received theory which dominates the discipline.

Neoclassical economists regard the theory of exchange value as the cornerstone of economic theory. They agree with the classical economists that theorists must study prices to understand how economic order arises from self-interested individual action. To understand production and distribution and consumption, one must understand both price fluctuations and long-run equilibrium prices or exchange values. In this chapter I hope in an informal way to make the neo-classical approach intelligible. Later, in chapters 5–7, I shall develop neoclassical theory more rigorously. My goal in this chapter is to show clearly how the problems of capital and interest arise within the general neoclassical program.

1. Marginal Utilities and Exchange Values

In developing an alternative theory of exchange value, neoclassical theorists relied on further generalizations concerning individual choices to exchange commodities. When a rational and self-interested individual, A, exchanges one unit of commodity x for q units of commodity y voluntarily, A wants q units of y as much or more than 1 unit of x. Since the early neoclassical economists were influenced strongly by utilitarianism (e.g., Jevons 1871, chs. 2, 3), they found it natural to say that q units of y just then gives A as much or more utility as one unit of x. Saying so, however, commits one neither to utilitarianism nor to the identification of utility with a mental state that is supposed to be the sole goal of action. One can stipulate rather innocuously that option 1 has more utility than option 2 for A if and only if A prefers 1 to 2. Obviously the above conditions depend on nothing peculiar to A; any rational and self-interested agent will engage voluntarily in an exchange only if doing so increases his or her utility thus defined. We can conclude that rational and mutually disinterested individuals are utility maximizers.

To say that individuals are utility maximizers is to say no more than that they do what they prefer. To coax more content out of this platitude, economists need to be able to discuss utility *functions*. These consistently relate options (which are identified with bundles of commodities) to levels of utility. Individuals can possess utility functions only if their preferences are complete and consistent. Moreover, economists suppose that agents are not satiated. A commodity bundle x possesses for all agents a greater utility than bundle y whenever x contains as much of each commodity as y does and more of at least one commodity. As utility maximizers, agents will always exchange a smaller bundle of commodities for a larger one if they can.

If economists are interested in how voluntary exchanges of informed, rational, mutually disinterested individuals can lead to an efficient and systematic organization of the economy, they can ignore the mistakes individuals make through irrationality, lack of information, or inadequacies in the assumption of mutual disinterest. As a first approximation, economists are thus perhaps justified in assuming away satiation. If one is interested in how an economy actually works, as opposed to how exchanges *can* lead to economic order, ignoring these complications is not obviously legitimate. Given these various strong assumptions, economists can specify for each individual a utility function which consistently relates larger bundles of commodities to higher levels of utility. As individuals grow and change, their utility functions will change, but we shall pass over these complications here.

I have not yet presented all the pieces of even a rudimentary theory of exchange. As Adam Smith noted long ago (1776, bk. I, ch. 4), exchange values are not proportional to utilities. All sane persons prefer lifetime supplies of water to lifetime supplies of diamonds, yet people regularly pay more for diamonds than for buckets of water. Neoclassical economists explain why by distinguishing the *total* utility that an agent's total stock of a commodity provides from the *marginal* or incremental utility which possessing another small unit of the commodity brings. Neoclassical economists offer the generalization that the marginal utility of a commodity is a decreasing function of the quantity of the commodity possessed. Unless people are satiated, consuming one more grain of rice will increase their total utility. One grain of rice will never make an enormous difference to people's total utility, but it will count more if they have almost no rice than if they have a great bowl of rice. The *disutility* of parting with a grain of rice will similarly be less if one has a great deal of rice than if one has very little. If utility functions are twice differentiable, one can simply say that their first partial derivatives with respect to the quantity of any commodity are positive and that their second partial derivatives are negative.[1]

Employing the principle of diminishing marginal utility, economists are much closer to being able to explain general properties of individual exchanging. If exchanging itself has no utility or disutility, individuals will agree to an exchange if and only if the marginal utility of what they are acquiring is equal to or greater than the marginal utility of

[1] If one graphs the utility function, one will have a surface in an $n + 1$ dimensional space (where n is the number of commodities). Each point on the surface represents a commodity bundle and its utility. The projection of any point on the surface onto n of the axes indicates how many of each of the n commodities are included in the given commodity bundle. The projection of the point on the remaining axis specifies the utility of the bundle. Moving away from the origin in any positive direction perpendicular to the utility axis, the curve will have a positive slope, but the magnitude of the slope will be smaller the further one is from the origin. If one holds the quantities of all commodities in a bundle except one constant, one can draw the graph in Fig. 2.1.

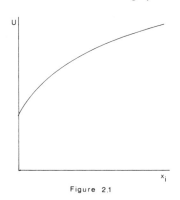

Figure 2.1

The quantity, x_i, of the variable commodity is represented by the horizontal distance from the origin. Total utility, U, holding the quantities of all other commodities constant, is represented by the vertical distance. The marginal utility of a commodity is in general a function of the quantities of all n commodities in a bundle. Holding the quantities of all but one commodity constant, one can represent marginal utility as a function of the quantity of that commodity alone. That function is the slope of the graph in Fig. 2.1.

what they are parting with. The exchange ratio between two bundles of commodities is not entirely determined by the utility functions of the exchangers. It also depends on the quantities of various commodities the exchangers already possess or expect to possess. If two people have almost no water and no expectations of having more soon, the first will have to offer a high price to induce the second to part with any water. Knowing *only* the utility functions or *only* the amount of water available, one could not explain why water could be exchanged for so large a bundle of commodities. One needs *both* bits of information. The "scarcity" of water is derived from these two pieces of information; it is not an independent fact. In neoclassical analysis, scarcity is not just a fact about quantities. Whether a good is scarce depends on the *relations* among its quantity, the quantities of other commodities, and preferences of individuals. Walras in fact identifies scarcity and marginal utility (1926, §22, §75). To make such an identification is reasonable since for a given agent (or in a given equilibrium state) x is scarcer than y if and only if the marginal utility of x is larger

---

One can draw the graph of this partial marginal utility function as in Fig. 2.2.

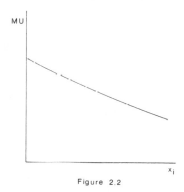

Figure 2.2

Here marginal utility, MU, not total utility, U, is measured in the vertical direction. The law of diminishing marginal utility asserts that the marginal utility curve will be downward sloping.

As is well known, economists can replace talk of marginal utilities with talk of marginal rates of substitution. The exposition here is intended to be simple and clear. Nothing of conceptual importance is lost by talking of marginal utilities. As recent work has shown, the use of calculus is avoidable. General equilibrium models can be formulated using weaker axioms than those in the calculus formulations I shall present. Calculus formulations are, however, historically significant, simple, and familiar. Given them, it is not necessary to go into the difference between marginal utility and marginal net utility. For an excellent discussion see Bliss 1975, part II, chs. 2–6.

than the marginal utility of y. Siamese cats (x) are scarcer than blind basset hounds (y).

Thinking in terms of utility functions suggests a different conception of cost. From the neoclassical perspective, the real cost in Adam Smith's parable of the deer and beaver is not a quantity of "exertion," but the disutility incurred in the effort to hunt deer or trap beaver. J. B. Clark says simply, "Cost is, in the last analysis, pain inflicted, just as utility is pleasure conferred" (1902:202n). Suppose individuals in Smith's parable happen to enjoy hunting deer and to hate trapping beaver. Those individuals who for some reason want a beaver will be willing to exchange many deer for one beaver. Even though it takes twice as much "toil and trouble" (as measured perhaps by expenditure of calories) to kill a beaver as a deer, the exchange value of a beaver will be much more than two deer.

Given the principle of diminishing marginal utility, neoclassical economists can begin to understand how the compensation of inputs into production is determined. A person who supplies some input into production suffers a disutility.[2] The disutility of parting with the input increases with the amount supplied. Individuals will supply more resources or labor only if they are given a larger bundle of commodities in return. Individuals will supply additional resources or commodities or services until the marginal disutility incurred in doing so becomes as large as the marginal utility of the additional commodities they can acquire with their income. Laborers who prefer consumption to leisure will work more and receive more income. Individuals whose resources have large marginal utilities or are relatively scarce as inputs into production, will also receive higher incomes; individuals whose resources have low marginal utilities and are relatively abundant as inputs into production will be poorly paid.

If cost is disutility, neoclassical economists not only have an alternative theory of cost, but they also have shown that the same factor influences both supply and demand. They can thus make the appealing claim that all prices are determined by supply and demand. All they have to do is to find a way of equating the disutility incurred in procuring something with the utility in consuming it.

---

[2] Some neoclassical theorists prefer to conceive of costs in terms not of disutility, but of alternative uses (Stigler 1941: 34, 231). The differences between the two approaches are small (Knight 1921: 73) and not relevant to my concerns.

2. Equilibrium

In order to show how the voluntary exchanges of utility maximizers result in a systematic organization of production and distribution, neo-classical economists have greatly sharpened the notion of economic order. The concept of economic equilibrium is the result of this sharpening. It is a development of the belief that an economy is working systematically and well when there is a balance between supply and demand. A closed economy is in equilibrium when the demand for commodities as constrained by the income individuals receive as compensation for their role in production is just matched by the supply of produced commodities. A state of equilibrium obtains when no one wants to carry out any further exchanges at the prevailing prices. The choices of individuals are thus reconciled. The notion of equilibrium crudely defined here is described by economists as general equilibrium, because it is concerned with the entire economy (See Arrow 1968:376–89).

The idea of a general economic equilibrium faces two immediate difficulties, since it appears to ignore economic changes and the importance of time and expectations. Marshall (1930:323) speaks of a number of balls resting at the lowest point of a hemispherical container as in stable equilibrium. If they are displaced, the force of gravity damped by friction will act to restore them to a stable configuration at the bottom. But capitalist economies are not balls in cups; they are constantly changing. How can the notion of an equilibrium apply to a constantly changing system? Furthermore, the utility function of a rational agent must rank both future and present consumption states, since present choices affect our future well-being. For George, the utility of a hammer depends on his knowing what he will do with it and what utilities the outcomes of his actions will have. Notice that this future reference of utility functions does not require that the utility functions themselves change. George's preferences for wood furniture may be entirely fixed. Scarcities also depend on expectations. Economists must bring time and expectations into the analysis of equilibrium. They can introduce time explicitly via the notion of an intertemporal general equilibrium. That notion, however, is quite recent and raises special difficulties. I shall discuss it below in chapter 5. The more traditional concept of a general economic equilibrium, which provides the setting for traditional difficulties with the role of capital, is of a stationary equilibrium.

In a stationary equilibrium, the future is exactly like the present, and the present is exactly like the past. People will continue to behave in the future just as they have in the past and the present. Change and expectations thus have no role in the analysis of a stationary equilibrium. Of course, no economy is in stationary equilibrium. Traditional neoclassical theorists instead regarded economies as if they were constantly on the verge of reaching it, in the hope that economists could profitably employ stationary equilibrium analysis. "Exogenous" changes (changes in the givens of the analysis) keep economies from actually reaching such equilibria. Neoclassical economists have thus greatly simplified the analysis of how individual exchange leads to economic order. Actual properties of economies can be regarded as the composition of two different kinds of causal factors: disequilibrating exogenous "shocks" and adjustments of the system (which is ever seeking and always approaching equilibrium) to those shocks. Neoclassical economists have considered the effects of changes in tastes or taxation or of other givens by comparing stationary equilibria.

The problem of showing how economic order results from individual choice and voluntary exchange has thus been made precise. The economist needs to show (1) how prices are determined by the efforts of individual utility maximizers constrained by their original endowments of resources and the technological possibilities and (2) that when certain conditions obtain, these prices are exchange values and the economy is in stationary equilibrium. Finally, in conformity with the sketch of capitalist economies of chapter 1, neoclassical economists would like to demonstrate (3) that this stationary equilibrium is efficient or in some way optimal.

In practice the first two tasks of the general equilibrium theorist are performed simultaneously. The constraints on maximization may be expressed in mathematical equations. The maximization conditions yield other equations by means of calculus techniques. One then demonstrates that these equations solve for vectors (ordered lists) of prices, outputs, and inputs that satisfy the conditions for a stationary equilibrium.

A. Simple Exchange Equilibrium

To solve for such a general equilibrium is a complex task which requires further theoretical assumptions. Let us follow the early equilibrium theorists (Jevons 1871; Walras 1926, Wicksell 1911 for example) and simplify the problem by assuming away production(!). Individuals are just exchanging commodities already in existence. Even in this simplified problem, no equilibrium solution can generally be determined unless we assume that commodities are infinitely divisible and that individuals must take prices as given. It is possible to have an equilibrium solution with indivisibilities and without perfect competition, but one will usually be unable to prove that such a solution exists. Economists have been concerned with sufficient conditions for the existence of economic equilibrium, not with necessary conditions.

Given these assumptions, one can set up a system of equations in which the unknowns are prices and the quantities of each commodity that individuals wind up with by exchanging their initial endowments. We know how much of each commodity each individual begins with and each individual's utility function. Depending on the mathematical form of the utility functions, these may be sufficient to solve for all the unknowns. A simple example may make this claim clearer.

Suppose we have two groups of agents, A and B, with 100 members each and only two commodities, x and y. All members of A begin with the same initial endowment and have the same utility functions. The same goes for the members of B. (I am not considering the apparently simpler case of only two individuals, because with so few traders, exchange ratios would be influenced by the bargaining powers of the traders.) Initially each member of A has $x_a/100$ and $y_a/100$ and each member of B has $x_b/100$ and $y_b/100$. After exchanging they have respectively $(x_A/100, y_A/100)$ and $(x_B/100, y_B/100)$. We have six unknowns; the final quantities of commodities each possesses and the two prices. Since no one profits we have the two equations:

$$(2.1) \qquad p_x x_a + p_y y_a = p_x x_A + p_y y_A$$

$$(2.2) \qquad p_x x_b + p_y y_b = p_x x_B + p_y y_B$$

Since utility is maximized we have two more equations:

$$(2.3) \qquad \frac{U_x^A(x_A, y_A)}{U_y^A(x_A, y_A)} = \frac{p_x}{p_y}$$

$$(2.4) \qquad \frac{U_x^B(x_B, y_B)}{U_y^B(x_B, y_B)} = \frac{p_x}{p_y}$$

$U_x^A(x_A, y_A)$ is the partial derivative with respect to x of the "A" utility function evaluated at (x_A, y_A).

Since no goods are lost in the process of exchange:

$$(2.5) \qquad x_B + x_A = x_b + x_a$$

$$(2.6) \qquad y_B + y_A = y_b + y_a$$

Among the four equations (2.1), (2.2), (2.5), and (2.6), only three are independent. If we set p_x or p_y equal to 1 we can apparently solve for the other price, x_A, x_B, y_A, and y_B. Equations (2.3) and (2.4) can be derived easily from the calculus conditions for maximizing a function, but they also possess an economic meaning. If the ratio of the marginal utilities of the two commodities is not for both agents equal to the price ratio, the economy is not in equilibrium. Someone will want to exchange. If, for example, the ratio of the marginal utility of x to the marginal utility of y for A is greater than the price ratio, then trading away some y for some x brings about a net gain in utility. In equilibrium both price ratios and marginal utility ratios must have adjusted themselves until (2.3) and (2.4) hold.

The analysis of a situation of a simple exchange economy is an extreme simplification of the problem of demonstrating the existence of an equilibrium for a capitalist economy. In this analysis economists have scarcely described an economy, since they are analyzing only a single exchange event. The notion of an equilibrium is greatly simplified here, since there seems to be no future at all. Actually one could consider the above "economy" as in stationary equilibrium—in each period the endowments simply appear and are exchanged. The example illustrates how little past and future there is to stationary equilibrium. In this simple exercise in equilibrium analysis, the theory of exchange value is simultaneously a theory of consumption and a trivial theory of the distribution of income. It thus promises to carry out completely the general program for economics. Notice that goods which are scarcer (i.e., have a higher marginal utility) will have higher prices.

B. Noncapitalist Production Equilibrium

To extend the neoclassical theory of exchange value to a capitalist economy, it is usual to make a theoretical detour. For examples of such detours see Wicksell (1911, vol. 1) or Walras (1926). Consider first an economy, unlike any real economy, in which none of the inputs into production are themselves produced and in which there is no interest (and in equilibrium no profits). We can think of the equations in this case as describing a single production-exchange event or a series of repeated events that constitutes a monotonous history of this hypothetical economy. Each year the same quantities of resources and unproduced factors of production are available at the same prices. Output and prices of output are constant. The only way in which to study the effects of a change, let us say an increase in population, is by comparing the stationary equilibrium that can be derived from the new system of equations with the original stationary equilibrium.

To set up the conditions for an equilibrium, economists need some way of expressing in mathematical equations the motivation of producers and the technological possibilities of transforming inputs into outputs. Walras initially presented a general equilibrium system in which fixed quantities of inputs are needed in production (1926, sec. 204). Technological possibilities have, however, usually been expressed by introducing production functions with special properties. I shall follow this usual course. The additional motivation assumption almost always made is that producers maximize profits.

The special features of production functions are the following. If the quantity of all inputs except one is held constant, and the quantity of the remaining input is increased, the quantity of output is increased. As successive increments of the one variable input are added, after a point, output increases at a decreasing rate. The returns to the successive input increments, which economists call the "marginal (physical) products," are diminishing. Production also exhibits constant returns to scale; if *all* inputs are increased or decreased in the same proportion, output is increased or decreased in exactly that proportion. If one can apply calculus to the production functions (if they are twice differentiable), these conditions mean that the first partial derivatives are positive, the second (after a point) negative,[3] and that the functions are homogeneous of degree one.

From the properties of production functions and the assumption that producers maximize profits, it can be shown (1) that the ratio of the "marginal products" of different inputs to the same output must be equal to the price ratio of the inputs; (2) that the value of the marginal product of an input must be the same in all its applications and (3) that profits must be zero in all enterprises. The last result may seem surprising, but it is what one should expect, since "production" is instantaneous and requires only unproduced inputs. Given constant returns to scale, consumers could always buy the inputs and "produce"

---

[3] For many variables the second order conditions are actually more complicated. Footnote 1, which discusses utility functions, may be useful to those uncomfortable with the calculus terminology.

the outputs themselves. In equilibrium there can be no profits. These three conditions provide the additional equations needed to solve for a noncapitalist stationary equilibrium. The givens are utility functions (whose domain includes factors of or inputs into production[4]), the original endowment of commodities and of factors of production, the distribution of that endowment, and the production functions. Given all the various assumptions needed to formulate these givens and to derive mathematical equations from them, one can solve for a stationary equilibrium.

3. Exchange Value as Determined by the Constrained Balancing of Marginal Utilities.

We can now understand better the marginal utility theory of exchange value. Prices of commodities and of factors of production are jointly determined by all the givens in an equilibrium system. So are the marginal utilities experienced in consuming different commodities and the marginal disutilities incurred in surrendering inputs to production. These marginal utilities and disutilities depend, like prices, on utility and production functions, the initial endowment of resources and commodities, and the distribution of this endowment. It is thus misleading to say that prices are causally determined by marginal utilities (or to say that prices are causally determined by scarcities). Marginal utilities (or scarcities) and prices are simultaneously determined. Within the constraints of the production functions and the distribution of the initial endowments, equilibrium prices bring individual preferences into relation with one another.

Neoclassical economics thus presents what might be called a "constrained balancing of marginal utilities" or a "constrained maximization of utility" theory of exchange values. Notice that, if other parameters are held constant, the price of a factor of production is a decreasing function of its quantity relative to the quantities all other commodities and factors of production.

It seems that neoclassical economists have nearly everything they need for the presentation of a rich and systematic foundation for economic theory. They have a single model which may show how the

---

[4] In speaking of "factors of production," economists sometimes simply mean "inputs into production." Sometimes they mean only general *kinds* of inputs into production, like capital or land. Sometimes they mean only those inputs into production which are themselves unproduced, like labor or land. I shall use "factor of production" as a synomym for "input into production."

choices of informed rational self-interested individuals whose only interactions are voluntary exchanges can give rise to economic equilibrium and thus to a determinate system of exchange values, outputs, and distribution of income. All neoclassical economists need to do is to extend the theory to the real life case in which agents employ produced means of production.

4. Problems with Capital and Interest

Applying this model of constrained balancing of marginal utilities to a capitalist economy presents serious difficulties. How can one explain profits within the framework of general equilibrium models? Profit or interest is apparently the return to capital, but how is this possible? What is capital? Can one speak sensibly of its marginal product or of the marginal disutility of parting with it? How can one determine what the quantity of capital is? Should one look for some way of accounting for the phenomenon of profits or interest which avoids talking about capital? Like the classical theories of value, neoclassical theories face their sternest test when they confront the problem of incorporating interest into price theory and explaining how interest is determined.

The most straightforward approach to these difficulties is that of J. B. Clark (1902: viii, 123, 190, 363, and *passim*). He sharply distinguishes capital, as a permanent "fund of productive wealth" which is successively embodied in various capital goods, from capital goods themselves.[5] Capital goods are factors of production that, like all factors of production, earn rents. Capital, on the other hand, earns interest. This permanent "fund of productive wealth" is measured in value terms, but it is not just the value of capital goods. It is, according to Clark, a real factor of production (1902:29f). Interest, as the return to capital, is determined in exactly the same way that the returns to all other factors of production are determined; it is equal to the marginal product of capital and depends on the quantity of capital available relative to the demand for it and the availability of other factors of production.

There are various difficulties with Clark's treatment of capital. He

---

[5] Citing Clark, Frank Knight (1936a: 460) maintains "that the capital of an economic society or system is a continuous organic whole, a fund measured in value units, though at any moment it is largely (not entirely) embodied in things of a sort which more or less regularly wear out. . . . This view is in harmony with all ordinary thinking and procedure in connection with capital quantity. The quantity of capital represented by any existing thing is simply its value, the capitalization of its yield."

seems to be saying that interest is determined by the marginal product of capital; but, as mentioned previously, it is misleading to say that the price of any commodity or factor of production is determined by its marginal utility or its marginal product. From the perspective of general equilibrium theory, prices are determined by all of the givens of the system of equations. This criticism, however, misses the central flaw in Clark's proposal. He is suggesting in effect that capital, as a "fund of productive wealth," be included among the constraints on the equilibrium solution. The endowment of capital (since it is measured as a quantity of value) is, however, itself a function of the exchange values for which economists attempt to solve. If one takes capital to be a fund of "productive wealth," the explanation of interest as the return to capital cannot take the same form as the general explanation of the return to factors of production. The problems of incorporating capital and interest into neoclassical value theory remain.

Unless neoclassical economists can find some way of incorporating the phenomenon of interest into the constrained balancing of marginal utility theory of exchange value, that theory of value cannot be correct. The viability of the fundamental structure of neoclassical economics depends on the success of neoclassical capital theory. Neoclassical economists must explain what capital is and how the quantity and rate of interest are determined. Perhaps the only sensible theory of exchange value is based on physical cost and distribution between wages and profits. Perhaps the whole project of explaining exchange values on the basis of constrained preferences is a mistake. The project cannot succeed until the puzzles of capital and interest are solved.

The viability of the opposing theory of value based on physical cost and distribution depends on the demonstration that physical cost and distribution can determine exchange value without bringing in utilities. Whether interest is a cost to be explained in terms of some disutility or whether interest is merely a portion of the social surplus apparently has implications for both positive and normative theory. Notice that it has not yet been established that these supposedly alternative theories of value exclude one another; perhaps interest can be regarded as both a cost in terms of a balancing of marginal utilities theory and as a portion of the social surplus in terms of a physical cost cum distribution theory.

Capital theory thus rests at the foundations of economic theory. Let us now examine and assess specific neoclassical attempts to deal with the problems that capital and interest pose.

CHAPTER THREE
Neoclassical Theories of Capital and Interest

In real economies reproducible inputs are used in production. Owners of these inputs earn interest. How, from a neoclassical perspective, is this income to be understood? Economists need to explain how the prices and rentals of capital goods are determined, what capital is, and how the interest on capital is determined. Within the neoclassical approach to economic theory there are two ways to tackle this complicated problem. Recently theorists have attempted to refine general equilibrium models until in principle they enable one to explain the rentals of all capital goods as well as all prices. Possessing such models one can then calculate the value of "capital" by adding up the value of all the capital goods. Adding up the rentals on all capital goods minus their depreciation, one would have the total amount of interest earned. Dividing the total amount of interest by the value of capital, one could say what the rate of interest was.

Such a general equilibrium approach to the problems of capital and interest has many virtues, but I shall focus first on earlier attempts to associate capital with some particular aspect of production and to interpret interest as the cost of this factor. The puzzles that capital and interest present are better understood if one follows their development in a roughly historical way. Associating capital with some aspect of production and interest with its cost, theorists attempted to explain the apparent productivity of capital and the existence of interest explicitly (see for example Wicksell 1911:149). Contemporary general equilibrium theories say nothing directly about capital or interest. In addition, those general equilibrium theories which have significant implications concerning capital and interest are too abstract to help with many important questions. When Robert Solow, for example, sought to discover how much of the growth of America's GNP in the twentieth century has been due to technological progress (1957:312–30), he could not turn to general equilibrium theories. Instead, he worked with an aggregate production function, in which the inputs were simply capital (measured by its value) and labor. Interest and wages were set equal to the respective marginal products. There are many serious economic questions which theorists cannot consider unless they employ such simplified models. Although simplified theories which link capital with an aspect of production face many difficulties, I shall argue that such theories may nevertheless be informative. Even though most contemporary theorists regard the general equilibrium approach as more rigorous and fundamental, we should not simply pass over more traditional theories of capital and interest.

The traditional approach is to associate capital with some feature of production and to regard the rate of interest as the price of this feature. There are several ways to carry out this idea. I have already mentioned that J. B. Clark regarded capital as a permanent "fund" of productive wealth. Clark hoped to treat capital as an input, in many ways on a par with lathes or steam engines. Clark's program requires that one measure this input, discover what its role in production is, and investigate its marginal productivity. The theorist should be able to explain why the rate of interest is positive by pointing to the scarcity of this factor of production (or its marginal productivity).

To speak of explaining interest in terms of the marginal productivity of capital is somewhat confused. As I have explained, marginal productivities or relative scarcities are not givens to an equilibrium system, but are calculable within such systems (see Bliss 1975, pp. 33–77 and ch. 5). Clark's work is confused, but, as I argued before, the principal difficulty does not lie in the attempt to explain wages or interest in terms of marginal productivity. Clark seeks to add another factor of production, capital, and another price, interest, to some equilibrium system. Charitably interpreted, Clark's claim that interest is determined by marginal productivity asserts only that the initial endowment of capital (relative to that of labor or land) and the known technology are crucial factors influencing the rate of interest. Even though the rate of interest is a function of all the unknowns, it is not equally sensitive to all of them. It is reasonable to focus on particular factors.

Having said this much for Clark, his theory of capital and interest remains unsatisfactory. One cannot coherently introduce as a given into an equilibrium system a quantity of capital measured as a quantity of value. Such a quantity will obviously depend on what the equilibrium prices are. Even if the account were not thus incoherent, it would be mysterious. What sort of an input into production is a "permanent fund of productive wealth"?

One might indeed question not simply Clark's particular theory, but any attempt to associate capital with some single feature of production. What Clark and others who have proposed simplified capital theories have attempted resembles partial equilibrium analysis. Just as one isolates for the purposes of analysis the market for shoelaces and considers demand and supply for shoelaces as (at least as a first approximation) functions only of the price of shoelaces, so one might isolate the market for "capital" and attempt to consider separately the supply and demand for capital. One has made a strong argument that interest can be explained in the same way as prices are, if the partial equilibrium tools apply to capital and interest in the same way that they apply to any other commodity and its price. The capital theorist wants, in Böhm-Bawerk's words, to show that "The exchange . . . in which interest has its origin, is only a special case of the exchange of goods in general. It goes, then, without saying that the formation of price in this case is subject to the same laws as [sic] govern the formation of price in economical exchange generally" (1888:375).

Such a project seems dubious, however. The market for shoelaces is relatively isolated. A shift toward a method of producing shoelaces that requires more synthetic materials and less cotton has limited consequences for the rest of the economy. A change in the price of shoelaces is unlikely to have appreciable ramifications in many other markets. A general shift toward more capital-intensive methods of production has, on the other hand, broad repercussions and reflects general economic changes.

Despite these apparent difficulties, many neoclassical economists have attempted to give such simplified theories of capital and interest. I shall consider in some detail one particularly intelligible effort, the "Austrian" theory of capital and interest, so-called, because it was largely developed by Austrian theorists, particularly Böhm-Bawerk (1888). See also (Menger 1871, 1:4 and 3: 3, 8) and (Jevons 1871, ch. 7). The Austrian theory is more sophisticated than Clark's work and, indeed, functions as a critique of Clark. It avoids introducing a mysterious physical something which functions as an input into production in addition to capital goods.

1. Capital and Waiting

One way of incorporating capital into neoclassical theory is to say, as Clark did, that capital earns interest because it is scarce and has a positive marginal product. To the Austrian theorists such a claim seemed naïve and unhelpful. According to them, to possess capital is simply to own, and thus to control, productive goods. Capital is not itself some productive stuff. Furthermore, regarding capital as an input leaves the crucial questions unanswered. Both capital and capital goods are augmentable. Why doesn't the quantity of capital increase to the point where profits are zero? Knut Wicksell, whose exposition I shall follow for the most part, objected that we cannot talk of the scarcity of capital without specifying the units in which we measure capital. The obvious choice of value units seems unsatisfactory. How could the scarcity of capital be a scarcity of a quantity of value? Surely competition would simply bid up the value of capital until it was no longer scarce (Wicksell 1911:146). Something physical and real must be involved.

According to Böhm-Bawerk and Wicksell, the real physical something involved is *time*. Capital goods can "be ultimately resolved into labor and land" (Wicksell 1911:149). Saving up labor and land and applying them indirectly increases their productivity. Capital is not itself a factor of production. Rather "capital is saved-up labor and saved-up land. Interest is the difference between the marginal productivity of saved-up labor and land of current labor and land" (Wicksell 1911:154). This difference shows the role of time or "waiting." "Waiting" is both deferring consumption and applying resources to activities that require longer intervals of time to produce consumption goods. Time or waiting makes it possible to apply land and labor in increasingly indirect or roundabout and thus (the crucial step) more productive ways (Böhm-Bawerk 1888:82–87). Interest is not the marginal product of capital. Capital is not an input and has no marginal product. Interest is a portion of the increased output that waiting makes possible paid to those who own the resources which permit the waiting. Indeed interest might be said to be the marginal product of time or waiting.[1]

As accumulation proceeds, more and more roundabout processes will be employed. The marginal contribution of waiting will decline. Waiting will no longer be so scarce. The role of time in production apparently provides a unified demystified treatment of capital and interest.

Time has a second important relationship to interest, which was

---

[1] Böhm-Bawerk would be hesitant about this particular formulation, since he objects to theories, like Nassau Senior's which regard the capitalists as performing a sacrifice which contributes to production when they abstain from consuming their wealth (1888:123).

pointed out by Böhm-Bawerk (1888, book V, ch. 3), but about which Wicksell has little to say. Böhm-Bawerk puts it as follows: "to goods which are destined to meet the wants of the future, we ascribe a value which is really less than the true intensity of their future marginal utility. We systematically underestimate future wants, and the goods which are to satisfy them" (1888: 253). If I now prefer present consumption to future consumption, then I must be paid a premium to save or invest. Time matters not only because the productivity of land and of labor are increased when land and labor are applied indirectly, but also because the utility of commodities (from a given time perspective) is decreased by deferring consumption. Time preference or "impatience," as Irving Fisher called it, is a function of the current level of consumption as well as of (expected) future levels of consumption. A person on the edge of subsistence will be unwilling to sacrifice any current consumption to increase future consumption. A person who expects to be better off in the future without any present sacrifices will be less willing to defer present consumption to add more to future consumption. When waiting is scarce, the productivity of land and labor are necessarily relatively low. Rents and wages which, in equilibrium, equal the respective marginal products of land and labor will also be low. Workers and landlords will be relatively unwilling to defer consumption. Time preference will likely be high. The rate of interest will be high both because the gains from waiting are large and because individuals will be unwilling to defer consumption and thus to wait. When, on the other hand, production has become extremely roundabout, the level of consumption will be high and the difference between today's and next year's level of consumption will be slight. People will be much less impatient. The gains from increasing the roundaboutness of production will be less dramatic. The rate of interest will thus be lower. With sufficient accumulation the rate of interest might vanish, but it need not. Time preference might choke off savings. We might never reach a point when production cannot be increased by increasing the roundaboutness of production.

The Austrian theory is an ingeneous attempt to provide a unified explicit theory of capital and interest without introducing into the analysis both capital goods and something called "capital." Of course, there is no denying that businessmen talk of their capital and the returns their capital earns. The Austrian theory attempts to reveal the truth behind the misleading appearances. The value of capital will be a rough indicator of the quantity of "waiting" or the degree of roundaboutness. The apparent productivity of capital is a reflection of the real productivity of more roundabout production processes with longer periods of production. We have a sketch of an intelligible theory of capital and interest.

2. Wine and Grape Juice

The above comments provide only a fragmentary sketch of a theory of capital and interest. Much more is needed. How is apparent capital accumulation related to the time-intensity of production? How can one measure the time-intensity of production? How can one find out whether the value of capital and the length of the average period of production do generally increase together? How can one test the claim that with increased roundaboutness come higher returns? How do market forces relate the rate of interest to the period of production?

Wicksell does surprisingly little to answer these questions. His presentation of the Austrian theory takes a different course. After merely sketching the general claims (1911:162–63, 184) he turns immediately to the construction of models of hypothetical simplified economies. He then employs these models to illustrate, develop, and vindicate his general claims concerning capital and interest.

Wicksell's discussion of simplified hypothetical economies raises difficult philosophical questions. What roles can discussions of hypothetical cases play in science? Can such discussions serve as evidence for or against theories? What structure do such "models" have? These questions are important ones in the philosophy of economics, because a large part of theoretical economics employs similar simplified models.

Let us begin by examining Wicksell's simplest model (1911:178–81). The notation used here is mine, not Wicksell's. One has an industry or a sector of an economy in which firms buy grape juice and store it as aging wine. The industry is competitive, and each firm attempts to maximize its profits. Since there are many firms, none can influence the price of grape juice or the rate of interest. To simplify my discussion, I shall assume (unnecessarily) that each firm buys a fixed amount of grape juice. The value of the stored wine (x) is a given increasing function of its age. The only choice a firm has is how long to store the wine.

There is thus a point input of grape juice of value w, which the firm takes as fixed. The task is to determine the equilibrium state of such a wine sector. In the equilibrium state there will be equal quantities of wine stored of every age up to and including the equilibrium period of storage, t^*. Notice that this model is of an economy in stationary equilibrium. Wicksell talks of "changes" and discusses the derivative of, for example, the value of grape juice with respect to equilibrium time of storage. This talk can be confusing. One is considering stationary equilibria only and is unable to say anything about *changes*. All Wicksell is doing is *comparing* stationary states. As Joan Robinson points out (1953–54:81–106), confusion on this point is one of the pitfalls of stationary equilibrium models.

The profit of any firm, P, is the value of the wine sold, x, minus the cost of the grape juice, $w(1 + r)^t$, where r is the rate of interest and t is the period of storage. The compound interest factor, $(1 + r)^t$, must be included because during the time period involved firms could have been earning interest on the money they invested in buying grape juice. If one allows a period to be extremely short one can approximate $(1 + r)^t$ by e^{rt} where r is now the momentary rate of interest and e is the base for the natural logarithms. Thus one has:

$$(3.1) \qquad\qquad P = x - we^{rt}$$

Since this is a perfectly competitive sector with no uncertainties or risks, there can be no profits in equilibrium. Another way to say the same thing is that each firm will earn only the normal rate of profit, which in this special case is equal to the rate interest on a secure loan. Wicksell treats "normal profits" as interest. There must be no other profit. Hence, for the equilibrium storage period t^* and the equilibrium value of wine x^*:

$$(3.2) \qquad\qquad x^* = we^{rt^*}$$

Each firm attempts to maximize profits. Taking the derivative of (3.1) with respect to t and setting it equal to zero (with w, r as constants) one gets in equilibrium

$$(3.3) \qquad\qquad r = \frac{1}{x^*}\left(\frac{dx}{dt}\right)^*$$

The rate of interest is equal to the proportional increase (in the neighborhood of the equilibrium storage period) of the value of wine with respect to time. (Compare Jevons 1871:241.) One cannot know whether (3.3) gives a condition for the maximization of profits until one examines the second derivative of (3.1). Wicksell specifies that the second derivative of $x - we^{rt}$ is everywhere less than zero:

(3.4)
$$\frac{d^2x}{dt^2} - \frac{1}{x}\left(\frac{dx}{dt}\right)^2 < 0$$

This is a reasonable stipulation. All that Wicksell requires is that the value of wine increase less than geometrically with its age. One can thus reasonably expect that profits can be maximized. Letting k be the equilibrium value of capital, one gets finally:

(3.5)
$$k = w \int_0^{t^*} e^{rt}\, dt = \frac{x^* - w}{r}$$

(3.6)
$$x^* = rk + w$$

(3.6) says that the value of the wine is equal to the payments for the grape juice plus the interest payments.

There are five variables in the model: x^*, w, r, t^*, and k, but only three independent relations besides the unspecified equation relating the value of the wine to its age. There is thus a degree of freedom and no account of what determines the rate of interest. J. Hirschleifer suggests that the system should be closed by introducing time-preference (1966–67:191–99). Wicksell draws a graph (Fig. 3.1).

Wicksell has plotted the log of the value of the wine and of the compounded value of the grape juice against time. (3.4) says that the log x curve is concave. (3.2) asserts that for any equilibrium period of storage that the log x and the log $w + rt$ curves intersect. (3.3) demands that the two curves be tangent at the point of intersection [recall that $(d\log x/dt) = (1/x)(dx/dt)$]; k is an increasing function of the trapezoid $[(0, \log w), (t^*, x^*), (t^*, 0), (0, 0)]$.

One can now determine directly from the graph that a longer equilibrium period of storage, t^*, goes with a higher price of grape juice, w, a larger equilibrium value of wine, x^*, a larger value of capital, k, and a smaller rate of interest, r. The greater productivity of roundabout processes benefits the sellers of grape juice (workers and landlords). x^* reaches a maximum when $r = 0$. The model does not specify whether for any finite t^* r will be zero and x^* reach a maximum. It is, for example, consistent with (3.1)–(3.6) to add the equation $r = 1/t^{*2}$ or the equation $r = (1/t^{*2} - 1/10,000)$.

Wicksell can now examine the relations between the apparent marginal product of capital, dx/dk and the rate of interest. Differentiating (3.6) with respect to k, he finds

(3.7)
$$\frac{dx}{dk} = r + k\frac{dr}{dk} + \frac{dw}{dk}$$

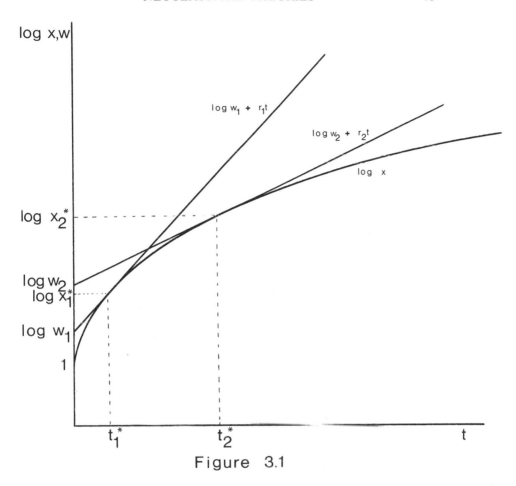

Figure 3.1

The apparent marginal product of capital is equal to the rate of interest plus the increased value of grape juice minus the decreased interest payments. In this model the rate of interest is larger than the apparent marginal product of capital.[2]

The relations in this simple model are as the Austrian theory says they should be. Let us briefly review and classify the assumptions of the model. Most are common in neoclassical or "equilibrium" models (see ch. 6, §2). Wicksell assumes that there are competitive conditions, that agents are price takers, that markets clear, that capital is mobile,

---

[2] Differentiating (3.2) with respect to t^* and using (3.3), one finds that $dw/dt^* = -wt^* dr/dt^*$. Differentiating (3.6) with respect to t^* and employing this last result, one finds, instead of (3.7) that $dx/dk = r + (k - wt^*)dr/dk$. We can see from (3.5) that k is larger than wt^*; dx/dk is thus smaller than r.

that commodities are infinitely divisible and that agents are perfectly informed. Furthermore, he assumes the "laws" that equilibrium is reached and that firms attempt to maximize profits. There are only three special assumptions : (1) The input of grape juice is fixed. (2) $dx/dt > 0$. (3) $(d^2\log x/dt^2) < 0$. (2) is a particular instance of Böhm-Bawerk's "law of roundaboutness" that increasing the waiting in production increases the value of the product. If we regard time as an input, (3) is a special instance of the "law" of diminishing returns to a variable input into production with other inputs held constant. (1) is just a simplification. The model shows that these assumptions entail (i) that r is the marginal product of the period of storage, (ii) that r is smaller while k and w are larger when that period is longer, (iii) that capital is not an independent factor of production, and (iv) that the apparent marginal product of capital is not equal to the rate of interest. The last implication can be disputed. It will be discussed further in chapter 4, §2.

The assumptions and theorems of the model should now be clear. What is not clear is what, if anything, Wicksell has accomplished by presenting the model. To understand the significance of the model demands some careful philosophical discussion.

3. Models and Theories in Economics

What has Wicksell accomplished? He has written a mathematical fairy tale incorporating the claims of the Austrian theory of capital. As fairy tales go, his is unexciting. What is the point of the exercise?

My answer will be roundabout (and thus, I hope more productive). Wicksell has developed a particular kind of model. To understand precisely what he has done, we must first understand what economic models are. There is, however, no way to understand the structure and significance of economic models without a definite conception of scientific theories. To appreciate the peculiarities of economic models we need to understand what theories are and what roles they play in science.

My view of theories and models is controversial. One way to evaluate my philosophical analysis is to employ it in case studies and to see how well it "works." As we shall see, my view of theories and models not only helps one to understand directly and simply how economists theorize, but it also refines and clarifies philosophical questions about this theorizing. I shall not argue that my view of theories and models is in general the only correct one. I claim merely that this conception simplifies and clarifies this philosophical inquiry into theories of capital and interest. The distinctions I shall need can be made in different terminology. Other conceptions of theories and models could have been employed, but they would have been further removed from economists' conceptions of their own work and they would have complicated the discussion.

My analysis of theories and models relies on the conception of scientific theories suggested by Patrick Suppes (1957, ch. 12). See also Sneed (1971) and Stegmueller (1979). In outline Suppes proposes that we regard scientific theories as *predicates*. The empirical claims of science consist of assertions that such predicates are true of actual systems. Suppes insists that scientific theories are *set-theoretic* predicates, because he hopes to provide formal restatements of scientific theories. Since I am doubtful about the prospects and merits of this program, I do not insist that theories be set-theoretic predicates. Once one drops the talk of set theory, the core of Suppes' conception of scientific theories can be presented very simply.[3] Giere (1979, ch. 5) provides just such a simplified presentation.

Giere takes scientific theories to be definitions of predicates, not to be predicates themselves, a difference not important here. Newton's laws of motion and his law of gravitation define, for example, what Giere calls "a classical particle system." The predicate, "is a classical particle system," is true of something if and only if Newton's laws of motion and of gravitation are true of it. On Giere's view of scientific theories, the basic claims of the Austrian theory of capital define a new predicate, "is an Austrian economy," or a new kind of system, "an Austrian economy." An economy is (at a time) an Austrian economy if and only if the basic assumptions of the Austrian theory of capital are true of it at that time.

On this view of scientific theories, there is no point to asking whether the claims of a theory are true or whether a theory provides reliable predictions. Mere predicates cannot be true or false or provide any predictions. Definitions are trivially true but also do not enable us to make any predictions.

Science, of course, does more than provide definitions. The proposing of scientific theories is, on this view, only one part of the theoretical enterprise. The other crucial part is the proposing of *theoretical hypotheses*, which assert that the new term is true of some actual system. In Giere's view, Newton's laws of motion and his law

---

[3] For a formal application to neoclassical economics of Sneed's conception of scientific theories see Händler (1980).

of gravitation only define a "classical particle system." Newton, however, did more. He also offered the theoretical hypothesis that the solar system is a classical particle system. The Austrian theorists similarly offered the theoretical hypothesis that actual competitive economies are (approximately) Austrian economies. We accommodate the conviction that theories say something about the world by dividing "theories" in some intuitive sense into *theories* (predicates or definitions of predicates) and theoretical hypotheses which employ these new predicates.

Although this account of scientific theories may appear cumbersome, it is useful in understanding the theoretical work of economists. First, however, I shall introduce a crucial terminological change. What Giere and Suppes call a "theory," I shall call a "model." I shall then use the term "theory" for something else. It is generally a bad idea to change terminology in this way, but I think in this case that the change is worth the dangers of confusion: I shall not only be better able to match the usage of economists, but I shall also be able to capture the intuition that theories say something about the world. Suppes in fact admits that scientists frequently use the term "model" as I shall, to mean what he means by "theory" (1957:254). Giere argues that the term "model" is in one of its senses more or less a synonym for "theory" (1979:81). I think that it clarifies matters to reserve the term "theory" for another use. Models define kinds of systems. The sentences in models, which I shall call "assumptions," are merely clauses in such definitions. It is a mistake to ask whether an assumption in a model is true or whether a model itself is true. We test theoretical hypotheses, not models.

Economists use the term "model" in many ways (Machlup 1960:569). Although some economic models are also models in other senses of the term, I know of none in theoretical economics which cannot be characterized as a predicate or as a definition of a predicate. Taking models as definitions permits one to develop an interesting and cogent interpretation of the nature and significance of economic models. Note that in philosophical and mathematical discussions of this century the term "model" has a different meaning. Philosophical discussions of models in this other sense of the term are of little use to economists or to philosophers interested in economic models.

The following two definitions summarize the discussion thus far:

A *model* is a predicate or a definition of a predicate (or of a kind of system). It is made up of assumptions.
A *theoretical hypothesis* states that the new predicate defined by a model is true of something.

Using models and theoretical hypotheses, economists can make claims about the world. In defining "an Austrian economy" by means of the claims of the Austrian model of capital and interest and offering the theoretical hypothesis that the United States has always been an Austrian economy, one can conclude, for example, that in the United States more roundabout production processes have always been more productive. One can infer from a theoretical hypothesis what I shall call "closures" of the assumptions of the model. The model Giere calls a "classical particle system" contains, for example, the assumption that any two bodies attract one another with a force inversely proportional to the square of the distance between them. The assumption does not say what it applies to. From the theoretical hypothesis that the solar system is a classical particle system, one can infer the "closure" of the assumption—that any two bodies in the solar system attract one another with a force inversely proportional to the square of the distance between them. In the closure of the assumption the domain is specified and in some cases the interpretation of the predicates in the assumption is limited or sharpened. From a theoretical hypothesis one in a sense "recovers" the assumptions of the model. A theoretical hypothesis entails the closures of all the assumptions of the model. Closures of assumptions are genuine statements which may be true or false.

Some theoretical hypotheses state that a particular real-world system, like the solar system, belongs to the extension of the predicate defined by the model. When a theoretical hypothesis is such a singular statement, I shall call the resulting set of closures of the assumptions of the model an *applied theory*. It is a theory of the particular individual hunk of the world referred to in the theoretical hypothesis. Philosophers are sometimes attracted to the predicate view of models (called in the literature "theories") because they seek to avoid judging general theoretical claims to be either true or false. On the predicate view of models one can apparently avoid judging whether Newton's law of gravitation, for example, is a universal law. Instead one considers whether it is true of particular ensembles of bodies.

Although one might employ a predicate view of models in attempting to avoid judging the truth of general theoretical statements, one need not use the predicate view of models in this way. Someone who claims that we do not need to consider whether Newton's law of gravitation, for example, is truly a universal law invites two critical questions. Why do scientists confidently employ the law in domains in which they have not tested it? How can one rationalize the *general* judgments scientists make concerning at least the *usefulness* of the purported law? I find these criticisms persuasive. In my view scientists *can* offer not only singular theoretical hypotheses ("The solar system is a classical particle system") but general theoretical hypotheses ("Everything is a classical particle system"). The distinction between singular and general theoretical hypotheses does not, however, capture precisely the distinction between general laws and a regularity in an individual system only, since the latter distinction is not a formal one. There are many difficult questions here that deserve further philosophical discussion. The only point I insist on is that theoretical hypotheses are not restricted to singular claims about individual systems and that the closures of assumptions they imply may be general laws. Adopting a view of models as predicates or as definitions of predicates does not itself commit one to any thesis concerning the aims of science or whether general theoretical claims may be true.

A theory is thus a set of assertions systematically related to one another which is derivable from a theoretical hypothesis. Equivalent reformulations of the assertions do not count as theory changes. If the theoretical hypothesis mentions only a particular system, we have an applied theory. If our theoretical hypothesis is universal (and our model does not itself mention spatiotemporal particulars), we have a pure or a general theory.

Let me summarize schematically. A model consists of a set of assumptions, $A_1, \ldots, A_n$. These assumptions define a new predicate, M. A theoretical hypothesis, H, is a statement like "X is an M" where X refers to something and M is the predicate defined by the model. From H one may deduce the set of statements $A_1^H, \ldots, A_n^H$, where A_i^H is the closure by H of the ith assumption of the model. The set of statements $A_1^H, \ldots, A_n^H$ is a theory.

4. Special Case Models

Given my definition of a "model," we can see that Wicksell's story about aging wine is a rather special kind of model. The sort of system it defines, an Austrian wine sector, is quite specific and extremely unrealistic. Any theoretical hypothesis asserting that a certain portion of an economy is an Austrian wine sector will be false. Yet, it is not only the falsity of theoretical hypotheses that distinguishes Wicksell's model from more usual scientific models: It is also an example or a description of a special case.

Special case models, like general theoretical models, can be regarded as predicates or as definitions of predicates. They have, however, their own peculiarities. Whether a model is a special case model depends on its relations to others and on how it is used. In special case models, various features of a more general theory or model are simplified and made less general and more vivid. The resulting model is used particularly for illustrating or evaluating the more general model. Special case models can be used both to support and to contest general models. A set of assumptions constitutes a special case model only if it simplifies and specifies the features of some more general model. In presenting a special case model, economists sometimes invite us, as Wicksell implicitly does, to believe that the assumptions of the model are true in some possible economic circumstances.

It is especially appropriate to call special case models "models," because they resemble descriptions of the actual physical models that scientists and engineers often build. Just as one can illustrate, develop, teach, and test general claims about the properties of airplanes by means of scale models, so one can illustrate, develop, teach, and test general claims about properties of economies by means of special case economic models.

To claim that economists can use special case models to illustrate, develop and teach general principles should not be controversial. All sciences employ models in these heuristic ways. Unless, like Duhem (1906, ch. 4), one sees this practice as evidence of a weak English mind, one should not object to the heuristic use of special case models. This role is of great importance. Integrating the Austrian theory of capital with the general neoclassical (equilibrium) approach to economics is quite difficult. Models like Wicksell's are a beginning. The implications of the claim that increased roundaboutness increases the product are not obvious. One can employ simple models like Wicksell's to see what the implications would be were its assumptions true. Examples like aging wine help one to appreciate the plausibility of the suggestion that "waiting" contributes to production. Wicksell's model certainly possesses heuristic virtues.

Philosophers have, however, contested the claim that special case models can be used to test or to provide evidence for theoretical claims. Since models are only predicates or definitions of predicates they are not themselves tests or evidence or anything. Special case models can, however, be used as part of reports of imaginary experiments. If one asserts that the assumptions of the model are true in some possible economic circumstances or that they could be true, one can regard the assumptions of the model and their implications as describing results of an imaginary experiment. When employed to report the results of an imaginary experiment, can special case models help one to test or to confirm general theoretical claims?

Carl Hempel, for one, thinks not. He points out that perfectly plausible, but entirely misleading imaginary experiments have been used in the past. He concludes, "Such experiments, then, cannot provide evidence pertinent to the test of sociological hypotheses. At best, they can serve a heuristic function: they may *suggest* hypotheses, which must then be subjected, however, to appropriate objective tests" (1965:165). By parity of reasoning, scientists ought never to rely on actual experiments, because they have been misleading, too. That imaginary experiments may mislead does not show that they have no evidential force.

Can one apply special case models to provide evidence that theoretical hypotheses employing the relevant general model are true? This question is particularly important for our purposes, since theoretical discussion and debate concerning capital and interest constantly employ special case models (see Dewey 1965, ch. 1). J. E. Cairnes, in contrast to Hempel, is quite unreserved about evidential applications of special case models. "There is, however, an inferior substitute for this powerful instrument [experiment] at his [the economist's] disposal, on which it may be worth while here to say a few words. I refer to the employment of hypothetical cases framed with a view to the purpose of economic inquiry. For, although precluded from actually producing the conditions suited to his purpose, there is nothing to prevent the economist from bringing such conditions before his mental vision, and from reasoning as if these only were present, while some agency comes into operation . . . the economic character of which he desires to examine" (1888:90).

Can we agree with Cairnes? Is it ever rational to rely on such special case models to support general hypotheses? I think so. We can at least grant, as Popper does (1968:442–56), that such models may have a *critical* function. One can use them to demonstrate that some more general model is inconsistent or that a theoretical hypothesis employing it conflicts with prior beliefs. One can employ special case models to point out possibilities previously overlooked. Furthermore, it seems to me that applications of such models may confirm theoretical hypotheses. The theoretical hypothesis that Wicksell's wine and grape juice model is true of some possible economic sector bears much the same relationship to the Austrian theory of capital that descriptions of experimental results bear to theoretical hypotheses. If one is prepared to assert that some possible economic sector is roughly a wine and grape juice sector, one has found in this possibility, in this imaginary experiment, an instance of Böhm-Bawerk's "law" of roundaboutness. One sees that the claims of the Austrian theory match in this instance what economists already expect. If, like many economists, one believes that in simple economic circumstances a larger value of capital will (other things being equal) go with a lower rate of interest, one can use Wicksell's model to test Böhm-Bawerk's law against this belief. One is not acquiring new beliefs about the world in the course of having new experiences. Instead one is learning about the logical relations between prior beliefs, simplifying assumptions, and a new hypothesis. It is thus misleading to speak of such applications of simple case models as a substitute for experiments. They are quite different. The special case model is being used to show that the implications of the theory being considered match the economist's prior beliefs. Economists can use such models to check the consistency of the propositions of the theory with accepted beliefs.

Although we can thus see that it is rational to invoke special case models to help criticize or confirm general theoretical claims, we can also understand why this practice makes philosophers like Hempel uneasy. So long as one contests or defends theories in only this way, one's theorizing is not directly subject to control by experience. Empiricist philosophers and economists want more than consistent beliefs. They want beliefs that are supported by observations and experiments.

Empiricists do not, however, need to reject the use of special case models when assessing theories. When economists measure their theories against their prior beliefs, they may be confronting their theories indirectly with the results of observations. The prior beliefs may be well confirmed. If the relations between the prior beliefs and the observations which support them are very simple, the theoretical hypothesis applying the special case model would virtually be an account of past experiments. One's belief that Wicksell's assumptions are true of some simple cases is not, however, directly related to observations or experiments. One thus has grounds to be skeptical concerning the evidential force of theoretical hypotheses applying special case models like Wicksell's. Yet, insofar as one is justified in believing that such a model does sometimes apply, one has evidence for the theory under consideration. We shall have to return to this topic later when we consider what role ideology has played in capital theory. The accepted beliefs economists rely on in using special case models for theory assessment may carry ideological distortions.

5. Wood and Axes: The Basic Model

Wicksell also developed a more complicated model in his treatment of Åkerman's problem (1911:274f). A point input of labor produces a capital good. The combined use of labor and the capital good during the lifetime of the capital good yields a continuous output of the consumption good. With two commodities and two sectors Wicksell's treatment of Åkerman's problem allows one to consider more of the difficulties of capital theory. I shall not, however, present Wicksell's model here. A much simpler, more versatile, and more interesting model proposed by Oskar Lange (1935–36:159–92) captures the important features of Wicksell's two-sector model (see the appendix to this chapter).

Lange's model is important to my exposition. In discussing general equilibrium theory in chapter 5 and Sraffa's work in Chapter 8 I will present special case models which are variants of Lange's model. I will use the various special case models to clarify the relations between the different theories of capital and interest. I will thus be proposing and using special case economic models to discuss general economic models. The function of the models in this book are expository and illustrative. I shall not rely on any of the features peculiar to the special cases to argue for or against any general theoretical hypotheses concerning capital and interest.

In Lange's model there are two commodities: a capital good (axes) and a consumption good (wood). Axes are used both in the production of axes and in the production of wood, while wood is not used in production at all. Both the production of axes and of wood takes one period (year). Although the period of production is not a variable in either sector, the roundaboutness of production is reflected in this simple model. Let x, m, and m' denote respectively the wood output and the quantity of axes used in the two sectors. $m + m'$ is the ax output. Lange assumes that all axes last exactly one year. Lange's model has two production functions, which are homogeneous of degree one with positive first partial derivatives, and, after a point, negative second partial derivatives.

(3.8) $x = f(m, L)$ (production function for wood)

(3.9) $m + m' = h(m', L')$ production function for axes)

where L and L' are the respective quantities of labor used in each sector. There is a constant and fully employed labor force. Thus:

(3.10)
$$L + L' = L^*$$

where L^* is a constant. If we let p_x be 1, maximizing profits in the wood sector gives:

(3.11)
$$p_m = f_m$$

(3.12)
$$w = f_L$$

where w and p_m are the wage and price of axes and f_m and f_L are the values of the partial derivatives of f with respect to ax and labor inputs when profits are maximized. Maximizing profit in the ax sector, one can derive

(3.13)
$$h_m = 1$$

(3.14)
$$w = h_L p_m$$

where h_m and h_L are the values of the partial derivatives of h when profits are maximized.

There are thus as many equations as unknowns and the system appears to solve. Lange does not himself set $p_x = 1$. He treats p_x as a variable and the model itself as having a degree of freedom (1935–36:172). It simplifies matters to take p_x as numeraire. Notice that there seems to be no room for interest (1935–36:172–73). Time preference is thus necessarily zero.

Interest enters Lange's model through a limitation on what Lange calls "money capital." Suppose that in the wood sector $mp_m + wL$ are in this stationary state limited for some reason, perhaps time preference, to some amount of $x = k^*$. Subject to the limitations on money capital k^* and (k'^* in the ax sector), one can again express the conditions for the maximization of profit:

(3.15)
$$p_m = \frac{f_m}{1 + i}$$

(3.16)
$$w = \frac{f_L}{1 + i}$$

(3.17)
$$(1 + i') = h_m$$

(3.18)
$$w = h_L \cdot \frac{p_m}{1 + i'}$$

where i and i' are Lagrange multipliers. (3.15)–(3.18) are the direct result of setting the partial derivatives of the two Lagrange functions equal to zero. If one assumes that there is a unified money market and just one economy-wide limit on money capital, $K^* = (k^* + k'^*)$, then, with the equalization of the rate of interest, $i = i' = (f_m h_{L'} - f_L)/f_L$, which is the rate of real interest or the real rate of return over the cost of transferring labor from the wood to the ax sectors. Notice that the interest is compounded on indirect labor: $w = h_{L'} \cdot p_m/(1 + i) = h_{L'} \cdot f_m/(1 + i)^2$.[4] Given the last equation, labor will be relatively cheaper in producing wood and more than the optimum quantity will be used. Thus the marginal productivity of direct labor and the wage will be lower because of the shortage of money capital.

Notice that, despite the fixed periods of production, Lange's model does support the Austrian view that capital is not an independent factor of production and that indirect processes are more productive. When money capital is scarce, less indirect and more direct labor per unit wood output will be used. Thus wood production is less time intensive than it is when money capital is abundant. The rate of interest is a steadily decreasing function of the time intensity as so construed. All the other relationships are as in Wicksell's treatment of Åkerman's problem. If time intensity is larger, w/p_m, K^*, m, L' and x are larger, while r is smaller. Furthermore (1935–36: 184), $x = rK^* + w(L + L')$. Thus

$$(3.19) \qquad \frac{dx}{dK^*} = r + L^* \frac{dw}{dK^*} + K^* \frac{dr}{dK^*}$$

The apparent marginal product of money capital divides itself into the rate of interest plus the marginal increase in wages minus the marginal decrease in interest payments. Thus one has the same relation as (3.7) above. The rate of interest is not equal to the marginal product of capital; it is not necessarily always larger or smaller than the apparent marginal product of money capital. Calculating a period of production is possible but messy, since axes are not made by unassisted labor. (See Dorfman 1959: esp.361–65).

A couple of words need to be said about demand and time preference. In the above I have tacitly assumed that one is dealing with a closed economy in which workers consume their wages and capitalists consume their profits. If profits are reinvested and there is no time pref-

---

[4] As Lange points out (1936–37:232), interest is also compounded on the indirect use of axes. Combine (3.15) and (3.17).

erence, the only stationary equilibrium is the state of maximum production and zero interest. Unless some quantity of profits is consumed, interest can only be a temporary phenomenon that reveals the shortage of money capital (and thus of waiting). Once one includes the consumption of capitalists and the variable factor of time preference, the shortage of money capital may be permanent. One can have an absolutely stationary state (like Marx's simple reproduction, 1967, vol. 2, ch. 20) with positive profits equal to the consumption of the capitalists.

6. The Austrian Theory

In order to assess the theory of capital sketched above, it is essential to state this theory explicitly. The following formulation is not refined, but it will serve. We can think of the basic statements of the theory as the following:

(3.20) Some general formulation of neoclassical equilibrium theory that does not itself provide any account of capital.

(3.21) Storing up the current services of land and labor increases their productivity at a decreasing rate.[5]

(3.22) Individuals prefer present consumption to future consumption.[6]

(3.23) The quantity of capital is measured by the quantity of services of land and labor stored up and the time during which they are stored. Capital is not an independent factor of production.[7]

(3.24) Interest is the return to this storing up or waiting.

(3.21) and (3.22) seem to be the fundamental "laws," while (3.23) and (3.24) define "capital" and "interest." The following are three important derivative claims:

(3.25) Interest is not the marginal product of capital.

---

[5] "On the whole it may be said that not only are the first steps more productive, but that every lengthening of the roundabout process is accompanied by a further increase in the technical result; as the process, however, is lengthened the amount of product, as a rule, increases in a smaller proportion" (Böhm-Bawerk 1888:84).

[6] Perishable commodities available only in certain seasons are the best known counterexamples.

[7] "Capital is an intermediate product of nature and labor, nothing more. Its own origin, its existence, its subsequent action, are nothing but stages in the continuous working of the true elements, nature and labour. They and they alone do everything from beginning to end in bringing consumption goods into existence" (Böhm-Bawerk 1888:96).

(3.26) The rate of interest is smaller when the time-intensity of production is larger.

(3.27) The quantity of wages and/or rent is larger when the roundabout-ness of production is greater.

Remember that in the above formulations we are comparing stationary states. (3.20)–(3.24), regarded as assumptions, define an Austrian competitive economy. The Austrian theorists believed that real economies are, to some degree of approximation, Austrian competitive economies. (3.20)–(3.24) can thus also be regarded as empirical generalizations true or false of actual economies.

The assumptions and implications of assumptions listed above are part of or consistent with the two models discussed. As roughly formulated above, the Austrian theory need not insist that waiting *is* precisely a factor of production, nor that interest is its marginal product, but only that larger stores of productive services involving more waiting are more productive and that interest results from the increased productivity to which waiting gives rise. The rate of interest is positive, because individuals prefer present consumption to future consumption and because roundabout processes of production are more productive.[8] Although I have not presented anything like a formalization of the Austrian theory of capital, its main claims and logical structure are clear enough that they can be assessed.

APPENDIX TO CHAPTER 3: Wicksell's and Lange's Austrian Models

Wicksell's treatment of Åkerman's problem (1911:274f) is designed to show that the claims of the Austrian theory of capital remain valid when one shifts to a more complicated time structure of production. In the model Wicksell presents, a point input of labor produces a capital

---

[8] Contrast these claims to Robinson's (1966:395). She argues that neither time preference nor the productivity of capital goods has much to do with profits, at least in modern economies. "Present purchasing power is valuable partly because under the capitalist rules of the game, it permits its owner . . . to employ labor and undertake production that will yield a surplus of receipts over costs. In an economy in which the rate of profit is expected to be positive, the rate of interest is positive. A positive rate of interest being established, for every individual owner of wealth the present value of purchasing power exceeds its future value to the corresponding extent. . . . This has nothing whatsoever to do with the subjective *rate of discount of the future* of the individual concerned, though it is true that a comparison between his subjective discount rate and the rate of interest obtainable may be said . . . to influence his savings habits."

good, axes, from which a continuous output of the consumption good, wood, is produced with the assistance of labor. The durability of axes is a function of the quantity of labor time it takes to produce them. Their efficiency is constant over their lifetime. Through some stipulations concerning cost and production functions and the labor force and some imprecise, but correct mathematical manipulations, Wicksell provides almost a complete specification of the simplified hypothetical wood and ax economy. One degree of freedom remains, but that might be eliminated, as J. Hirschleifer (1966–67) suggests, by including some role for time preference. Wicksell's model makes no reference to utility functions or to demand.

As a result of his various manipulations, Wicksell shows that, in stationary equilibrium states in which the equilibrium durability of axes, t^*, is larger, the labor input per ax, a, the output of wood, x, the wood wage, w, and the wood value of capital, K, are all larger. The rate of interest, r, and the (wood) rental cost for axes, b, are smaller. One thus finds, as the Austrian theory asserts, that increased roundaboutness goes with increased output, a higher wage, a lower rate of interest, and a larger value of capital. In this two-commodity model, we still find the so-called "Wicksell Effect." Part of the increase in capital is absorbed in higher wages; only part of it increases output. The rate of interest is generally larger than the marginal product of capital, although Wicksell notes the puzzling possibility that they may diverge in the opposite direction (1911:292–93). As in his simpler wine and grape juice model, Wicksell illustrates, elaborates, and perhaps even supports his general theory of capital by means of a mathematical model.

Yet certain features of the model are disquieting. With a larger equilibrium durability of axes, the distribution of the labor force between sectors and the distribution of income between interest and wages remain constant. Moreover, with a given technology and labor force, there is neither a maximum output nor a maximum feasible lifetime for axes. These results seem counterintuitive. One wants to know whether they are an implication of the Austrian theory for two-sector models generally. If so, it seems that Wicksell's wood and ax model would count *against* the Austrian theory of capital that he presents. Moreover, Wicksell's model has a feature that is of ideological importance: there is no possible stationary equilibrium in which the rate of interest is zero. Is it in fact impossible for interest to disappear?

None of the above counterintuitive or contestable conclusions can be derived when one replaces the particular cost function Wicksell employs with a more reasonable one. The model that results has important affinities to the model discussed in §5 and helps to see precisely the relationship between Lange's work and Wicksell's.

In a model that has one degree of freedom, we can consider the various economic variables as functions of some parameter, z. To simplify matters, Wicksell treats t^*, the lifetime of the axes produced in the given static equilibrium, as itself the parameter on which the other economic variables depend. What Wicksell does, which shortens the exposition at the cost of some mathematical clarity, is to take a, the input of labor per ax as a function of t^*, the equilibrium lifetime of the axes. The particular function he proposes, about which more will be said later, is:

$$(3.28) \qquad\qquad a = k\, t^{*v}$$

where k and v are positive constants with v less than 1; t^* is being used as a surrogate for some parameter upon which the static equilibrium depends, but a does *not* depend upon any specific equilibrium or, indeed, even on the existence of an economy. Let t be the lifetime of some given ax. Then (3.28') $a = k\, t^v$ expresses a technological fact wholly independent of any other features of the economy. If the given ax happens to have the lifetime t^*, then the value of a, for $t = t^*$, is $k\, t^{*v}$, but a is function of t, not of t^*. Similarly the discounted value of the rentals of an ax over its actual lifetime t is $(b/r)(1 - e^{-rt})$, where b and r are functions of the parameter t^*.

If the lifetime of the given ax, t, is equal to the equilibrium lifetime, t^*, then the price of an ax is $(b/r)(1 - e^{-rt^*})$. Zero profits in competitive equilibrium tells us that

$$(3.29) \qquad\qquad \frac{b(1 - e^{-rt^*})}{r} = wa.$$

Maximizing profits, $(b/r)(1 - e^{-rt}) - wkt^v$, with respect to t, we get as the first order condition:

$$(3.30) \qquad\qquad be^{-rt} = wkvt^{v-1}.$$

For $t = t^*$, we have (3.30') $be^{-rt^*} = wkvt^{*v-1}$.

From here on we can investigate the parametric dependence of the various variables on t^*. Although in stationary equilibrium the longevity of axes is taken as the parameter upon which the variables depend, the difference between a change in the longevity of axes and a change in the parameter upon which the variables depend should be kept clear. The same issue arises in the simpler wine and grape juice model, where it is important to distinguish between the parameter which determines which equilibrium one is in (which is taken to be the equilibrium storage period) and the time interval during which a certain batch of wine has aged.

The basic equations of Wicksell's model are the following eight:

$$(3.28) \qquad a = kt^{*v}$$

$$(3.29) \qquad \frac{b(1 - e^{-rt^*})}{r} = wa$$

$$(3.30'') \qquad e^{rt^*} = 1 + \frac{rt^*}{v}$$

$$(3.31) \qquad L + L' = L^*$$

$$(3.32) \qquad x = CL^c \left(\frac{L't^*}{a}\right)^d$$

$$(3.33) \qquad b = \frac{dxa}{L't^*}$$

$$(3.34) \qquad w = \frac{cx}{L}$$

$$(3.35) \qquad K = \frac{L'b(e^{-rt^*} - 1 + rt^*)}{ar^2}$$

(3.30") is a consequence of (3.29) and (3.30'). It implies that rt^* is a constant, which is a great mathematical convenience. L is the quantity of labor devoted to wood production, L', the quantity devoted to ax production. L^* is a constant. The wood production function is a Cobb-Douglas production function with c and d positive constants adding to 1. C is another positive constant. The wood and ax production processes require negligible time intervals. According to (3.33) and (3.34), ax rentals and wages are equal to the marginal products of axes and labor respectively in producing wood. The value of capital is obtained by integrating the value of the stock of axes of each age.

If we do not include the price of wood, which is taken as the numeraire (equal to one), there are nine variables, a, x, w, b, r, t^*, L, L' and K. There is thus one degree of freedom. Varying t^* parametrically, the results summarized earlier can be obtained straightforwardly. Those results support the general claims of the Austrian theory of capital.

Two special features of Wicksell's treatment of Åkerman's problem are primarily responsible for the more disquieting conclusions mentioned earlier: the Cobb-Douglas production function for wood and the particular cost function for axes. I shall not discuss the virtues and pitfalls of the Cobb-Douglas production function here. More interesting is Wicksell's cost function for producing axes, $a = kt^v$. Wicksell argues that this function should be considered as a general form of a cost function for capital goods (1911:288), but it is in fact quite counterintuitive. It specifies that more labor per ax is needed to produce more durable axes, but that as axes become more durable (no matter how durable they already are), it becomes easier (requires less additional labor) to make them last still longer. There is no limit to the durability of an ax, given a large enough labor input. I suggest replacing (3.28) and (3.28') above with

$$(3.28a) \qquad a = \frac{k}{N - t^*}$$

$$(3.28a') \qquad a = \frac{k}{N - t}$$

N here is a constant which is the limit of the possible durability of an ax with finite labor input; k is, as before, a positive constant. I make no general defense of (3.28a) as a cost function for capital goods, except to point out that it is more plausible than Wicksell's. Notice that da/dt is positive and that, until $t (= t^*) = \frac{1}{2}N$, t^* increases more than proportionally to a and thus that there would be a tendency for t^* to be larger in static equilibria in which there is a larger wood output. Equations (3.29) and (3.31)–(3.35) remain as before. (3.30″) changes as follows: Since $t^* = t$, one can derive from (3.28a') and (3.29)

$$(b/r)(1 - e^{-rt}) = wk(N - t).$$

Maximizing profit and substituting t^* for t, one gets,

$$be^{-rt^*} = wk(N - t^*)^2.$$

Substituting $wke^{rt^*}(N - t^*)^2$ for b in the first expression and rearranging, one derives:

$$(3.30a) \qquad e^{rt^*} = 1 + r(N - t^*).$$

Although the derivations involve some tedious calculus, it can be shown that, just as in Wicksell's model, x, K, w, and a are all larger when t^* is larger (provided t^* remains less than $\frac{1}{2}N$), while r and b are smaller (Hausman 1978:98–103).[9] On the other hand, there are three new results. When one compares static equilibria in which t^* is greater than $\frac{1}{2}N$, not all of the above relations still hold. With a given fixed

[9] The derivation in Hausman (1978:101–2) that purports to show that K must increase with t^* contains an error. A valid derivation follows. I shall not repeat the proof that dx/dt^* is positive, even though I use the result, since it is tedious and available in my (1978:100).

(a) First I shall show that $d(rt^*)/dt^*$ is negative for $t^* < \frac{1}{2}N$.

(1) let $u = rt^*$, $n = \dfrac{N}{t^*}$

(2) $e^u = 1 + u(n - 1)$ (1), (3.30a)

(3) $\dfrac{du}{dn} = \dfrac{u}{(e^u + 1 - n)}$ differentiating (2)

(4) $\dfrac{du}{dn} = \dfrac{u}{e^u + 1 - (1/u)(e^u + u - 1)}$ (2), (3)

(5) $\dfrac{du}{dn} = \dfrac{u^2}{(ue^u - e^u + 1)}$ (4)

(6) let $g(u) = ue^u - e^u + 1$

   $g(0) = 0; \quad \dfrac{dg}{du} > 0$ if $u > 0$

   hence $g(u) > 0$ if $u > 0$

(7) $\dfrac{du}{dn} > 0$ if $u > 0$ (5), (6)

(8) if $n > 2$, $e^u = 1 + u(n - 1)$ has a positive solution for u use Taylor's expansion or graph

(9) $\dfrac{du}{dn} > 0$ if $n > 2$ (7), (8)

(10) $n > 2$ if and only if $t^* < \frac{1}{2}N$ (1)

(11) $\dfrac{dn}{dt^*} < 0$ (1)

labor force and a given technology there is, as one would expect, a maximum output which is reached when capital goods are plentiful and the rate of interest is zero. This is the case when $t^* = \frac{1}{2}N$. Second, L' (the labor used in producing capital goods) increases with t^*. The proportion of the worker population employed in the consumer goods industry is smaller when capital goods are more durable (and capital or waiting is more abundant). As t^* approaches $\frac{1}{2}N$, L/L' approaches c/d. Third, the distribution of income between wages and interest is no longer constant. rK/wL^* is a monotonic decreasing function of t^*, reaching zero when $t^* = \frac{1}{2}N$. Thus the existence of a Cobb-Douglas production function for consumption goods does not itself insure constant factor shares. A simulation is provided at the end of the appendix.

The modified Wicksellian model bears a close relationship to Lange's model presented in §5 and clarifies the relationship between Lange's and Wicksell's work. The major relations among the parameters are the same. The only striking differences between Lange's model and the modified version of Wicksell's are that in the latter axes are still

---

(12) $\dfrac{d(rt^*)}{dt^*} < 0$ if $t^* < \frac{1}{2}N$ (9), (10), (11), (1)

(b)   Now to show that $\dfrac{dK}{dt^*} > 0$

(13) $K = \dfrac{L'b(e^{-rt^*} - 1 + rt^*)}{ar^2}$ (3.35)

(14) $b = \dfrac{dxa}{L't^*}$ (3.33)

(15) $\dfrac{1}{d}\dfrac{K}{x} = \dfrac{e^{-u} - 1 + u}{ru}$ (1), (13), (14)

(16) $D_{t^*}\left(\dfrac{1}{d}\dfrac{K}{x}\right)$ differentiating (15) and rearranging

$$= \dfrac{r(1 - e^{-u} - ue^{-u})\dfrac{du}{dt^*} + u(1 - u - e^{-u})\dfrac{dr}{dt^*}}{r^2u^2}$$

(17) $e^u = 1 + rN - u$ (1), (3.30a)

(18) $\dfrac{dr}{dt^*} = \dfrac{e^u + 1}{N}\dfrac{du}{dt^*}$ differentiating (17)

produced by unassisted labor and are of variable durability. There are three points to be made concerning these differences.

(1) Money capital is abundant in Lange's model when it is equal to the value of the maximal products of both sectors, while in the modified Wicksellian model, the total capital when r is zero (if one assumes, as in Lange's model, a one-year production period for axes and wood) is the maximum total product plus $L't^*p_m/2a = L't^{*2}b/2a$—the value of the stock of axes. Much more "accumulation" is needed before r is zero. Lange's model understates the contrasts between stationary equilibria where money capital is scarce and those where it is abundant.

(2) If there is any factor which upsets the equilibrium position, adjustment appears more difficult and time-consuming in the modification of Wicksell's two-sector model than in Lange's.

(3) The greater realism of Lange's model—its avoidance of the use of unassisted labor in the production of capital goods—is a considerable advantage. Realism here comes with a bonus rather than a cost in terms of applicability and simplicity.

---

(19) Let $F = Nr^2u^2D_{t^*}\left(\dfrac{1}{d}\dfrac{K}{x}\right)$

(20) $F = [rN(1 - e^{-u} - ue^{u})$ (16), (18), (19)

       $+ \quad u(1 - u - e^{-u})(e^u + 1)]\dfrac{du}{dt^*}$

(21) $F = [(e^u + u - 1)(1 - e^{-u} - ue^{-u})$ (20), (17)

       $+ \quad u(1 - u - e^{-u})(e^u + 1)]\dfrac{du}{dt^*}$

(22) $F = [(1 - u^2)(e^u + e^{-u})$ (21)

       $+ \quad u(e^u - e^{-u}) - (u^2 + 2)]\dfrac{du}{dt^*}$

(23) $F = 2\left[\displaystyle\sum_{j=1}^{\infty} \dfrac{u^{2j+2}(1 - 4j - 4j^2)}{(2j + 2)!}\right]\dfrac{du}{dt^*}$ (22) adding the Taylor's series

(24) $F > 0$ for $t^* < \frac{1}{2}N$ (23), (12), (1)

(25) $\dfrac{dx}{dt^*} > 0$ for $t^* < \frac{1}{2}N$ Hausman 1978.100.

(26) $\dfrac{dK}{dt^*} > 0$ for $t^* < \frac{1}{2}N$ (19), (24), (25)

On the whole, it seems to me that, having modified Wicksell's treatment of Åkerman's problem in order to avoid its implausible and unfounded implications, one might as well drop Wicksell's model altogether unless one is particularly concerned with questions of variable durability (see Solow 1961). If one still wants to make use of a two-sector Austrian model, one can, I think, more profitably employ Lange's work. While seeking better theoretical tools, economists in need of a good two-sector model for investigations of the effects of different durability of one's capital stock may still find Wicksell useful. For other investigations, they are well-advised to pass over Wicksell's treatment of Åkerman's problem and turn instead to Lange's simpler and more versatile presentation.

Table 3.1 Simulation of the Modified Wicksellian Model
$N = 100; \quad c = 1/4; \quad L^* = 1000$

t^*	r	L	L'	$x[(k)^d/C]$	$w[(k)^d/C]$	$b[1/C(k)^c]$	$K[(k)^d/C]$
5	.89	600	400	45,000	18.8	.177	29,500
10	.35	546	454	78,000	35.7	.143	121,000
15	.19	502	498	106,000	52.8	.125	280,000
20	.12	468	532	130,000	69.4	.115	505,000
25	.077	427	573	152,000	89	.106	818,000
30	.050	392	608	169,000	108	.0994	1,220,000
35	.032	357	643	183,000	128	.0933	1,710,000
40	.019	322	678	193,000	150	.0886	2,280,000
45	.0086	287	713	199,000	173	.0847	2,960,000

CHAPTER FOUR
The Cambridge Criticisms of Neoclassical Capital Theory

The Austrian theory may be ingenious, but is it true? Can one, for example, explain in part why real wages increased steadily in the United States from the end of World War II until the late 1960s by pointing to an increase in the average period of production? Is the rate of interest determined by preferences for present consumption and the larger productivity of more time-intensive production processes? Apart from illustrative special cases, we have not yet seen any evidence. Most orthodox economists believe that there is *something* to the story the Austrians tell about the relations between time, interest, and capital. Theorists have from time to time articulated and defended certain aspects of the theory.[1] Yet there is little evidence for its truth, and many distinguished neoclassical economists have criticized it harshly.[2]

Before turning to general equilibrium models and the alternative neoclassical approach to capital and interest, I shall consider some recent criticisms of explicit theories of capital and interest like Clark's or the Austrian theory. The issues I shall discuss are the subject matter of a now dead controversy between critics of neoclassical theory (most of whom were associated with Cambridge University) and defenders (whose chief spokesmen were associated with MIT). Thus the controversy was appropriately labeled "The Cambridge Controversy." The main points in the controversy were settled by 1966 with the critics carrying the day, although the significance of the criticisms is still disputed.[3]

---

[1] For example Kaldor (1937), Hayek (1941), Dorfman (1959; 1959–60), Solow (1961), and Hicks (1973).

[2] Especially Knight (1936–37, 1938). Hayek (1941) is as much a critique as a development of the Austrian theory. Metzler (1950) and Lerner (1953) are sympathetic critics.

[3] The literature on the Cambridge Controversy is by now immense. Listed below are those contributions that are most interesting or important with respect to the issues that

Beginning with Robinson (1953–54), a number of economists, most of whom have had some association with Cambridge University, have enunciated criticisms, of neo-classical theories of capital, interest and economic growth.[4] I shall not consider the theory of growth. This restriction conceals some of the motivation for economists' concern with production functions and the theory of capital and interest, but it will not distort the theoretical issues. The Cambridge economists do not espouse a uniform doctrine. Neither do they all criticize the same aspects of neoclassical theory. Nevertheless, it is fair to identify them as a school, since they make use of similar analytical techniques and since almost all look to Marx and Ricardo for inspiration.

Some of the Cambridge critics believe that their work reveals the bankruptcy of the whole neoclassical approach to economic theory. Most neoclassical theorists believe, on the other hand, that the Cambridge critics have mistaken the inadequacies of certain parables or simplifications for flaws in fundamental theory. If the critics are right, they have largely overturned established economic theory. If the defenders are right, the critics have merely seized on superficial difficulties. To assess the Cambridge controversy, several different questions must be addressed. In this chapter I shall ask, "What flaws in explicit neoclassical theories of capital and interest like the Austrian theory have the Cambridge critics revealed?" In Chapters 5 and 6 I shall consider how theories like the Austrian theory fit into neoclassical theorizing and whether other kinds of neoclassical theory avoid the Cambridge criticisms. Showing that these other (general equilibrium) theories avoid the Cambridge criticisms does not, however, close the discussion, since general equilibrium theories have their own problems. The critics, whose work I consider in this chapter, look to Sraffa's work as a foundation for their own. This foundation will be developed and assessed in chapters 8 and 9. Only at the end of this book will we be fully able to judge the force of the Cambridge criticisms.

I shall be considering. For further bibliography and for extensive discussion see Blaug (1975) and Harcourt (1975a). Other contributions are Bhaduri (1966, 1969), Bliss (1970), Bruno, et al. (1966), Champernowne (1953–54), Collard (1973), Dixit (1977), Dougherty (1972), Ferguson and Nell (1972), Garegnani (1966, 1970), Hahn (1975), Harcourt (1969, 1975b, 1975c, 1976, 1977), Laibman and Nell (1977), Morishima (1966), Pasinetti (1966, 1969, 1970, 1972), Robinson (1953–54, 1966), Samuelson (1961–62, 1966), Sen (1974), Solow (1963, 1967, 1970), Stiglitz (1974), Yeager (1976). Two collections of relevant articles are Harcourt and Laing (1971) and Hunt and Schwartz (1972). Other relevant articles will be mentioned in chapters 8 and 9 in connection with my discussion of Sraffa's work.

[4] The principal economists are Robinson, Pasinetti, Garegnani, Kaldor, Nuti, Harcourt, Dobb, Eatwell, Bhaduri and Nell.

1. Outline of the Criticisms

The Cambridge critics have been dissatisfied with many different aspects of neoclassical economic theory. Robinson (1953–54) accused neoclassical theorists of misusing stationary equilibrium analysis. Her criticism was cogent and forceful. Yet few other participants in the Cambridge Controversy have been concerned with whether economists should compare stationary states. Apart from growth theory, there have, I think, been three major objects of criticism: (1) neoclassical applications of aggregate production functions, (2) neoclassical theories of the relations between capital, interest, and exchange values, and (3) neoclassical theories of the distribution of income. These three objects are not completely distinct, but the division helps in deciding where the various Cambridge critics are aiming their critical arrows and whether they hit their mark.[5] One warning to avoid later misunderstanding: the controversy has focused on extremely unrealistic comparisons of different stationary states in which the production *possibilities* are identical, but in which, because of the differences in wages, different production *processes* or *techniques* are employed. The special case models discussed are of no practical interest. They are only important for the light they shed on economic theory.

Much of the Cambridge criticism has been directed to the use of aggregate production functions in empirical and historical studies. I have already referred to Solow's use of such a function (1957:312–30). In an aggregate production function total output is regarded as a function of a few aggregate variables, such as land, labor, capital, or time. Robinson (1953–54:81, 90) and Pasinetti (1969) object, however, that factors of production are not easily substitutable for one another and that the proportions in which factors are available are less important in explaining output or the distribution of income than neoclassical economists suggest. One cannot use less of some malleable stuff called "capital" in production and compensate by employing more of some homogeneous stuff called "labor." Changes in factor proportions are changes in the technology employed. They are expensive, time-consuming, and have broad economic effects. One can provide simple hypothetical examples in which such discreteness of technologies limits the validity of neoclassical results (Pasinetti 1969:520–23).

The Cambridge economists have also objected explicitly to including

---

[5] In this chapter I shall not discuss separately criticisms of neoclassical theories of the distribution of income. Some of these criticisms follow directly from points I shall discuss. Others rely on Sraffa's work and are best considered later in Chapters 8 and 9.

the quantity of capital as an argument in an aggregate production function. In denying that output should be regarded as a function of the quantity of capital, where the quantity of capital is a quantity of value, the Cambridge critics echo Böhm-Bawerk, Wicksell, and Lange. Capital is not an input into production. Differentiating an aggregate production function with respect to the quantity of capital does not tell one what the marginal contribution of capital to production is, since capital makes no contribution at all. The apparent marginal product does not equal the rate of interest and does not help one to understand the distribution of income. On all these points the Cambridge theorists are at one with the Austrian theorists. The reasons for these conclusions differ, however. The Cambridge critics agree that capital is not an input into production whose cost is interest, because they do not believe that there are any inputs into production apart from various resources, labor, and capital goods and because they believe that interest is not a cost at all. They are thus no better disposed to an Austrian aggregate production function with time as a variable than they are to more common aggregate production functions. Austrian aggregate production functions are seldom encountered and rarely discussed, because they are not suitable for most empirical studies.

Objections to aggregate production functions thus lead directly to objections to neoclassical theories of the relations between capital, interest, and exchange values. If the Cambridge criticisms were only directed to particular aggregate production functions or with production functions which involve smooth substitutability, the criticisms would not strike deeply at neoclassical economic theory. The aggregate production function is at best a useful device to answer empirical questions. Contemporary theory can dispense with continuous differentiable production functions. Modern linear programming techniques can even replace such functions in practice. To explain interest as the cost of waiting or of capital does not require that one make use of any aggregate production functions.

Criticisms of neoclassical accounts of the relations between capital, interest, and exchange values go deeper. Both Clark's theory and the Austrian theory assert that interest is the return to a scarce element in production. Expanding on a curiosity noticed by Ruth Cohen in the early 1950s and discussed by Sraffa in 1960, the Cambridge critics have provided perfectly plausible special case models with no technological innovations in which the rate of interest—at all but its lowest values— is an *increasing* function of the value of capital. It seems that without technological change capital can be more abundant and yet command a higher rate of interest. This possibility implies that at least one of the following four claims must be false:

(1) Capital is a factor of production.
(2) The value of capital is a measure of its quantity.
(3) The apparent marginal productivity of capital is a decreasing function of its quantity.
(4) The rate of interest is an increasing function of the marginal productivity of capital.

If all of these claims are true, a higher value of capital must go with a lower rate of interest. Since the Austrian theorists have already challenged (1) and (2) and have shown how (4) could be false, one might wonder whether the Cambridge critics have added anything. If one examines their arguments, however, one finds that they apply equally to the Austrian theory. Indeed, the Cambridge criticisms apply to any theory that associates capital with some single aspect of production. In the next two sections I shall develop these criticisms.

2. The Wage-Profit Frontier

To discuss the Cambridge criticisms of the relations between capital, interest, and exchange values, one needs a further theoretical tool. That tool, the wage-profit frontier, or as Samuelson (1961–62) calls it, "the factor-price frontier," is ingeniously simple (see Bhaduri 1966, 1969). Suppose one has an economy with no unproduced factors of production except homogeneous, fully employed labor. There is thus no rent. One has for a given method of production, some net output, Y, and net income, Yp_Y, which is distributed between wages, wL, and profit, rK, where K is the value of the produced means of production. For simplicity assume that there is no depreciation. Since Yp_Y is net income, it does not particularly matter whether K involves fixed capital, circulating capital, or both. Since income is divided between wages and profits,

$$(4.1) \qquad Yp_Y = rK + Lw$$

where L is the number of workers, which is taken to be a constant. Dividing through by L and writing yp_y for $Y \cdot p_Y / L$ and k for K/L, one obtains

$$(4.2) \qquad yp_y = rk + w.$$

Setting $p_y = 1$ and rearranging,

(4.3) $w = y - rk.$

One may then graph (4.3) (see fig. 4.1). One must, however, interpret figure 4.1 and equation (4.3) carefully. They *do not* depict the true relations between wages and profits. Figure 4.1 represents the tradeoff between wages and interest *if* the proportions between capital and labor are held constant despite the differences in wages and interest. In reality, unless this is an absolutely fixed-proportions economy, the production process employed will differ depending on wages and interest. If capital and labor are infinitely substitutable for one another in a Clark-like smooth aggregate production function, only one point of the wage-profit line in figure 4.1 will represent an actual combination

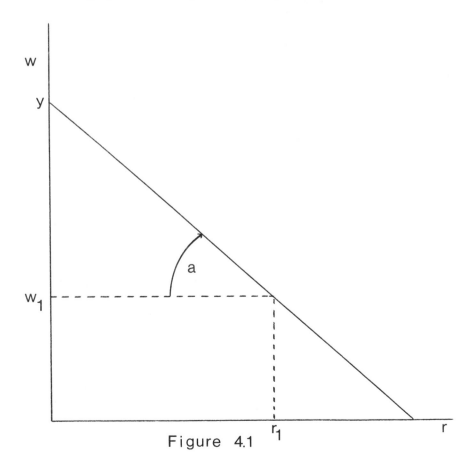

Figure 4.1

of wages and interest. If there are a finite number of techniques of production, a segment of that line will be on the wage-profit frontier.[6] The actual wage-profit relationship (excluding technological changes) will be the outer envelope of such graphs since, for a given wage, entrepreneurs will employ that technique which will maximize profits. Figure 4.1 has some convenient properties. When interest is zero the wage and the per capita net income are equal; $k = (y - w)/r = \tan a$. If the wage-profit line is a straight line, $k = -dw/dr$. If $k = -dw/dr$ at (r_1, w_1), then the wage-profit line must either be a straight line or it must be tangent at (r_1, w_1) to a straight line through that point and $(0, y)$. The importance of these last observations is the following:

$$(4.4) \qquad \frac{dw}{dr} = \frac{dy}{dr} - k - r\frac{dk}{dr} \quad \text{[differentiating (4.3)]}$$

$$(4.5) \qquad r\frac{dk}{dr} = \frac{dy}{dr} \quad \text{if and only if } k = -\frac{dw}{dr}$$

$$(4.6) \qquad r = \frac{dy}{dk} \quad \text{if and only if } k = -\frac{dw}{dr}$$

Thus one can say, roughly, that the rate of interest is equal to the apparent marginal product of capital if and only if the wage-profit lines, (which are by definition tangent to the wage-profit frontier at one or more points or coincide with it over some interval) are straight lines.

The economic meaning of a straight wage-profit line is simple: the line will be straight if and only if the value of capital is independent of the distribution of income between wages and interest. In that case the value of capital acts like a physical measure of capital, and one can regard the rate of interest unproblematically as the price of capital. Of course no one believes that when the production process used is held fixed, the value of capital remains the same no matter what the distribution of income is.

Let us now consider the wage-profit frontier (fig. 4.2). Since the frontier is either tangent to wage-profit lines or made up of segments of such lines and since such lines have negative slope, the slope of the frontier is everywhere negative. Both wages and interest can increase simultaneously only through the discovery of some new technique of production. Furthermore at any switchpoint between two techniques,

[6] The wage-profit frontier does not necessarily represent the actual wage-profit trade-off, because switching techniques will typically bring about or be accompanied by technological innovation, which will cause the frontier to shift. See Hicks (1975:367).

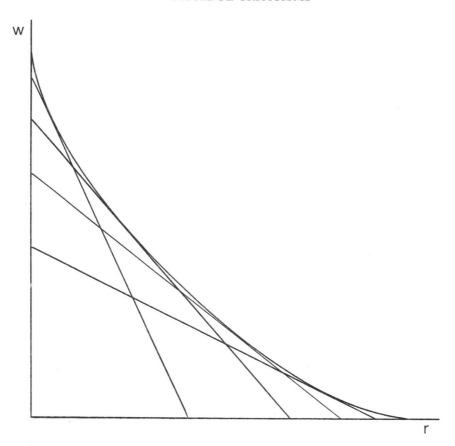

Figure 4.2

T_1 and T_2, $k_1 > k_2$ if and only if $y_1 > y_2$ and $k_1 > k_2$ if and only if $k_1/y_1 > k_2/y_2$. A higher per-capita value of capital always goes with a higher capital-output ratio and a higher per-capita income. These results match what a Clark-like theory demands. The proof of these claims is simple.

(4.7) $y_1 - rk_1 = y_2 - rk_2$ since w and r for the two techniques are equal at a switch point

(4.8) $y_1 - y_2 = r \cdot (k_1 - k_2)$ from (4.7)

Since r is positive $y_1 > y_2$ if and only if $k_1 > k_2$. (4.8) seems to provide a shortcut to a proof that $r = dy/dk$ at least at all switch points and to contradict the argument that $r = dy/dk$ if and only if the wage profit lines have constant slope (Solow 1967:32–33). Although (4.8) is not a trivial result, it only shows that $r = dy/dk$ if we hold wages and interest (and thus prices) constant. If prices are constant, an increase in the value of capital is truly an increase in the quantity of capital goods and dy/dk behaves like a physical rate of return.[7] (4.8) cannot serve as part of a theory of the causal determination of the rate of interest by the marginal productivity of capital; but, as already discussed above, the notion that the marginal productivity of capital *causally determines* the rate of interest is misleading.

Proving that $k_1 > k_2$ if and only if $k_1/y_1 > k_2/y_2$ is also simple.

(4.9)
$$k_1 \left(\frac{y_1}{k_1} - r \right) = k_2 \left(\frac{y_2}{k_2} - r \right) \quad \text{from 4.7}$$

(4.10)
$$\frac{k_1}{k_2} = \frac{\dfrac{y_2}{k_2} - r}{\dfrac{y_1}{k_1} - r}$$

(4.11)
$$k_1 > k_2 \quad \text{if and only if} \quad \frac{y_2}{k_2} - r > \frac{y_1}{k_1} - r$$

$$k_1 > k_2 \quad \text{if and only if} \quad \frac{y_2}{k_2} > \frac{y_1}{k_1}$$

$$k_1 > k_2 \quad \text{if and only if} \quad \frac{k_1}{y_1} > \frac{k_2}{y_2}$$

[7] Pasinetti (1969:508–31) makes the same point, although more polemically. He objects to Solow's claim, which is technically correct, that "the interest rate is an accurate measure of the social rate of return to savings" (Solow 1967:30). Because of reswitching, an investment can have more than one rate of return. While this does not falsify Solow's claim, it makes Pasinetti skeptical of the significance of the equality between the rate of return and the constrained derivative of income with respect to the value of capital. See also Solow (1970:423–28 and Pasinetti (1970:428–31). Dixit (1977:20–23) accuses Wicksell of a bad confusion in attempting to link what Wicksell considered to be the marginal product of capital [see (3.7)] to the rate of interest. Keeping prices constant as in (4.8), the difficulties disappear: "stock appreciation should never be included . . . in the first place" (p. 20). "Of course we now know how they [the paradoxes] arise from mistaken concepts, and we have seen how the general framework of intertemporal equilibrium explains or resolves them" (pp. 22–23). Although the Austrian theory is unsatisfactory, it is not such a muddle as this, nor is intertemporal equilibrium theory such a successful resolution.

The wage-profit frontier enables one to depict simply the relations among wages, profits, and techniques of production. Thus far we have seen that, unless there is a technological innovation which shifts the frontier, wages and profits are inversely related. At different wage rates different techniques of production will be most profitable. At switch points between different production processes (points where two processes are, at a given wage, equally profitable), the process that has the larger value of capital and the higher capital/output ratio will have the larger output.

3. Reswitching and Capital Reversing

How is this analytical device converted into a tool of criticism? The geometry of wage-profit lines suggests the theoretical possibility of reswitching or double-switching depicted in fig. 4.3. Technique 1 is most profitable both at very high and very low values of the rate of interest, while technique 2 is most profitable at intermediate values. For $r > r'$ technique 1 will be in use. For $r'' < r < r'$ technique 2 will have the highest wage for a given rate of interest or the highest rate of interest for a given wage. At still lower interest rates it is profitable to switch from technique 2 back to technique 1. In itself the possibility of reswitching is not very important.[8] What is important is what happens at point B: (r', w') on the graph. Remember that nothing is actually *happening*. We are only comparing stationary states. What is peculiar about figure 4.3 is that for $r'' < r < r'$ the technique chosen has a lower per capita value of capital, a lower per capita income (consumption), and a lower capital/output ratio than does the technique in use for $r > r'$. When technique 2 is employed, there is less capital than when technique 1 is (unless the value of capital is not a measure of its quantity), yet the rate of interest is *lower* than it is in some equilibrium states in which technique 1 is employed. This phenomenon is sometimes called "capital reversing." The "normal" inverse relation between the rate of interest and the quantity (value?) of capital is re-

[8] Both critics and defenders of neoclassical theory agree with this assessment. Some defenders of neoclassical theory see nothing but confusion in the whole notion of reswitching. As Bliss points out (1975:239), the set of prices at which a technique would be chosen is unconnected only if we restrict ourselves to stationary states or to semi-stationary growth and to constant price vectors: "it seemed that the set of values at which a technique might be chosen was not connected. *But this is an optical illusion.* Firms . . . choose plans in the light of complete intertemporal price systems." The difficulty with Bliss' vision and with Dixit's restatement (1977) lies in making sense of the intertemporal equilibrium theory presupposed.

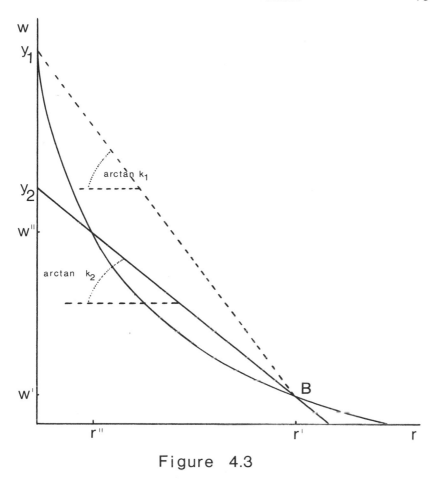

Figure 4.3

versed. Reswitching is sufficient for capital reversing, but not necessary, as fig. 4.4 illustrates.

In fig. 4.4 there is no reswitching. Each technique is most profitable for only one range of wages. Yet the switch from technique 3 to technique 2 is a capital reversing switch. Technique 2 is employed at rates of interest lower than those at which technique 3 is employed, yet it has a lower per capita output and a lower value of capital; k_2, the magnitude of the slope of the straight line from $(0, y_2)$ to B, is less than k_3, the magnitude of the slope of the straight line from $(0, y_3)$ to B. The only limit the geometry of such graphs places on capital reversing is that the switch to the technique employed at the lowest rates of interest cannot be capital reversing.

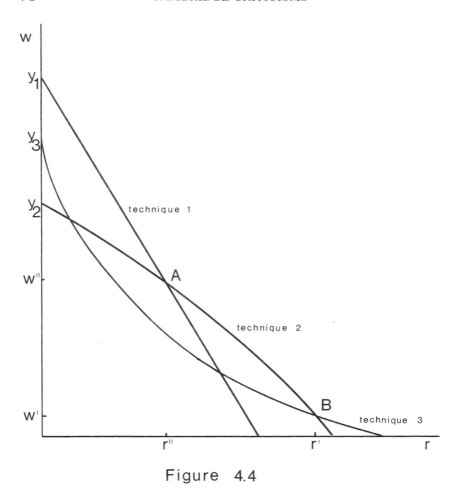

Figure 4.4

Capital reversing implies that at least one of the four claims listed above in §1 is false. If capital is an input into production whose value measures its quantity and whose marginal product decreases with its quantity, and if the rate of interest is proportional to the marginal product of capital, then the rate of interest and the value of capital must be inversely related. How can one regard capital as a factor of production if, in the models of the critics, firms find it profitable to use *less* capital when its price (the rate of interest) declines? When an input becomes cheaper one should expect firms to find it profitable to use relatively more of it. Something is drastically awry.

One can also give algebraic models of reswitching. Bliss provides the following simple one (1975:91). One is comparing stationary states which employ respectively the following techniques:

I: $1L$ and $2x$ make $5x$

II: Process 1: $1L$ and $1m$ make $5x$ and $1m$
Process 2: $4L$ make $1m$.

From these equations, setting $p_x = 1$, one can easily calculate the two wage-profit lines: $w_1 = (3 - 2r_1)/(1 + r_1)$ and $w_2 = 5/[(1 + 4r_2) \cdot (1 + r_2)]$. The two curves intersect at $(.25, 2)$ and $(1, \frac{1}{2})$[9] and their graph resembles figure 4.3, except that for Process II r is not bounded. There is nothing less plausible about algebraic examples of reswitching and capital reversing than there is about the sort of model that Wicksell or Lange present and discuss.

Precisely the same sort of algebraic hypothetical counterexample can be posed to the Austrian theory. Suppose that we have two methods of producing some consumption good, x. Let t be the time when x is available for consumption. One method requires the application of 3 units of labor at $t - 11$ and 10 units of labor at $t - 1$. The other requires the application of 10 units of labor at $t - 6$ and 2 units of labor at $t - 1$. Setting $p_x = 1$, the equations of the two wage profit lines are $w_1 = 1/[3(1 + r)^{11} + 10(1 + r)]$; $w_2 = 1/[10(1 + r)^6 + 2(1 + r)]$. The second technique will produce x at a lower cost (and thus be the technique with the higher wage or higher rate of interest for $r < 6\%$ or $r > 15\%$).[10]

---

[9] Bliss miscalculates the intersections.

[10] Calculations for the Austrian reswitching model are as follows:

technique 1: $p_1 = w_1[3(1 + r_1)^{11} + 10(1 + r_1)]$

technique 2: $p_2 = w_2[10(1 + r_2)^6 + 2(1 + r_2)]$

at the switch points: $w_1 = w_2$; $r_1 = r_2$. Thus

$$w[3(1 + r)^{11} + 10(1 + r)] = w[10(1 + r)^6 + 2(1 + r)].$$

Assuming that $r \neq -1$, one gets $3(1 + r)^{10} - 10(1 + r)^5 + 8 = 0$.

$$(1 + r)^5 = 4/3 \qquad (1 + r)^5 = 2$$

$$r \doteq 5.97\% \qquad r \doteq 14.9\%$$

Böhm-Bawerk suggests that we calculate the average period of production, T, as follows:[11]

$$T = \frac{\sum_{j=1}^{n} L_j t_j}{\sum_{j=1}^{n} L_j}$$

where L_j is the point input of labor in the period t_j periods before the one in which the output is available. L_n is the most ancient labor input. If one applies this formula to the given techniques, one finds that $T_1 = (33 + 10)/13 = 43/13$. $T_2 = 62/12$. The second technique has the longer average period of production. Stationary equilibrium states for a rate of interest between 6% and 15% compared with stationary equilibrium states for $r > 15\%$ have a lower rate of interest, a higher wage, and a *less* roundabout method of production. Either the marginal contribution of waiting is larger when more roundabout processes are already employed, or the rate of interest is not the price of waiting.

We can also calculate the value of capital.

$$K_1 = 3w_1 \left[\sum_{i=1}^{11} (1 + r_1)^{i-1} \right] + 10w_1$$

$$K_2 = 10w_2 \left[\sum_{i=1}^{6} (1 + r_2)^{i-1} \right] + 2w_2.$$

K_2 is larger than K_1 at both switch points. The switch from technique 2 to technique 1 at $r \doteq 15\%$ is a capital reversing switch. The reswitching cannot be explained in terms of a reversal of the capital intensities of the two techniques at different interest rates.[12]

[11] Böhm-Bawerk 1888, p. 89. See also Kuenne 1971, p. 45. This formula presupposes that the rate of interest does not affect the period of production.

[12] When $r = 5.9\%$, $K_1/w = 10 + 3\left[\left(\sum_{i=1}^{10} (1.059)^i \right) + 1 \right]$

$$= 13 + 3[(1.059)^{11} - (1.059)] \div .059$$

$$\doteq 55.$$

$K_2/w = 12 + 10[(1.059)^6 - (1.059)]/.059$, which is about 72. when $r \doteq 14.9\%$, K_1/w is about 83 and K_2/w is about 89.

If one modifies Böhm-Bawerk's measure of the average period of production, as some authors have suggested, to take account of compounding of the effects of roundaboutness, the period of production for process 2 remains longer than the period of production for process 1.[13] Modifying Böhm-Bawerk's measure of the average period of pro-

[13] There are possibilities for disagreement concerning how to calculate the average period of production in a way which takes account of the compounding of roundaboutness. See Kuenne (1971:69) for a simple exposition. The most reasonable formula seems to me the following:

$$T = \frac{\sum_{i=1}^{k} L_i \left[\sum_{j=1}^{n_i} (1 + r)^{j-1} \right]}{\sum_{i=1}^{k} L_i}$$

k is the number of different point inputs of labor; n_i is the number of periods before the output is available that the labor input L_i is added. Applying this formula,

$$T_1 = \left[3\left(\sum_{j=1}^{11} (1 + r_1)^{j-1} \right) + 10 \right] \bigg/ 13$$

and

$$T_2 = \left[10\left(\sum_{j=1}^{6} (1 + r_2)^{j-1} \right) + 2 \right] \bigg/ 12.$$

For r_1 and $r_2 = 0$, one gets the same values as from the simpler formula that ignores interest. For $r \doteq 5.9\%$, $T_1 \doteq 4.2$ and $T_2 \doteq 6$. For $r \doteq 14.9\%$, $T_1 \doteq 6.4$ and $T_2 \doteq 7.4$.

Leland Yeager (1976:328–29) shows that reswitching need not always establish capital reversing, if one is willing to calculate the average period of investment in a particular way. He discusses a simple model due to Samuelson in which there are two techniques: A, employed at low and high rates of interest and B employed at intermediate rates of interest. Let r_1 and r_2 be the rates of interest at the two switch points with $r_1 < r_2$. For $r < r_2$ the average period of investment of B, calculated in Yeager's way, is less than that of A, but for $r > r_2$, A becomes the less time intensive technique. Yeager finds this result comforting, "Preconceived insistence on measuring all factor quantities in purely physical terms clashes with the fact of reality—or, of arithmetic—that the amount of waiting, requiring in accomplishing a physically specified purpose depends on its own price." (p. 337). I find Yeager's conclusion unpalatable and, in any case, mistaken. Yeager calculates the average period of investment of labor and waiting as follows:

$$T = \frac{\sum_{i=1}^{k} L_i \left[\sum_{j=0}^{n_i-1} (n_i - j)r^j \right]}{\sum_{i=1}^{k} L_i \left(\sum_{j=0}^{n_i-1} r^j \right)}$$

duction in this way makes that period a function of the rate of interest. One then wonders what role the average period of production is supposed to play in an explanation of the rate of interest.

In this algebraic special case model the fundamental claims of the Austrian theory do not hold. Contrary to (3.26) the rate of interest is not always smaller when the time-intensity of production is larger. If the quantity of waiting or the average period of production measures the increased productivity of the stored up services of land and labor (3.23) and the marginal productivity of such storing up is a decreasing function of its quantity (3.21), and interest is the cost of this storing up or waiting (3.24), then it cannot be the case that a lower rate of interest goes with a shorter average period of production. Contrary to (3.27), wages are also not always larger when the roundaboutness of production is greater. The Cambridge critics have produced a *story* that falsifies any capital theory which takes interest to be the cost of some input which yields diminishing returns.

4. Interpretation and Tentative Conclusions

The Cambridge critics have presented simple special case models in which certain techniques employ more roundabout methods of production and have a higher value of capital yet have a higher rate of interest than do others. If interest increases with the marginal productivity of "capital" and the marginal productivity declines with the quantity of "capital," there should be an inverse relation between the rate of interest and the period of production or the value of capital. The Cambridge critics have thus presented simple hypothetical cases in which things do not work as neoclassical capital theories say they should.

What should one conclude? The possibilities explored by the critics show that the Austrians' claims are not *necessary*; but mere possibilities will never prove that those claims are false. Surely one can argue

---

where k is the number of different labor inputs and n_i is the number of periods before the output is available that the input L_i is added. For the example I have been considering in the text, one finds that $T_1 = [3(\sum_{j=0}^{10} (11 - j)r^j) + 10] \div [10 + 3(\sum_{j=0}^{10} r^j)]$; $T_2 = [2 + 10(\sum_{j=0}^{5} (6 - j)r^j)] \div [2 + 10(\sum_{j=0}^{5} r^j)]$. For $r \doteq .059$, $T_1 \doteq 3.4$, $T_2 \doteq 5.15$. For $r \doteq .149$, $T_1 \doteq 3.6$, $T_2 \doteq 5.12$. The capital reversing does not disappear. Whatever the merits of Yeager's aspirations and of his method of calculating the period of investment, he has found no general answer to the problem of capital reversing. Comparing stationary equilibria with $r > 14.9\%$ to stationary equilibria with $5.9\% < r < 14.9\%$ one finds that with a higher rate of interest a more time intensive productive technique is employed.

that, until the Cambridge critics have shown that the peculiarities of the special case models are true of the real world, they have not revealed any flaw in neoclassical capital theories. Although there is some justice in this objection, I do not think that the Cambridge criticism can be so easily dismissed. The Cambridge critics have not shown that capital reversing is a real phenomenon, but neither have neoclassical economists given us reason to believe that there is usually an inverse relation between the rate of interest and the quantity of capital. Measuring the various theoretically relevant quantities, particularly the time-intensity of production, is impractical, perhaps impossible. There is no experimental way to know whether the anomalous phenomena occur. Bruno, et al. have investigated the conditions which logically rule out reswitching and have shown that they are so strong that no real economy is likely to meet them (1966, esp. pp. 543–46). The conditions which rule out capital reversing are even stronger: The Cambridge critics have not merely presented some strange possible cases; they have revealed that the neoclassical theorist has no good reason to believe what traditional capital theories assert.

There is a second consideration that reinforces the importance of the mere possibilities the Cambridge critics have discussed. The Austrian theory was not intended as a calculating device which enables economists to make predictions about the behavior of certain economic quantities when they have measured others, but was supposed to *explain* what capital and interest are and, to some extent, to justify the existence of interest. Although the normative and the descriptive issues are distinct, they are explicitly related. Böhm-Bawerk asserts, "In the essence of interest, then, there is nothing which should make it appear in itself unreasonable or unjust" (1888:360). If one cannot discount the possibilities revealed in the counter-models or explain them away in terms of Austrian concepts of capital and interest, one cannot claim to have explained what capital and interest are or to have justified the earning of interest.

Some neoclassical economists have argued that, even if capital reversing does occur, it is no more important to capital and interest theory than are the existence of Giffen goods and upward-sloping demand curves to the theory of demand (Blaug 1975:42–43; Stiglitz 1974:896). This argument is a mistake. It is fair to say that rough supply and demand theory states that demand curves are downward sloping, just as the Austrian theory of capital and interest states that interest is a decreasing function of the quantity of "waiting." Thus far the analogy carries one. There are, however, three important conditions that are not analogous. Demand theorists know there are few Giffen goods. They know why there are Giffen goods. They can successfully predict that certain goods in certain economies (potatoes in Ireland, rice in China, or yams in New Guinea) are likely to be Giffen goods. Capital theorists, on the other hand, do not know whether capital reversing is common or rare. Until recently they possessed no theory which made sense of the phenomenon. The status of that fundamental theory remains, moreover, questionable. From the perspective of the Austrian theory or of Clark's theory, capital reversing is nothing but a disconfirmation. Capital theorists are also unable to predict when capital reversing will occur. They cannot point to some feature of an economy and say, "Ah, we can see that this is one of the exceptional cases in which we should not expect our simpler capital theories to work." There is no justification for the claim that capital reversing demands only minor qualifications in simplified capital theories.

The criticisms of the Cambridge economists, even though they involve only the construction of special case models, should not be dismissed. Yet the critics have not accomplished nearly so much as some of them think. The Cambridge critics have shown, as Wicksell did, that the value of capital may depend on the distribution of income between wages and interest, and have thus made clear that the quantity of capital, as measured by its value, cannot be regarded as an economic primitive on a par with iron ore deposits. Perhaps, they have thus refuted J. B. Clark. Yet there is little new in this refutation. I know of no theorist of the past generation who has denied that the value of capital might differ with a different distribution of income. The Cambridge critics, on the other hand, have not refuted the Austrian theory. They have revealed no logical inconsistency in it, nor have they shown that there is any error involved in using either Clark's or the Austrians' theories in empirical studies like Solow's. One may lack evidence for the Austrian theory; Clark's theory may be ultimately incoherent. Yet there is no way to prove, a priori, that nothing can be learned by employing these theories. It is preferable not to base one's investigations on such shaky foundations, but there may be no better choice. Remember that the Cambridge criticisms do not rule out the possibility that (other things being equal) the rate of interest is in fact always smaller when the value of capital and the roundaboutness of production are larger.

The important conclusion established by the Cambridge critics is that the Austrian theory of capital is *unfounded*. One has no reason to believe the claims of the theory. Whatever good reasons we have to accept other neoclassical theories, those reasons do not support the Austrian theory. Since economists have no reason to believe the Austrian theory, they have no reason to believe that it explains the phenomena of capital and interest. *If* orthodox economists have nothing better than the Austrian theory, they cannot justifiably assert that they know why there are profits or what determines whether profits are, on average, large or small. The Cambridge critics thus raise serious questions about the ability of neoclassical economics to deal with the phenomena of capital and interest.

CHAPTER FIVE
Intertemporal General Equilibrium Theory

The Cambridge criticisms show that neither Clark's nor the Austrian approach provide any warranted theory of the rate of interest. Whatever general justification neoclassical theories possess, that justification does not carry over to simplified capital theories. Economists have no reason to believe they can measure capital by time in such a way that the rate of interest is a decreasing function of the period of production. Since, holding all other factors constant, the rate of interest can increase when the quantity of capital, no matter how one tries to measure it, increases, theorists are unjustified in conceiving of interest as a payment to a factor of production. It thus appears that marginal utility theory fails to give any warranted coherent account of the nature of capital and interest.

Such a conclusion is not yet justified. Neoclassical economists have another arrow in their quiver. Samuelson (1961–62) begins with these comments:

> Repeatedly in writings and lectures I have insisted that capital theory can be rigorously developed without using any Clark-like concept of aggregate "capital," instead relying on a complete analysis of a great variety of heterogeneous physical capital goods and processes through time. (1961–62:193)

Solow seconds Samuelson on this point:

> The highbrow answer is that the theory of capital is, after all, just a part of the fundamentally microeconomic theory of the allocation of resources, necessary to allow for the fact that commodities can be transformed into other commodities over time. Just as the theory of resource allocation has as its "dual" a theory of competitive pricing, so the theory of capital has as its "dual" a theory of intertemporal pricing involving rentals, interest

rates, present values, and the like. In both cases, a complete price theory is also a theory of distribution among factors of production, if not among persons. (1963: 14)

According to Samuelson and Solow the Cambridge critics have been attacking parables and simplifications; their comments do not touch the rigorous theory. I shall now examine this "highbrow" answer—the theory of intertemporal pricing.

One must thus look beyond the simple parables to the more general models developed by contemporary theorists. Walras' own models, or even their refinement in Lindahl's work (1939, part III) will not be discussed, because both face serious criticisms (Eatwell 1975c, Collard 1973, and Jaffe 1942) and have been superseded by intertemporal general equilibrium models as developed by Arrow, Debreu, and Malinvaud. I know of no acceptable treatment of the rate of interest or profit which employs a model of a stationary general equilibrium.

1. Intertemporal General Equilibrium

In this chapter I shall largely follow Malinvaud's lucid exposition (1972, ch. 10).[1] Equilibrium theorists distinguish commodities both by their nature and by the time period in which they are available. Thereby they reinterpret the atemporal production equilibrium (ch. 2, §2) as an intertemporal equilibrium. "Goods" are commodities of the same nature. Malinvaud is concerned with the organization of the economy (of production, distribution, and consumption) during a time period from $t = 1$ to $t = T$. The date $t = 1$ is "now." All the individuals involved make all their decisions now for the entire period up to T. Each agent thus decides on a "program" of activities during each period. These decisions, which are, of course, constrained by the initial endowment and its distribution and the technical possibilities, will determine the complete course of the economy over the time interval $(1, T)$. By distinguishing commodities according to the time period in which they are available, intertemporal equilibrium theorists are automatically embedding time and expectations in utility and production functions. Uncertainty is simply assumed away. Obviously these theorists are operating at a ferociously high level of abstraction.

At $t = 1$ agents operate with "discounted" prices. If the equilibrium

[1] See also Koopmans (1957, esp. pp. 105–26); Debreu (1959), Arrow and Hahn (1971), and Bliss (1975, ch. 3).

exchange ratio is three eggs in period 4 for one custard pie in period 2, $p_{c,2}/p_{e,4} = 3$. The double subscripts specify respectively what good the commodity is and what period it is available in. Notice that nothing has been said about what eggs will cost *during* the fourth time period. Agents complete all exchanges of current commodities and of titles to commodities of all other dates entirely within period 1. Imagine a commodity futures market in which exchangers have perfect information about the future. Such a market differs from the construction of the equilibrium theorists in one minor respect. "The 'price' [on real futures markets] to be paid is also specified now (it is the 'price' prevailing on the floor of the exchange), but it is understood that this 'price' shall be paid *at the delivery date, at the delivery location*. This difference from the price concept which will be used here is inessential" (Debreu 1959:33). In period 1, the agents are actually carrying out exchanges (although for future commodities only contracts can be currently transferred). Prices are those (discounted) prices that are current in period 1.

The determination of economic equilibrium proceeds just as in ordinary general equilibrium theory. Each consumer has a utility function which he or she maximizes by adjusting purchases of commodities (and sales of resources or services) until the ratio of the marginal utilities of commodities (and resources and services) equals the (discounted) price ratio. Production functions or production sets specify what commodities in what quantities can be made available in each period. These production functions can most conveniently be represented as relating output in period k to input in period $k - 1$. Processes of production that require more than one time period are regarded as creating a series of intermediate products (like a partly built dam) at the end of each period. These production functions are homogeneous with constant returns to scale, positive first partial derivatives and (beyond a certain quantity), negative second partial derivatives. The result of perfect competition will be that the value of the marginal product of a commodity in each of its uses will be the same, and the marginal products of different commodities combined in the production of any commodity will be proportional to their prices. These conditions, plus the nonexistence of profit in profit-maximizing competitive equilibrium and the specification of the original endowment and its distribution, are sufficient for the existence of an equilibrium solution for the system. For a proof see Debreu's *Theory of Value*. For an intuitive explanation of the principle of such proofs, see Arrow (1968). A simple general equilibrium model is developed below in §5.

Intertemporal equilibrium models rest on the reinterpretation of the notion of a commodity. Once commodities are distinguished by the date at which they are available, atemporal production equilibria (which have no produced inputs) are transformed into intertemporal equilibria, which can have intermediate products and capital goods. With a simple reinterpretation of the notion of a commodity, models apparently without any relevance to the phenomena of capital and interest become (at least in the view of equilibrium theorists) the key to capital theory!

2. Own Rates of Return

How does interest enter? Malinvaud defines what he calls the "own rate of return" as follows:[2]

$$r_{q,t} = \frac{p_{q,t}}{p_{q,t+1}} - 1$$

If the discounted price of a good q at $t + 1$ is less than the discounted price of q at t, then the own rate of return of q at t is positive: people are willing to exchange one unit of q at t only for more than one unit of q at $t + 1$. Own rates of return express how a single good exchanges with itself over time. A good available today which exchanges for more of itself next year has a positive own rate of return this year. A good available in two years which exchanges for less of itself three years from now has a negative own rate of return two years from now.

Given the utility functions of consumers one can define a one-period own subjective interest rate for each good:

$$r_{q,t}^s = \frac{S'_{q,t}}{S'_{q,(t+1)}} - 1$$

where S is the utility function and $S'_{q,t}$ is the value of its partial derivative with respect to commodity q at t. $r_{q,t}^s$ is likely to be positive for most goods because of "time preference" and the fact that consumption plans in a progressive society involve the consumption of more of q at $t + 1$ than at t.

Malinvaud defines the (own) one-period technical interest rate as

[2] Malinvaud puts it differently. First he defines what he calls the "own discount factor," $p_{q,t}/p_{q,1}$, and then defines the own rate of interest in terms of the own discount factor (1972:232).

follows:

$$r^t_{q,t} = \frac{f'_{q,t}}{f'_{q,t+1}} - 1$$

where $f'_{q,t}$ is the value of the partial derivative of the production function with respect to commodity q at t. The technical interest rate will be greater than zero if using x in production today produces more of x in the next period. Growing trees will have a positive technical interest rate, while picked strawberries may have a negative technical interest rate.

Maximization of utility insures that the ratio of the marginal utilities equals the price ratio. Maximization of profits insures that the ratio of the marginal products also equals the price ratios. In competitive equilibrium $r^s_{q,t} = r^t_{q,t} = r_{q,t}$. Thus own rates of return reflect both subjective and objective factors of interest determination.[3] One must again be careful in speaking of "determination." $r^s_{q,t}$ or $r^t_{q,t}$ or $f'_{q,t}$ or $S'_{q,t}$ are not more primitive than are $r_{q,t}$ or $p_{q,t}$. All of these are simultaneously determined by the givens to the intertemporal equilibrium system.

3. The Rate of Interest.

Nothing, however, has been said about the rate of interest. The various own rates of return will not be equal and even if they were we would still not have all the pieces of a theory of the rate of interest, because we have not yet learned anything about contemporary prices—the prices of goods *within* any of the time intervals.

If the current price of tomatoes is $110 and the discounted price of tomatoes to be delivered in one year is $100, the own rate of return for tomatoes in period 1 is 10%. But this says nothing about the rate of interest or the rate of return on investing the tomatoes. The rate of interest can be any number at all larger than -1. In prices actually ruling one year from now, tomatoes might be worth $330 and the rate of interest 200%, or tomatoes might be worth in next year's prices $99, in which case the rate of interest is -10%. Nothing said so far specifies what the rate of interest is.

In fact the general equilibrium solution is completely independent

---

[3] Irving Fisher stresses these two factors. Although his terminology was somewhat different, one can regard Böhm-Bawerk as stressing them, too. Intertemporal equilibrium models can plausibly be regarded as the "dovetailing" of Fisher's theory of the determination of the rate of return with price theory to which Fisher looked forward (1930:131n). See also Dougherty (1972:1324–49).

of the rate of interest and asserts nothing explicit about it. The rate of interest has no role whatsoever in the general equilibrium solution. This sounds more paradoxical than it is, since the rate of interest and contemporary prices (which also are not part of the general equilibrium solution) are dependent on one another. Economists can stipulate whatever rate of interest they want, but if their stipulation is too large, the price level will increase. A changing price level shows that the nominal interest rate specified differs from the real rate of interest. Furthermore, it can easily be shown (and will be later in this section) that whatever rate of interest is stipulated, each investment earns exactly that. The characteristic property of a capitalist economy, that in equilibrium there is an equal rate of return on all investments, is preserved.

The general equilibrium solution provides implicitly a theory of the rate of interest. Malinvaud suggests that one pick a numeraire good which is such that when its price is set equal to 1 in each period, the general price level will remain steady (1972:233, 240–41). The own rate of return on this numeraire good is (for each period and investment term) the rate of interest. There are, of course, problems in defining a suitable price index. The more the goods available in different periods differ, the more difficult it is to say whether the price level has remained steady. That the numeraire commodity in each period be the same good is only a notational convenience. To simply my discussion, I shall consider only the one-period rate of interest, r_t. If Q is the numeraire good and $\bar{p}_{q,t}$ is the contemporary price of good q in period t, $p_{q,t}/p_{Q,t}$, then one can derive the following:

$$\frac{1 + r_{q,t}}{1 + r_t} = \frac{p_{q,t}}{p_{q,t+1}} \div \frac{p_{Q,t}}{p_{Q,t+1}} \quad \text{by definition}$$

$$= \frac{\bar{p}_{q,t}}{\bar{p}_{q,t+1}}$$

The prices of all those commodities whose own rate of return is larger than the rate of interest will decline, while the price of all those whose own rate of return is less than the rate of interest will increase. General stability in the pricing system shows that one has picked the numeraire well and correctly determined the real rate of interest.

4. Is There Such a Thing as the Rate of Interest?

C. J. Bliss argues that thinking in terms of intertemporal equilibrium theory should lead economists to stop talking about the rate of interest altogether. "Our idea is nearly the exact antithesis of Solow's proposal.

It is that capital theory should be liberated from the concept of the rate of interest, meaning by that one rate. . . . Instead, we will find the concept of intertemporal prices to be fundamental and will see that working with the rate of interest is a clumsy groping for that concept'' (1975:10). Notice in fairness to Solow that he too regards highbrow theory as concerned with intertemporal pricing (1963:14). In so far as Bliss is only arguing that economic theory should be developed in terms of intertemporal prices, his claim depends on the relative adequacy of intertemporal general equilibrium theory. If such theories are indeed superior, economists should agree with Bliss that intertemporal prices are theoretically fundamental.[4]

But Bliss wants, I think, to go further and to assert that there is something mistaken or incoherent in talking about a single rate of interest. Of the traditional neoclassical view that capital accumulation results in a falling rate of interest, he says:

> In the first place, as we have had reason to remark and underline above, the rate of interest is not a legitimate concept outside the particular and special conditions of semi-stationary growth with a constant-rate-of-interest price system. The orthodox vision includes the statement that the rate of interest will decline as capital accumulation proceeds. Strictly, in the present case, that statement cannot be interpreted. We have a whole structure of interest rates, even in one week, not a single rate of interest. Which rate of interest should decline to validate the orthodox vision? The question is otiose. . . . All that one can reasonably say with regard to the rate of interest is that as a description of an optimal development . . . the orthodox vision fails to make sense. (1975:294)

Two separate questions need to be considered. First, Bliss asserts that there is no single n-period rate of interest at a given time. This assertion is misleading as the informal comments above suggest and as will be proved below.[5]

Frank Hahn makes the same assertion more emphatically:

> For most specifications it will not be the case that the equilibrium price of a good for future delivery in terms of the same good for current delivery

---

[4] The "superiority" here is problematic as is the notion that intertemporal theory is more *fundamental*. See chapters 7, 9, and 10.

[5] There may be terminological difficulties; I have been speaking indiscriminately of the rate of interest and the rate of profit. $r_t = r_{Q,t}$ is called by Malinvaud (1972:240–41) "The rate of profit." I doubt that Bliss would concede the existence of a single rate of profit.

will be the same for all goods. But then, as all the world knows, there is no such thing as "the rate of profit." If general equilibrium analysis takes the special case of an economy with constant returns to scale and linear Engel curves, then it is easy to show that for a special set of initial conditions there will be a uniform equilibrium rate of profit. To say that a very extreme specialization of a general model somehow shows the latter to be inapplicable requires the very summit of incomprehension. (1975, p. 360)

Bliss and Hahn are exaggerating. Hahn is right that contemporary prices and the rate of interest are entirely irrelevant to decision-making at the beginning of the initial period. The rate of interest and the numeraire for each time period can be regarded as entirely arbitrary. *In the basic model* "there is no such thing as 'the rate of profit,'" but one should not leap to any conclusions about real economics.[6] In real economies there are, of course, a large variety of different rates of return on different financial and real assets, but neither this fact nor the possibility of setting up intertemporal models that do not mention single (*n*-period) rates of interest shows that there is in fact "no such thing as 'the rate of profit.'" For any real economy one can add up the values of the returns on investments after subtracting out rents, risk premiums, and depreciation that turn up nominally as profits. One can also add up the values of the various investments for a period. After correcting for price changes, since different periods are involved, one can calculate the rate of profit.

Intertemporal equilibrium theory *does not* say that the rate of profit is entirely arbitrary and without any systematic relation to the functioning of the economy (Malinvaud 1972:240–41). Let me first show that the rate of return is equal on all investments of the same length and then argue that it is not arbitrary. That the rate of profit is equal on all investments is a perfectly general result, a trivial implication of the zero-profit condition. I shall only prove it for one-period investments. Consider any investment in period t resulting in a commodity bundle b in period $t + 1$. Let the input be the vector a. Let p_t and p_{t+1} be row vectors of discounted prices in periods t and $t + 1$. Then, from

---

[6] Robinson (1961:57) jumps to a related, but equally misleading conclusion: "in a market economy, either there may be a tendency towards uniformity of wages and the rate of profit in different lines of production, or prices may be governed by supply and demand, but not both. Where supply and demand rule, there is no room for uniform levels of wages and the rate of profit. . . . each [producer in a Walrasian system] can have a prospective rate of return on investment in his own line, but there is no mechanism to equalize profits between one line and another."

the zero profit condition, one knows that

$$p_{t+1} \cdot b = p_t \cdot a$$

Let the actual rate of return on the investment be $r_{y,t}$. Thus

$$\bar{p}_{t+1} \cdot b = \bar{p}_t \cdot a\,(1 + r_{y,t})$$

If $p_{Q,t}$ is the discounted price of the numeraire commodity in period t and $p_{Q,t+1}$ is the discounted price of the numeraire commodity in period $t + 1$,

$$\bar{p}_{t+1} = \frac{p_{t+1}}{p_{Q,t+1}} \quad \text{and} \quad \bar{p}_t = \frac{p_t}{p_{Q,t}}$$

Substituting in the production equation containing contemporary prices,

$$(p_{t+1} \cdot b)\,\frac{p_{Q,t}}{p_{Q,t+1}} = p_t \cdot a\,(1 + r_{y,t})$$

Since

$p_{t+1} \cdot b = p_t \cdot a$ and $p_{Q,t}/p_{Q,t+1} = (1 + r_t)$, $1 + r_t = 1 + r_{y,t}$ and $r_t = r_{y,t}$. The return on all investments equals the rate of interest.

Not only is the rate of profit on all investments of the same length which are made in the same period identical, but it is not arbitrary. This point was already briefly made above. The rate of interest will depend on the choice of a numeraire, but if one chooses badly, the general price level will increase or decrease. The real rate of profit or interest after one corrects for inflation or deflation is determinate. There is no perfect measure of price stability, but there are usable and nonarbitrary standards. To give a simple criterion: the price level in period 2 is equal to the price level in period 1 if and only if $\bar{p}_1 \cdot q_1 = \bar{p}_2 \cdot q_1$ where $\bar{p}_1$ and $\bar{p}_2$ are row vectors of the contemporary prices in the two periods and q_1 is the column vector of the commodities available in period one. What this means is that the price level is roughly stable if it costs the same this year to buy the goods that one bought last year. Other, and possibly preferable, standards of price stability are available.

Bliss has, however, a second point to make, which is valid. The rates of interest between any two time periods will in general differ.[7] To regard this proposition as a difficulty for previous theories of interest does not seem fair. Economists did not need intertemporal equilibrium models to tell them that rates of interest on investments of different lengths differ or that rates of interest in different time periods differ. Indeed the thesis of a falling rate of interest or profit is incoherent without a recognition of such differences. That interest rates thus vary does not constitute a decisive objection to theorizing in terms of a single average rate of interest on investments of different terms. Stationary state or proportional growth models in which such a single rate of interest figures are highly unrealistic. But can one do any better? If one wants to deal seriously with the term structure of interest rates, intertemporal equilibrium models are not yet a great improvement, since the crucial factor, uncertainty, is still usually assumed away.

Furthermore, Solow is right to stress the importance of the rate of return to actual entrepreneurial decisions. A theoretical construct in terms of intertemporal prices, in which the rate of return has no explicit role to play, may or may not be a valid approach. It should, however, give one some way of relating these prices to the rate of return on investments involving various risks, if the model is to be relevant to the actual operation of the economy.

An intertemporal equilibrium solution implicitly determines rates of return in each period on investments of any length. Such returns are not explicitly mentioned in the solution, but as soon as one specifies a numeraire which holds the price level constant, one can calculate the rates of return. Only in stationary or proportional growth equilibria will there be only one rate of interest for investments of any length.

5. An Intertemporal Model

One can better appreciate what intertemporal equilibrium models are and how they implicitly provide theories of capital and interest by considering a simple example. The following model is far more restrictive than it needs to be, but the restrictions add to its simplicity and make it easier to compare with the models presented in Chapters 3, 4, and 8.

[7] At period t the returns on one- and two-period investments need not be equal. No forces of competition demand that they be. Competition does, however, demand that the discounted sum of the returns on a one-period investment at t and on a one-period investment at $t + 1$ equals the discounted return on a two-period investment at t.

Assumptions of the model: I have tried to distinguish those assumptions which are peculiar to the particular model from those which are common in models of intertemporal general equilibrium.

A: Setting

A1. Time period: There are only two time periods, $t = 1$ and $t = 2$. (In the general case there can be any finite number of time periods and the analysis can even be extended to an infinite time horizon.)

A2. Consumers and owners of resources and endowments: There are n consumers, divided into two disjoint classes—owners of the initial endowments and laborers. (In general there will be no such simple division of agents.)

A3. Services, resources and endowments: At $t = 1$, we have the vector of original endowments (x_1, m_1) where x represents wood and m represents axes. We also have a fixed quantity of homogeneous labor, L^*. x_2 and m_2 represent the commodities in period 2. All commodities, services, and resources are infinitely divisible. (In general, besides original endowments, each period may have its own vector of primary resource inputs. Labor can be heterogeneous and the vector of labor inputs from period to period may vary exogenously or as the result of production and consumption decisions. One can also specify all the possible commodities that may (but need not) exist in some period or other.)

B: Production

B1. The production functions: There are two of these, $x_2 = f(x_1, m_1, L)$ and $m_2 = h(x_1, m_1, L)$. Each is homogeneous of degree 1. The first partial derivatives are positive and the second partial derivatives are, after some quantity of x_1, m_1, or L, negative. (In general economists specify a single implicit production function from which some explicit production functions can be derived or a set of implicit production functions, one for each period. These functions are homogeneous of degree one with positive first and, after a point, negative second partial derivatives. Not every commodity in any time period need be an input at all, let alone an input into the production of all commodities. Joint products are also perfectly acceptable. As was mentioned in chapter 2, these calculus formulations are largely outdated.)

B2.   Entrepreneurs or firms aim to maximize profits.

C: Consumption

C1. Utility functions: Each consumer has a utility function that has (up to an unreached point of satiation) positive first and negative second partial derivatives. Moreover, in the specific example, I shall assume that aggregate utility functions, U^l, for laborers and U^C for owners of non-labor resources are known in advance. Both commodities are consumption goods. Taking the aggregate utility functions as given in advance is equivalent to assuming that all owners of like original endowments have the same utility functions, so that the aggregate is not affected by prices or incomes. (In general, aggregate utility functions cannot be known independently of the equilibrium solution and are not theoretically useful. Not every commodity need be an argument in each utility function.)

C2. Consumers maximize utility as constrained by their initial holdings of commodities or resources.

D: Market Conditions

D1. There is no excess demand.

D2. No one is able to influence the prices of what he or she buys or sells.

D3. There is free mobility of labor and all commodity inputs.

D4. All parties on the market have complete and accurate information concerning quantities and prices of commodities and technological possibilities.

D5. All parties are perfectly creditworthy and have limitless access to credit.

D6. Total expenditure equals total income.

D7. Total expenditure equals total income in each period.

D8. All available labor is expended.

D9. The wage is paid at the beginning of $t = 1$. (Assumptions D7–D9 are special assumptions which are made only with respect to the special model I am developing. No use of D-5 nor mention of credit will figure in this special model.)

Assumptions of group A or of group D would not (when asserted of actual economies) be counted by anyone as laws. They are merely simplifications needed to set up a system of equations or inequalities for which one can prove that an equilibrium solution exists. The specification of initial conditions by assumptions of groups A or D gives rise to philosophical perplexity, because many of these simplifications are not only false with respect to most modern economies, but false with respect to all known economies. As idealizations they are numerous and extreme. Assumptions B and C, on the other hand, seem to involve lawlike claims. These issues will be discussed in chapters 6 and 7.

The Intertemporal Model

On the basis of the assumptions above, one can set up the following system of equations that have an equilibrium solution:

$$(5.1) \qquad\qquad x_2 = f(x_1, m_1, L) \quad (B1)$$

$$(5.2) \qquad\qquad m_2 = h(x_1, m_1, L_1) \quad (B1)$$

$$(5.3) \qquad L^x + L^m = L^* \quad (A3, D8)$$

where the superscript indicates the good into which the labor is an input.

Maximization of profits ($B2$) plus the features of production functions ($B1$) and some calculus manipulations insure that the marginal products of inputs bear the same ratio to one another as do their prices.[8]

$$(5.4) \qquad\qquad \frac{{}^*f_{m_1}}{{}^*f_{x_1}} = \frac{p_{m,1}}{p_{x,1}}$$

$$(5.5) \qquad\qquad \frac{{}^*f_L}{{}^*f_{x_1}} = \frac{w}{p_{x,1}}$$

$$(5.6) \qquad\qquad \frac{{}^*h_{m_1}}{{}^*h_{x_1}} = \frac{p_{m,1}}{p_{x,1}}$$

$$(5.7) \qquad\qquad \frac{{}^*h_L}{{}^*h_{x_1}} = \frac{w}{p_{x,1}}$$

[8] For an exposition of these calculus techniques, see Henderson and Quandt (1971). By ${}^*f_{x_1}$ or ${}^*U^L_{x_1}$, I mean the value of the partial derivative of f or U^L with respect to x_1 evaluated at the equilibrium. f_{x_1}, the partial derivative, is a function ${}^*f_{x_1}$ is a number.

The utility functions are $U^L = U^L(x_1, m_1)$ and $U^C = U^C(x_1, m_1, x_2, m_2)$. Maximizing utility, one can derive by straightforward calculus techniques four more independent equations ($C1$, $C2$):

(5.8)
$$\frac{{}^*U^L_{m_1}}{{}^*U^L_{x_1}} = \frac{p_{m,1}}{p_{x,1}}$$

(5.9)
$$\frac{{}^*U^C_{m_1}}{{}^*U^C_{x_1}} = \frac{p_{m,1}}{p_{x,1}}$$

(5.10)
$$\frac{{}^*U^C_{m_2}}{{}^*U^C_{x_2}} = \frac{p_{m,2}}{p_{x,2}}$$

(5.11)
$$\frac{{}^*U^C_{x_2}}{{}^*U^C_{x_1}} = \frac{p_{x,2}}{p_{x,1}}$$

Furthermore, market clearing ($D1$) implies:

(5.12)
$$m_1 = m_1{}^L + m_1{}^C + m_1{}^x + m_1{}^m$$

(5.13)
$$x_1 = x_1{}^L + x_1{}^C + x_1{}^x + x_1{}^m$$

Since the income of workers must equal their expenditures ($D6$ and denying $D5$),

(5.14)
$$wL^* = p_{x,1} \cdot x_1{}^L + p_{m,1} \cdot m_1{}^L$$

Finally zero profit in competitive equilibrium (which follows from f and h being homogeneous of degree one and D2–4, 7) requires that

(5.15)
$$p_{x,2} \cdot x_2 = p_{x,1} \cdot x_1{}^x + p_{m,1} \cdot m_1{}^x + wL^x$$

(5.16)
$$p_{m,2} \cdot m_2 = p_{x,1} \cdot x_1{}^m + p_{m,1} \cdot m_1{}^m + wL^m$$

There are 16 independent equations and 17 unknowns ($x_1{}^x$, $x_1{}^m$, $x_1{}^L$, $x_1{}^C$, x_2, $m_1{}^x$, $m_1{}^m$, $m_1{}^L$, $m_1{}^C$, m_2, L^x, L^m, $p_{x,1}$, $p_{x,2}$, $p_{m,1}$, $p_{m,2}$, w). Taking $p_{x,1} = 1$, the system is perfectly determinate. The general existence proof for intertemporal equilibrium systems proves that this system is solvable.

The two own rates of return are by definition:

$$(5.17) \qquad r_{x,1} = \frac{p_{x,1}}{p_{x,2}} - 1$$

$$(5.18) \qquad r_{m,1} = \frac{p_{m,1}}{p_{m,2}} - 1$$

Since the actual rate of return, whatever it is, must be equal on all investments

$$(5.19) \qquad r_{x,1} = \frac{p_{x,1}}{p_{x,2}} - 1 = \frac{p_{x,1}(1 + r_1)}{\bar{p}_{x,2}} - 1$$

$$(5.20) \qquad r_{m,1} = \frac{p_{m,1}}{p_{m,2}} - 1 = \frac{p_{m,1}(1 + r_1)}{\bar{p}_{m,2}} - 1$$

If r_1 is larger than both $r_{x,1}$ and $r_{m,1}$, $\bar{p}_{x,2}$ is larger than $p_{x,1}$ and $\bar{p}_{m,2}$ is larger than $p_{m,1}$. If r_1 is less than both of the own rates of return, the price of both wood and axes will decline. If r_1 is the real rate of interest in period 1, then it must be between or equal to $r_{x,1}$ or $r_{m,1}$.

The model presented in this section, despite its extreme simplicity, exemplifies the structure of intertemporal models generally. Given preference structures, production possibilities, the initial endowment, and its distribution, one proves that there exists at least one intertemporal equilibrium for the economy. In such a proof, one derives discounted prices, outputs, discounted incomes, consumption, actual technology employed, and the distribution of income. All of these quantities are independent of contemporary prices or the rate of interest. Given a numeraire for each period, one can derive contemporary prices and the nominal rate of interest. If one chooses the numeraires so that the price level remains steady, the nominal rate of interest will equal the real rate of interest.

6. Austrian and Intertemporal Models

Abstract intertemporal general equilibrium models help one to appreciate the relations among various economic models. Austrian models of capital and interest can be regarded as models of intertemporal general equilibrium to which additional restrictions have been added. Most previous economic models can be regarded as special versions of intertemporal equilibrium models.[9] To convert the simple model of §5 into Lange's model, one need only specify that the contemporary prices of goods are unchanging, and that output and its distribution is the same in all periods and equal to the initial endowment and its distribution and give x no role in production. The resulting model is still more powerful than Lange's, since the utility functions provide additional information. They would make it possible to determine the value of Lange's k and to 'explain' what limits money capital and restricts production from reaching its maximum. Dropping the utility functions, one has Lange's model. Lange's model, like the model of §5, is an equilibrium model to which particular consistent additional constraints have been added. In Lange's model, some information has also been omitted.

The two major contributions that arise from Böhm-Bawerk's work are the two "laws": (3.21) more roundabout processes increase the output from the services of land and labor at a diminishing rate; and (3.22) agents prefer present to future consumption. These generalizations need not be part of intertemporal equilibrium models in general, although in fact they are partly embodied in almost all intertemporal models. In reaching an intertemporal general equilibrium constrained by (nonaggregate) production functions and utility functions, it need not be the case that own technical and subjective interest rates are positive for all commodities. Prices of individual commodities can change over time. The weighted average must, however, be positive, if there is a positive rate of return. In the model of §5, for example, it need not be the case that the marginal product of an ax in ax making be larger than one ax or that the capitalist prefer present axes to axes in period 2. The own rate of interest for axes may be negative. In that case, speaking loosely, wood must follow Böhm-Bawerk's "laws" or else the rate of return for the whole economy would be negative. Since x and m are inputs into the production of both goods, there is no general way to measure capital or time intensity. Some of the relations between time, utilities, and production that the Austrians were looking for at the aggregate level are preserved in certain averages and at the level of individual commodities; but no simple conclusions concerning aggregate capital, an average period of production, or the rate of interest can be reached. Only by further restrictions does it become possible to speak of a period of production and to achieve a simplified model of capital and interest.

[9] I shall argue in chapter 7 that intertemporal general equilibrium models ought not themselves to be regarded as the fundamental theoretical constructions of neo-classical theory. The basis of neo-classical theory lies in what I shall call "equilibrium theory."

What distinguish Austrian models of capital and interest from equilibrium models in general are these further restrictions. These restrictions include not only Böhm-Bawerk's two basic insights, but also simplifications which permit one to state these insights as generalizations concerning "the average period of production" and "the preference for present commodities" and "the rate of interest." Three simplifications are essential: (1) the analysis is confined to stationary equilibria; (2) consumer goods are not inputs into production, and (3) the time structure of production permits calculation of the time intensity. Models which exemplify or embody the Austrian theory of capital and interest are models which are simplified in this way and which behave in accordance with Böhm-Bawerk's two generalizations.

We can now understand better how the Cambridge criticisms bear on the Austrian theory and on the whole neoclassical approach to capital and interest. The Cambridge counter-models can be regarded as special case general equilibrium models. None of the assumptions of the Cambridge models is inconsistent with those of the most abstract intertemporal general equilibrium model. The reader can verify this claim by comparing the Cambridge counter-models of chapter 4 with the most general form of the assumptions of intertemporal equilibrium models discussed in the last section. The point will be much more obvious after we consider the basic conceptual structure of neoclassical economics in chapter 6. If the assumptions of the Cambridge models are, as I have asserted, consistent with those of abstract general equilibrium models, it follows immediately that the Cambridge economists have not produced even hypothetical counter-examples to abstract general equilibrium theories of capital and interest.

The difficulties the Cambridge critics have identified lie entirely with the addition to intertemporal equilibrium models of Böhm-Bawerk's lawlike assumptions and the three simplifications listed above. In adding these five assumptions, one is going beyond what general equilibrium theories warrant. The Cambridge critics have not revealed any flaw in general equilibrium models, nor have they shown that Böhm-Bawerk's lawlike assumptions ought not to be partly embodied in them. Even general equilibrium models which assume that in equilibrium own technical and subjective interest rates are positive give one no reason to believe that there is any simple relation between interest and the value of capital or the time intensity of production. Consider Bliss' comment:

> Even people who have made no study of economic theory are familiar with the idea that when something is more plentiful its price will be lower,

and introductory courses on economic theory reinforce this common presumption with various examples. However, there is no support from the theory of general equilibrium for the proposition that an input to production will be cheaper in an economy where more of it is available. All that the theory declares is that the price of the use of an input which is more plentiful cannot be higher if all other inputs, all other outputs and all other input prices are in constant proportions to each other (1975:85).

On the basis of abstract general equilibrium models we have no reason to exclude capital reversing or reswitching.[10] Partial equilibrium analysis of capital and interest—attempting to isolate supply and demand for capital and consider them separately—is not merely applying routinely the standard neoclassical tools. The assumptions such analyses depend on are not well founded.

Showing that the Austrian theory of capital and interest is unfounded and that its claims to explain the phenomena of capital and interest are unwarranted does nothing to undermine general equilibrium theories of capital and interest. At this point we can understand why many neoclassical economists are exasperated with the Cambridge critics. Examining the shadows of the real theory, the critics have declared the theory insubstantial. But how substantial are intertemporal equilibrium theories? In what real economy do omniscient agents choose the whole future? Perhaps the Cambridge critics have only mistaken the shadow for the ghost.

---

[10] Reswitching and capital reversing are, however, ruled out of the simple model of §5 because of the properties of f and h and because all commodities are inputs into the production of at least one commodity. See Stiglitz (1973:123–25).

CHAPTER SIX
On the Interpretation of General Equilibrium Models

In chapter 5 we saw that intertemporal general equilibrium models make claims about rates of interest without mentioning any aggregate quantity of capital or period of production. From the perspective of such models, the Cambridge criticisms are of little interest. Perhaps neoclassical economists have at least arrived at a rigorous, coherent theory of capital and interest and their relations to exchange values. Yet intertemporal equilibrium models like the one in §5 of chapter 5 are puzzling. Do they truly provide an adequate account of capital and interest? Can they help one explain the principal phenomena of interest or profits? We have many different questions to consider.

The elegant models of general equilibrium which have been developed during the past three decades have puzzled even their makers, since they appear to have little to do with real economies. Some, like Debreu (1959:ix) and Malinvaud (1972:242), believe that these models help explain or analyze prices. Others, like Arrow and Hahn (1971:vi–viii) deny that general equilibrium models can be used to explain. To assess general equilibrium models as models of capital and interest, one needs to understand clearly what these models are and whether they have the characteristics models must have when they are used in explanations. In this chapter, after dismissing some misconceived criticisms of general equilibrium models and emphasizing their flexibility, I shall offer a philosophical interpretation of these models. My goal in this chapter is to make the conceptual structure of general equilibrium models and the relations between these models and the whole neoclassical approach to economics as clear and intelligible as possible.

1. Some Misconceived General Criticisms

Intertemporal general equilibrium models are elegant and the existence proofs which employ them are formally valid. Yet these models do not bear their economic meaning on their face. As I have described them thus far, they are liable to several objections. In this section I shall consider some apparent difficulties with the concepts, logical structure, and testability of general equilibrium theories. The three criticisms discussed here all rest on a misunderstanding of general equilibrium theorizing. Clearing away these *apparent* difficulties helps sharpen one's understanding of this theorizing. I offer here no assessment of general equilibrium theories.

In intertemporal equilibrium models, the quantities which affect the day-to-day operation of an economy—contemporary prices and the expected and actual returns on investments—need never even be mentioned. One has a model of the progress of an economy over time in which there are no decisions or choices made over time and in which no commodity lasts more than one time period. Can such models depict the real course of an economy? (Harcourt 1976, p. 33).

They can. The basic features of a time sequence are present in general equilibrium models. The production functions implicitly embody causal-temporal constraints on production; the utility functions implicitly embody sequences in consumption. The utility functions depend upon the recognition that different commodities are the same good, even though the notion of a good plays no role in the equilibrium solution. Given the assumption of perfect information, there is no difference between deciding on December 1, 1960, or on June 3, 1999, what to do on June 3, 1999. If there is anything strange here, it lies with the assumption of perfect information rather than with the notion of an intertemporal equilibrium.

But, a critic might continue, how can a theory in which contemporary prices and the rate of interest are not even mentioned possibly be correct? As Smith recognized and Ricardo stressed, capital tends to flow into sectors where large profits are being made and out of sectors in which the rate of profit is low. For Ricardo it is this tendency toward the equalization of the rate of profit that explains the uniformity of the wages paid to labor of a given quality or of the rent paid on the land of a given fertility and convenience. The reactions of capitalists to changes in profit margins are fundamental organizing forces. The capitalist's search for profits is the mainspring of economic life. Economists concluded that the rate of interest (or profits) is a crucial theoretical variable in any fundamental economic theory applicable to a capitalist economy. Yet the rate of interest has no explicit role in an intertemporal equilibrium model. How can such models possibly be adequate?

What takes the place in intertemporal equilibrium models of any mention of a general rate of interest is the condition that pure economic profits be zero. What Ricardo called the average rate of profit is regarded as a sum of interest costs for each of the various commodities. This cost is completely determined by knowledge of the various own rates of return. In fact one can easily recast Ricardo's original corn model (1815:9–42) in the concepts of intertemporal equilibrium models. In that model there is one commodity, corn, which, along with labor is used as an input into its own production. From corn output one subtracts corn input, the corn wages and the corn rent to get net corn output. If the rate of profit (net corn output divided by corn costs) is higher on one piece of land than on another, capital tends to move and rents will be bid up or down. The same story can be told in terms of an intertemporal equilibrium model. The technical interest rate for corn and the own corn rate of interest are positive. The discounted price of next year's corn is less than the price of this year's corn. The discounted net returns from corn production must be zero in equilibrium. If they are not zero, exactly the same processes of bidding up or down of rents and shifting of capital will take place. The notion of interest as a cost rather than a return has merely been taken seriously, and this cost has been disaggregated.

But can this story be told in terms of intertemporal equilibrium, in which the future holds no unexpected changes? Can the notion of an intertemporal equilibrium help one understand real economies, which are never in equilibrium at any moment, let alone in an intertemporal equilibrium? Every economics student learns that with changes in the conditions of production or with changes in tastes, the quantity supplied or demanded at what had been the normal price changes. The result is a bidding up or down of the price and an increase or decrease in the profits in that industry, which will, given competition, cause a movement of capitals until the market clearing price is an equilibrium price at which only normal profits are made. Since economies are never in equilibrium, such processes are always occurring and are central to the subject matter of economics.

Such a critic might go on to argue that stationary equilibrium models cohere, although uneasily, with this model of disequilibrium processes. Initially an economy is near a stationary equilibrium state. That equilibrium is then disturbed by changes in tastes or in production possibilities. As a result of the process of adjustment, a new stationary equilibrium would be achieved, were it not for other disruptions. It has been widely believed that short-run stationary equilibrium models provide a frame of reference or point of comparison for the analysis of actual economies.

An intertemporal equilibrium, on the other hand, is not an economic state toward which an economy can move. There is no sense attached to the notion of *restoring* an intertemporal equilibrium. If such an equilibrium does not exist during all periods of the relevant time interval, it does not exist at all. Can one tell the story of adjustments to price fluctuations within intertemporal equilibrium models? One might conclude that intertemporal general equilibrium models have no applications.

This criticism is, I think, mistaken. Considering and refuting it helps clarify the logical structure of equilibrium models. First, the assertion that atemporal general equilibrium models cohere or fit in with the story of economic adjustment is incorrect. As Robinson points out (1953–54), it is difficult to imagine any economy *getting into* a stationary equilibrium. In a stationary equilibrium, both the future and the past are identical to the present. The invidious comparison between stationary and intertemporal equilibrium models is unjustified.

The more important difficulty with this criticism is that it misunderstands the project of the general equilibrium theorist. Intertemporal equilibrium models are fundamentally accounts of the clearing of markets for both current commodities and for titles to future commodities and of the efficient allocation of resources over time. In order for the theory to explain how an economy actually behaves over a whole time period (if anyone has such grand ambitions), the notion of a full intertemporal equilibrium is essential. If, on the other hand, one is interested in discussing the reactions of markets for current and future commodities to changes in givens, one can focus on variants of the basic notion of intertemporal equilibrium.

Suppose, for example, one surrenders the condition that everybody has perfect information about future commodities, their prices, and the production possibilities. Suppose instead that individuals have some way of ranking every bundle of commodities that anybody believes will exist at any time and that all have beliefs concerning future utilities and technological possibilities. The easiest, although not the most plausible, way of describing such a situation is to suppose that subjectively every agent is in exactly the same state as in an intertemporal general equilibrium model.[1] Perfect certainty, but not omniscience, rules. The markets for current commodities and commodity futures are assumed to come rapidly to equilibrium. The proof of the existence of an intertemporal equilibrium demonstrates that such an equilibrium will exist, since it will be identical to an intertemporal

---

[1] This is not the only way in which theorists have dealt with failures of expectations. Debreu (1959, ch. 7) has a different treatment. Arrow (1974a:268–69) introduces uncertainty intuitively via a notion of contigent commodities.

equilibrium. The difference is not in the determination of equilibrium, but in what happens at the end of the first period. Without perfect information, expectations will be disappointed. The economy will not be in the state individuals would have predicted at the beginning of the time interval. A new market equilibrium will need to be established.

The variation on intertemporal equilibrium models sketched above provides us with what are called "temporary" equilibrium models.[2] Unlike either stationary or full intertemporal equilibrium models, they have elements of disequilibrium built into them. They can be meshed easily with the simple story of how an economy responds to changes in tastes and in conditions of production. In leading so directly to temporary equilibrium models, the efforts of the general equilibrium theorists may lead toward a better treatment of disequilibrium rather than, as the criticism above alleges, away from understanding actual (disequilibrium) economic states.

But why then does chapter 5 focus on intertemporal equilibrium models rather than temporary equilibrium models? First, theoretical discussions of capital and interest generally rely on full intertemporal general equilibrium models. Temporary equilibrium models do not have nearly the same range of acceptance. They require further elaboration. Second, temporary equilibrium models, as they currently stand, can provide no theory of actual returns. They are only a fragment of a theory of interest and profits. The markets for current commodities and commodity futures come to equilibrium. There is a going market rate of interest, which is determined by the same factors as in intertemporal equilibrium models. At the end of the period, however, expectations are disappointed. There is no reason why the sum of the actual returns on investments divided by the value of the investments should be the same, even in sign, as the market interest rate of the previous period.

This feature of temporary equilibrium models may turn out to be a great virtue. It might be argued that one should not expect to find any general theory of the actual rate of return. Uncontrolled, irregular exogenous political, sociological, or even meteorological factors perhaps have such a large role to play that no general account will be of any use. Alternatively, one might argue that temporary equilibrium models represent a step toward a more sensible theory of the rate of profit. All one needs is some account of the relations between expectations and past experience which relates expected and actual returns.

[2] The idea was first introduced explicitly to English-speaking economists by Hicks (1946:122–23). See Bliss 1975:57f) and Grandmont (1977:535–72).

Both of these positions are plausible. But economic theorists do not yet possess a more sensible theory of returns and distribution that employs temporary equilibrium analysis, nor are they generally willing to give up attempting to explain actual returns and actual distribution. It thus seems sensible to focus on intertemporal equilibrium models. They purport, at least, to explain more and they remain central to theoretical discussion.

Notice also that the theoretical gains in shifting to temporary equilibrium models are small at present. Temporary equilibrium models avoid the objectionably strong assumptions that all agents have complete knowledge of the economic future and that the economy is in intertemporal equilibrium. Yet the models still stipulate that agents have perfect information about the availability of all current commodities. Second, temporary equilibrium models must assume that at least one complete commodity futures market exists. Third, they assume that individuals are willing and able to rank all possible future consumption bundles. Fourth, they assume that markets come to equilibrium at the beginning of each time period. Either time periods are short and this last assumption is a particularly strong one, or time periods are quite long and the perfect information requirement concerning the present period must bear the theoretical burden. In focusing on intertemporal general equilibrium models, as the basis for a theory of capital and interest, I am not overlooking a clearly superior option. When asking how neoclassical economists explain distribution or interest, one should concentrate on intertemporal general equilibrium models.

As we have seen in this section, several of the apparently counterintuitive features of general equilibrium models are much more reasonable than they seem. To understand these models clearly and to appreciate their importance to neoclassical economics, we must now consider carefully what the foundations of neoclassical economics are and how they are related to general equilibrium models. Only then will we be in a position to offer a balanced assessment of these models.

2. Equilibrium Theory and the Basic Equilibrium Model

To understand what general equilibrium models are, it is helpful to distinguish them from what I shall call "the basic equilibrium model," of which general equilibrium models are "augmentations" (and refinements). The basic equilibrium model is constituted by those assumptions which are common to most microeconomic and general equilibrium models. Having already described the basis of equilibrium models in an informal and intuitive way (chapter 2), I shall now be more rigorous. Rigor can be deceptive, however: the rough descriptions are in some ways more revealing. As a fundamental model or as a foundation to a whole approach to economics, the basic equilibrium model cannot be captured precisely in any given formulation.

Most modern economists (although they do not use my terminology) regard the basic equilibrium model as fundamental to virtually all economic theory. They hope to be able to reduce, or at least relate, macroeconomic theories to the equilibrium model. They hope to be able to augment the basic equilibrium model to deal with questions of economic growth and change. This is the model they rely on in empirical research and in many welfare recommendations. When one has succeeded in saying what equilibrium models are, one has largely succeeded in saying what neoclassical economics is. General equilibrium models, whether abstract or practical, are not themselves the foundations of neoclassical economics. Those assumptions common to most equilibrium models, be they partial or general, are fundamental.

Looking back at the model in §5 of chapter 5 one can distinguish a number of assumptions which are common to most equilibrium models. These are of different kinds. The assumption that individuals are utility maximizers (C2) is perhaps an economic "law." Assumptions concerning information and the divisibility of commodities are ubiquitous simplifications, but are certainly not regarded as assertions or discoveries of economics. Although such simplifications are essential in most economic theorizing and are common constituents of economic models, they are neither assertions of economics nor, I suggest, part of the fundamental economic *theory*. I think we can better understand model building in economics if we focus on that subset of the assumptions common to equilibrium models which consists of basic assertions or principles.

"Equilibrium *theory*" is my name for the fundamental theory of microeconomics and indeed of neoclassical economics generally. Equilibrium theory consists of the basic principles or assertions of neoclassical economics. It asserts closures of some of the assumptions common to equilibrium models. Equilibrium theory is basically utility theory coupled with some generalizations concerning production and the motivation of firms or entrepreneurs. It may be formulated roughly as the following nine lawlike statements. Many qualifications are needed and will be discussed below.

(1) For any individual, A and any two options, x and y, one and only one of the following is true: A prefers x to y; A prefers y to x; A is indifferent between x and y.

(2) A's preferences among options are transitive.

(3) A chooses that option he or she believes maximizes his or her utility. (The utility of option x is greater than the utility of option y if and only if A prefers x to y. The utilities of options are equal just in case A is indifferent between them.)

(4) If option x is acquiring commodity bundle x' and option y is acquiring commodity bundle y', and y' contains as much or more of each commodity as x' and more of at least one commodity, then all agents prefer y to x.

(5) The marginal utility of a commodity c to an agent A is a decreasing function of the quantity of c that A has.

(6) When we increase any input into production with other inputs held constant, output increases, but, after a certain point, at a decreasing rate.

(7) Increasing all the inputs into production in the same proportion increases output by that proportion. The production set is weakly convex and additive.

(8) Entrepreneurs or firms perform those actions which they believe will maximize their profits.

(9) Through exchange the economic choices of individuals become compatible.

The talk of marginal utility in (5) and the supposition that utility functions are cardinal (that differences in levels of utility are significant) are easily eliminable. Economists generally prefer to talk in terms of marginal rates of commodity substitution. The conceptual issues can be addressed more directly if one continues to speak in terms of marginal utilities. Everything I shall say can be translated into more usual terminology.

Many economists would say that (1)–(3) assert that people are rational and that (1)–(4) assert that people are economically rational (Hausman 1979b:120–21). Notice that (4) has the effect of identifying options and commodity bundles. Diminishing marginal utility is supposed to be a psychological law, which is sometimes (implausibly in my opinion) regarded as part of what it means to be economically rational. Constant returns to scale and diminishing returns to variable inputs are supposed to be in some sense natural laws or technological givens (Rosenberg 1976b:29–30). I think that it is a mistake to regard (6) or (7) as natural laws. Production functions, unlike chemical formulae, are implicitly assertions about our *knowledge*. To say that firms attempt to maximize profits is supposed to be a lawlike claim concerning motivation, possibly deducible from other features of our theory. If this deduction were carried through, (8) could be dropped from the list. Since entrepreneurs are also consumers, it actually seems that

(8) may conflict with (3). (9) is special. It is not usually an axiom, but is a consequence of (1)–(8) and further simplifications in particular models. Yet (9) is not merely a derivative result. Economists set up their models and organize their theories in order to get this result. Although often *not* an axiom, (9) should be included among the fundamental "laws."

This set of lawlike statements is disquieting, since, even with qualifications, most of the claims appear to be false. Economists have, of course, recognized this peculiarity of (1)–(9); it is one of the reasons they prefer to think of their work in terms of models. Controversy concerning these purported laws has been extensive. Debate has focused on (or floundered around) four questions. Are these purported laws analytic or synthetic? Are they *a priori* or *a posteriori*? Are they theoretical laws or are they observational (that is, subject individually to direct observational confirmation or refutation)? Are they well confirmed or often falsified? Commentators on economic theory have disagreed drastically. These purported laws have been regarded as synthetic *a priori* (Von Mises 1960:12–13), (Hollis and Nell 1975, esp. ch. 9); analytic (Hutchison 1938, ch. 2), false (Friedman 1953), and not fully interpreted (Machlup 1955, 1960). Thinking in terms of models demands a reformulation of the issues, but resolves none of the questions. I will offer my interpretation of these fundamental "laws" in §2 & §3 of chapter 7.

Notice that some of these generalizations seem reliable only in certain circumstances, given a certain institutional setting. One reason why it is reasonable to claim that individuals generally prefer more commodities to fewer (4), is that there is a market on which excess commodities can be easily traded. (4) is not however *derivable* from (1)–(3) and (5)–(8), conjoined with auxiliary hypotheses and statements of initial conditions concerning the existence of markets. There are, alternatives to (4) from which (4) may be derived, but none of these alternatives is appreciably weaker or more reasonable than (4) itself. (1)–(9) do not exhaust the general "laws" of microeconomics. They (or some reformulation of them) are, however, the basic "laws." Other important lawlike claims (e.g., the price of a commodity will rise when demand for it exceeds its supply) can be derived from (1)–(8) and various stipulations concerning markets, information, and so forth. The above nine statements, however, express the fundamentals of neoclassical economics.

To assert that equilibrium theory is well formulated by (1)–(9) is rough and somewhat misleading. The assertion is rough because (1)–(9) are not a very precise statement of the theory; it is somewhat misleading, because neoclassical economists do not always make use of *all* of the above lawlike statements [(7) and (8) are the most likely to be dropped or replaced by contrary generalizations, while revealed preference theory is supposed to supplant (1)–(5)].

Formulating equilibrium theory as (1)–(9) may also be incomplete. My suggestion that one should exclude other common assumptions of equilibrium models from the fundamental theory can certainly be questioned. To understand what equilibrium models are, one must also make reference to commonly used mathematical techniques and standard characterizations of the institutional, informational, and material background. These characterizations may themselves be lawlike to some extent. The notion of a "law" is sufficiently problematic that I do not want to stake my contrast between (1)–(9) and the other assumptions common in equilibrium models on the greater lawlikeness of (1)–(9). Other common assumptions differ in three ways from (1)–(9). First, they have a narrower scope; the assertion that there are many buyers and sellers is not supposed to be true of every market in every economy. Second, these simplifications are not regarded by economists as discovered or asserted by their theory; the simplifications sketch the circumstances in which the theory is applied and are crucial to the derivation of important theorems, but they are not themselves assertions of the theory. Finally, although these claims concerning markets, resources, information, and the like are important to equilibrium models, they are less important than are (1)–(9) or some reformulation of them. Neoclassical economic analyses, like the model in chapter 5, generally assume that commodities are infinitely divisible. This assumption has, as the result of employing better mathematical techniques, become avoidable in certain circumstances. Were it to become fully dispensable, economists would not, I believe, conclude that there had been any great revolution in their fundamental theory. If, however, a number of the mathematical techniques and assumptions concerning prevailing circumstances were to change, one might well regard the fundamental theory as changed.

Replacing any of (1)–(9) with a nonequivalent generalization would, on the other hand, count by itself as a change of theory. The distinction between the fundamental laws and simplifications concerning background conditions is not, however, sharp. (7) for example is a borderline case (Samuelson 1947:84). Most economists would regard it as a simplification rather than as a "law," yet its scope is wide. It is not so crucial to the identity of equilibrium theory as is, for example, (3). Despite these many qualifications, it still seems to me enlightening to regard (1)–(9) as the fundamental theory of neoclassical economics.

3. General Equilibrium Models and General Equilibrium Theories

Given this analysis of equilibrium theory and of equilibrium models, we can now see that general equilibrium models are *augmentations* of the basic equilibrium model.[3] The assumptions of a general equilibrium model like that of chapter 5 fall into three groups: (a) reformulations of (1)–(9); (b) assumptions like perfect information or infinite divisibility of commodities, which are common to equilibrium models generally; and (c) assumptions that there are many commodities and that there is a general interdependence among the various markets. Assumptions of the third class are what distinguish general equilibrium models from other equilibrium models. What I mean by calling general equilibrium models "augmentations" of the basic equilibrium model should be clear. Further assumptions are added to reformulations (with occasional revisions) of assumptions common to equilibrium models generally.

As mentioned above, there is no non-trivial set of assumptions which is part of every equilibrium model. There is scarcely an assumption which is even *consistent* with the assumptions of every equilibrium model. There are models without perfect competition, without infinite divisibility of commodities, without perfect information, without constant returns to scale, and so forth. All I am claiming is that almost all neoclassical theories assert most of (1)–(9) and that almost all equilibrium models assume most of them. The basic equilibrium model also includes such simplifying assumptions as perfect information, infinite commodity divisibility, and so forth.

Partial equilibrium models augment these assumptions with further axioms of two distinctive kinds. First, certain economic magnitudes

---

[3] Ernst Händler (1980) agrees that general equilibrium theory is not fundamental. In Händler's and Sneed's terminology, general equilibrium theory is not a "basic theory element." Instead it is a "specialization" of the basic theory element of the theory net. What is basic to neoclassical economics, according to Händler, is not equilibrium theory, but a weak characterization of an economy which is common to all neoclassical analyses. This characterization contains only three generalizations (pp. 37–38): (a) production and consumption are respectively technologically and physiologically possible; (b) the weak preference relations ("is at least as preferred as") governing production and consumption are reflexive and transitive, (c) There is no excess "mean demand" on any market. Händler's and Sneed's "specialization" relation demands that models (in the logician's sense) which satisfy the axioms of a specialization of a theory element must also satisfy the axioms of the theory element itself. The basic theory element must thus, speaking loosely, be included in all of its specializations. The basic theory element of neoclassical economics must thus contain only axioms which are consistent with *all* neoclassical theories. While Händler's work is interesting, I think that my informal approach is much more flexible, intuitive, and informative.

like prices, incomes, quantities produced—which are in fact influenced by the workings of the market and which are sensitive to other factors in the economy—are taken as constants whose values are given. This permits independent consideration of single markets and permits one to consider factors influencing supply separately from those influencing demand. Supply and demand are principally partial equilibrium concepts. Second, to simplify matters, one works with certain sorts of aggregates. Instead of considering the complex changes in prices that result when one employs different techniques of production, one might assume as Lange does that all consumption goods can be treated as one commodity and all capital goods as another single commodity. If one is concerned with certain aspects of consumer choice, one might assume that all but one or two commodities which are of particular interest can be considered as a single composite commodity. It is thus incorrect to assert that microeconomics never deals with aggregates. These isolating and aggregating assumptions distinguish partial equilibrium models. In each case the state of mutual adjustment or equilibrium economists are considering is only partial, since they are ignoring adjustments in other markets and in other choices.

General equilibrium models avoid these isolating and aggregating assumptions. In general equilibrium models there are many commodities and a general interdependence among the various markets. There can, of course, be equilibrium analyses which are hard to classify as either partial or general. There are also two quite different varieties of general equilibrium models which need to be sharply distinguished. One of these is of practical use, while the other (like the model of chapter 5) is quite abstract. The first kind is exemplified by input-output models. By assuming, for example, that there are constant production coefficients and ignoring influences of demand, one can set up a model of an economy with perhaps a hundred different commodities and industries and, with the help of a computer, investigate how it operates. Practical general equilibrium models raise no other philosophical questions than do partial equilibrium models.

Models of the second kind, which I shall call "abstract general equilibrium models," place no limitations on the interdependence of markets or on the nature of production and demand beyond those implicit in the lawlike claims. When economists speak of general equilibrium models, it is usually this second, abstract variety that they have in mind. In the quotations near the beginning of chapter 5 it seems to me as if Samuelson and Solow are thinking of both kinds of general equilibrium models at the same time. They are thinking of practical general equilibrium models, since they believe that these models actually have explanatory and predictive uses (which, as I shall argue in chapter 7, abstract general equilibrium models do not have). Yet they must also be thinking of abstract equilibrium models, since practical models like input-output analysis provide no theory of the relations between interest and prices. With fixed input coefficients one cannot explain own rates of interest in terms of own technical interest rates. Without reference to utility functions, one cannot invoke own subjective interest rates in explaining the rate of interest. Demand and technology cannot be fixed if one wishes to account for the rate of interest as the equilibrium theorists wish to. Only abstract general equilibrium models can provide theories of capital and interest.

To assess what neoclassical economics has to say about capital and interest, one must thus focus on abstract general equilibrium models. It is important to stress that such models are not the fundamental models of neoclassical economics. As I argued in §2, the fundamental theory is equilibrium theory. Paradoxically, the basic equilibrium model is much more general than a general equilibrium model. General equilibrium models are augmentations of the fundamental model. General equilibrium *theories* (which follow from theoretical hypotheses employing general equilibrium models) are not the fundamental theory. These claims are not arbitrary stipulations. When scientists have some explicit explanatory or predictive purposes or when they want to develop a theory of a specific subject matter, they often augment the axioms of some fundamental model (or theory). Adding further assumptions to Newton's laws, one can set up a model of a solar system. Such augmentations are precisely what general equilibrium models are. They are unlike fundamental models in the natural sciences. Equilibrium theory serves much of the same role in economics that fundamental theories in the natural sciences serve in their respective domains.

Intertemporal equilibrium models, have the form of specialized models or of potential explanatory arguments. Yet the assumptions of such models concerning information, markets, and the like seem ill-suited for the purposes of explaining or predicting economic phenomena. Models like the one in §5 of chapter 5 assume that agents have complete and accurate knowledge concerning the availability and prices of commodities as well as the present and future production possibilities. They also stipulate that there is a complete set of commodity futures markets on which present commodities (or titles to future commodities) can be freely exchanged for titles to future commodities of every kind and date. Such assumptions render the models so obviously inapplicable that one cannot confirm theoretical hypotheses employing them.

Furthermore, since the assumptions of such models are not even approximately true in real economies, the models have almost no predictive worth. This explains why theorists like Milton Friedman are so unsympathetic to the "Walrasian viewpoint" (1953:89–92). Given the near absurdity of such stipulations as perfect information, one wants to know what the point is of abstract general equilibrium models. Can they really provide a fundamental theory of capital and interest as Samuelson, Solow, and Bliss believe? Can economists employ such models to explain the phenomena of profits? To this crucial problem we must now turn.

CHAPTER SEVEN

Philosophical Assessment of General Equilibrium Models

In assessing the models we have just studied, we face many questions. Theories and models serve many different purposes. A model may efficiently guide research, although no theoretical hypotheses employing it are of predictive or explanatory value. Like Ptolemy's account of planetary motion, a theory may make accurate predictions without actually explaining anything. My main concern here is whether general equilibrium models enable economists to explain adequately the principal phenomena of capital and interest. Those who deny that explanation is an important aim of economics or of science generally will find this question misguided. But it remains a question that economists and laymen ask. I shall implicitly defend its importance.

To assess the explanatory power of general equilibrium theories, we need to know what criteria scientific explanations must satisfy. Unfortunately there is no well-supported consensus among philosophers of science concerning these criteria. I cannot thus simply list a number of conditions which general equilibrium theories must satisfy and then check whether the theories do satisfy them. We must proceed cautiously and sensitively. General equilibrium theories apparently fail to satisfy criteria some philosophers have argued that explanations must satisfy. Some of these failures reveal the inadequacy or misapplication of the philosophical criteria. I shall argue, however, in §4 that the *simplifications* general equilibrium theories employ cannot legitimately be used in explanations. For this reason general equilibrium models cannot yet provide the basis for an explanatory theory of capital and interest.

1. Explanation

The much abused starting point for modern philosophical discussions of explanation is Carl Hempel's deductive-nomological model (1965:331–496). According to Hempel, a necessary condition for giving a scientific explanation is deducing a description of the event or state of affairs to be explained from a set of true statements, some of which are lawlike. Schematically we have:

laws
true statements specifying the circumstances
statement of what is to be explained

where the line represents a deductive inference. There is, according to Hempel, a second kind of explanation, an "inductive-statistical" explanation, which one employs when the laws are not deterministic. In statistical explanation one does not deduce what one wants to explain. Instead, one only shows it to be highly probable. For simplification, I shall focus on the deductive-nomological model. Most of my discussion, however, applies (with some rephrasing), to both models. That one deduces in a nonstatistical explanation the description of the event or state of affairs to be explained from a set of true statements, some of which are lawlike, is only a necessary condition. Sufficient conditions are not well understood and are sensitive to the particular context. Hempel is, of course, not just proposing a "model" in the sense discussed in chapter 3.

The deductive-nomological model has been much criticized. Indeed, one familiar with these criticisms might wonder why I focus on deductive-nomological explanation. I have two reasons. First many of the major criticisms of this model challenge its demand that scientific explanations be explanatory *arguments* (Scriven 1959, 1963; Salmon 1971). These criticisms are not germane here, since purported explanations of phenomena of capital and interest that employ general equilibrium models are arguments. As a set of necessary conditions on explanatory arguments, the deductive-nomological model has faced fewer criticisms and has fewer rivals. My major reason for focusing on the deductive-nomological model is that I know of no better analysis of explanatory arguments.[1] The grounds for this assessment of Hem-

[1] The criticisms Salmon and others have made of Hempel's model of statistical explanation are serious and Salmon's alternative is attractive. I shall, however, discuss neither these criticisms nor Salmon's model. Since apparent explanations employing general equilibrium models are arguments (proofs) and since the statements in such explanations are not statistical in form, it is simplest to focus on nonstatistical explanation and the deductive-nomological model. Ignoring statistical explanations and their many difficulties will create strains in my exposition, particularly since I shall argue in §3 that ultimately one must regard many economic explanations as statistical. The only alternative would be an elaborate and largely irrelevant discussion of statistical explanation. Purported explanations of phenomena of capital and interest that rely on general equilibrium theories are inadequate on any reasonable model of explanation I know of. This chapter employs the simplest model of explanatory arguments.

pel's analysis will not be clear until §6. Despite the difficulties I shall discuss in §2 and §4, I shall defend the deductive-nomological model as an analysis of explanatory arguments and shall use it to assess general equilibrium accounts of capital, interest, and exchange values.

Talk of scientific models does not fit gracefully into Hempel's analysis of explanations. I have argued (chapter 3) that we should regard models as sets of assumptions that define a new predicate. Theoretical hypotheses assert that the new predicate is true of something. From those hypotheses we may derive the closure of the assumptions of the model. The derived set of statements is a theory. Models thus contribute nothing to explanation until theoretical hypotheses are offered. The laws which are needed in a deductive-nomological explanation will be closures of assumptions of a model. The detailed specification of the relevant circumstances will usually not be derivable from a theoretical hypothesis, yet closures of assumptions of models need not always be lawlike. Models may contain only lawlike assumptions, like the model of a classical particle system, or they may also contain simplifying assumptions. If one were to assert that some actual economy is in intertemporal general equilibrium, one would not only be making lawlike claims. One would also be claiming the commodities are infinitely divisible, that agents have perfect information about the economic future, and so forth. Let $S_1, \ldots, S_n$ be the statements in a deductive-nomological explanation, not including the statement of what is to be explained. Let $S_1, \ldots, S_j$ be the laws and $S_1, \ldots, S_k$ be statements in the explanation implied by theoretical hypotheses. I am claiming that $1 \leq j \leq k \leq n$.

If explanatory arguments must be deductive-nomological (or inductive-statistical), must we not conclude immediately that general equilibrium theories cannot be used to explain the phenomena of capital and interest, or, for that matter, anything else? In Hempel's models, all of the statements must be true. Suppose one were to take the general equilibrium model of chapter 5, add the theoretical hypothesis that the economy of the United States in 1978 and 1979 was an equilibrium economy of the sort defined by the model, fill in initial conditions somehow, and deduce a real rate of interest which happens by some miracle to agree with the actual one-period real rate of interest. Surely one would not have provided a deductive-nomological explanation of the rate of interest. The theoretical hypothesis in this case is obviously false. Moreover, the difficulties are not confined to the particular case. All current general equilibrium theories contain statements that appear to be false. Some, like the model in chapter 5, will falsely assert that all individuals have perfect information concerning the prices and availability of commodities and concerning the production possibilities.

Many will falsely assert that the preferences of all consumers are transitive.

To conclude, without further analysis, that general equilibrium models can have no role in explanations would be to misapply pedantically the deductive-nomological model. Employing that model in this finicky way, one can criticize virtually all explanatory arguments scientists offer. Either the deductive-nomological model is much too demanding and needs replacing, or one must find a more flexible way to apply it.

Consider what happens when natural scientists attempt to deal with complicated everyday phenomena. Take the trite example of the path of a leaf's fall. In what sense can it be explained by physicists? Precise deductive-nomological explanation seems out of the question. Scientists cannot get exact information concerning all relevant initial conditions and cannot do all the complicated calculations that would be necessary if they did have the pertinent data. If the only stumbling blocks were these problems of knowing the initial conditions and of calculation, physicists would have what I shall call "an explanation-in-principle" of the leaf's path. Scientists would know all the relevant laws and causal factors. Even though they could not now and never could explain the path in detail, there would be nothing mysterious about the trajectories of falling leaves and nothing general or theoretical to learn about them. Explanations in principle appear to be genuine explanations.

Scientists justify their explanations in principle by developing theories they test in simpler circumstances. In the case of the falling leaf, one tests the theoretical hypothesis that the model of gravitation applies to ordinary bodies falling in evacuated chambers or that it applies to the motion of the planets. Theories of fluids and of resistance are also developed and tested with respect to simpler situations. It is difficult to know whether one has taken account of all the laws which bear on a leaf's tossing and gliding. Perhaps telekinesis is a significant phenomenon with leaves. Scientists have good reason to believe they know all the relevant laws when, with simplifications concerning initial conditions, they can make roughly correct predictions concerning falling leaves and are able to cite the factors responsible for any appreciable errors.[2] Philosophers must grant that such explanations in principle are truly explanations. If the deductive-nomological model does not

---

[2] Achieving a theory of falling leaves in this way is employing what J. S. Mill called the deductive method (1843, bk. III, ch. 11; bk. VI, ch. 9). Mill believed that economic laws are established inductively by psychology and the natural sciences and that economists then develop economic theory deductively (1843, bk. VI, ch. 9, §3; Cairnes 1888:71f).

permit this recognition, it is inadequate. The best evidence for or against a model of explanation is the congruence between the model and the achievements of scientists.[3]

Even explanation-in-principle is a tall order. I doubt that physicists can now explain in principle the path of a falling leaf. Economists certainly cannot explain in principle local or overall characteristics of real economies. Not only are the purported laws of economics difficult to confirm—perhaps because of the difficulties of setting up simplified experimental situations—but theorists know these "laws" are inadequate. Economists are ignorant of many relevant laws. They leave out of account significant causal factors. At best theorists believe that they have got what, following J. S. Mill, I shall call an "inexact science"—an account of the principal causal factors involved.

Inexact sciences appear to be explanatory. We believe that physicists can explain the paths of falling leaves even if they cannot give a full explanation in principle. The theory of gravitation explains some of the characteristics of tides, even though theorists remain ignorant to what Mill calls the "minor causes" (1843, bk. VI, ch. III, §1). We need to understand what such "inexact explanation-in-principle" is and when scientists are justified in believing that they have given one. I shall argue that, appearances to the contrary, one may regard many such explantions as deductive-nomological. I shall, moreover, show that even when one appreciates such inexact explanation-in-principle, one is still forced to conclude that current general equilibrium models do not enable economists to explain the main phenomena concerning capital and interest.

2. Inexact Laws

Economists have long recognized that they are unable to give precise explanations and that the general statements they rely on are, if interpreted naïvely, false. In defense of these general statements (and thus of the explanations which employ them), most economists would offer one or both of the following claims:

> (1) The lawlike assumptions of the basic equilibrium model are not precisely true of actual people and technologies, but in the relevant circumstances they are sufficiently correct and the failures (with certain exceptions) sufficiently random and insignificant that one may nevertheless rely

---

[3] Within this sentence lurk puzzles which I discuss in the postscript.

on equilibrium theories and consider them to be explanatory (Hicks 1946:11, 22, 34; Koopmans 1957:142).

(2) The assumptions of the basic equilibrium model are idealizations. Equilibrium models reveal the logic of economic relations in simplified ideal cases and neither are nor are meant to be precisely true of real economies. (Schumpeter 1954:1049–50n, 884, 889; Koopmans 1957:142f; Gibbard and Varian 1978, esp. pp. 673f).

These claims, as I have stated them, are vague and ambiguous. Various economists and philosophers have attempted to provide a firmer defense for the basic "laws" of equilibrium theory by refining these claims or by substituting what they regarded as philosophically more sophisticated views. Before discussing the views of others or the claim that economics is concerned with idealizations, we must analyze the inexactness of equilibrium theories. Not only, as we have suggested, may lawlike generalizations in explanatory theories be inexact or incomplete, but also many economists already believe that economic theory should be understood as somehow inexact or close to the truth.

In considering the inexactness of various economic theories, I am not merely calling attention to the fact that economists are able to make only inaccurate or imprecise predictions. They may be unable to make accurate predictions or to explain in detail merely because of difficulties in specifying the initial conditions or because of limitations in their mathematical powers. Not only are the implications of economic theories inaccurate or imprecise, but the basic generalizations, the nine "laws" of equilibrium theory, themselves appear to be inexact.

There are several different ways in which one might attempt to analyze inexact laws. Sometimes generalizations are inexact because they are approximate. They are not true as stated, but they can be made true merely by specifying a margin of error in a certain domain. Kepler's Laws are in this sense approximate. Within a certain percentage of the calculated angular velocities or periods of revolution, these laws appear to be true. By "blurring" what the laws assert (and thus imply) one gets exceptionless true generalizations. It seems unpromising, however, to interpret basic economic generalizations as approximate laws principally in this sense. Suppose in a recession it maximizes profit for several companies each to lay off 1000 workers. If no company laid off fewer than 800 or more than 1200, then the evidence would confirm (within a margin of error of 20%) that firms attempt to maximize profits. Economic behavior is, however, more complicated. One can reduce, but not eliminate, the disconfirmations of economic generalizations by specifying a margin of error. Some firms feel responsible for their employees and accept losses rather than lay them off. Other sorts of inexactness are involved.

Second, one might regard the lawlike claims of inexact sciences as probabilistic or statistical claims. Such an interpretation is implicit in the claim economists often make that only the aggregate consequences of the basic "laws" are significant (Hicks 1946:11). Yet this interpretation is problematical. To regard all empirical laws as probabilistic, as McClelland does (1975, ch. 1), seems to confuse the results of testing with what laws assert. The basic "laws" of equilibrium theory do not appear to involve elements of chance or randomness; they merely appear to have counterexamples. To construe all generalizations that face counterexamples as probabilistic is merely to rechristen them. Although I shall argue in the next section that we must regard some of the basic "laws" of equilibrium theory as statistical, this conclusion is not a happy one. It is best, for the reasons given, to attempt to construe the inexactness of economic "laws" in some other way. I shall make that attempt, but it does not fully succeed.

Perhaps one should deny that the basic generalizations of equilibrium theory are laws. They are rough generalizations which in certain applications work well enough. They are useful oversimplifications. Calling the inexact "laws" of equilibrium theory rough generalizations is appealing, but it is not informative until we know what a rough generalization is. If rough generalizations are to be analyzed in the various ways in which I am interpreting inexact "laws," "rough generalization" turns out to be only another term for "inexact law." What I have in mind in suggesting that one might attempt to *analyze* inexactness in terms of rough generalizations is that one might try to understand an inexact claim as something quite different from a law. Perhaps philosphers need to recognize that scientists sometimes employ in place of laws in their explanations a different kind of assertion, which may not be true.

This suggestion is problematic. One can appreciate that a false statement may help one to predict and control a certain range of phenomena, but how can a false statement *explain* anything or help one to understand how things truly are? What special features distinguish rough generalizations from simple falsehoods and permit one to use them in giving explanations? A philosopher might suggest, for example, that a rough generalization has explanatory worth only if it possesses a certain reliability, does not appear accidental, and enables scientists to systematize phenomena. These are plausible conditions. A generalization which satisfies them no longer appears, however, decisively unlike a law. No one has yet offered a cogent model of explanatory arguments that employ rough generalizations which is clearly different from established models of explanations employing laws. Until we have such a model, we are driven to interpret these inexact generalizations as laws of some sort. To say that inexactness is a matter of roughness is not to offer an incorrect analysis; it is not to offer any analysis at all.

Inexactness is, I believe, often not a matter of approximation or of statistics. Inexact laws are instead often qualified with implicit *ceteris paribus* (other things being equal) clauses. Scientists may assert some lawlike statement only with the proviso that other things are equal or that there are no unspecified interferences. Approximate claims may involve *ceteris paribus* qualifications in addition to a margin of error or a statistical restriction. Rosenberg has recently defended *ceteris paribus* qualifications in economics and in sciences generally (1976b:134–38). I agree with him that *ceteris paribus* qualifications may be legitimate. We shall see, however, that the inexactness of equilibrium theory goes beyond implicit qualification with *ceteris paribus* clauses.

A law which contains a *ceteris paribus* clause need not be inexact if the clause can be replaced by precise qualifications. Such replacement is not, however, possible in any inexact science. In this regard equilibrium theory is typical of inexact sciences. In asserting that, *ceteris paribus*, the preferences of consumers are transitive, economists are saying that in the absence of "interferences" or if the "interfering factors" are held constant, consumer preferences are transitive. Economists can enumerate some of the interfering factors from which they abstract. One should, for example, assume that the consumer's tastes do not change. One should assume that the consumer's memory is unimpaired. Theorists cannot, however, list all the possible interferences and replace the *ceteris paribus* clause with a precise qualification.

Is it sensible to regard statements so vaguely qualified as laws? (See Hutchison 1938:40f). Statements with such qualifications are dubious candidates for laws. It is not the case that *ceteris paribus*, we are all immortal; or *ceteris paribus*, that ravens are pink. Not all appeals to *ceteris paribus* qualifications to explain away apparent disconfirmations are legitimate or perhaps even make sense. One who regards the laws of inexact sciences as vaguely qualified claims must make clear what they assert and must distinguish legitimate from illegitimate uses of ineliminable *ceteris paribus* clauses. What do sentences with such clauses say? When, if ever, can one justifiably regard them as laws?

John Stuart Mill's discussion of inexact sciences is suggestive here.

According to Mill, in an inexact science

> the only laws as yet accurately ascertained are those of the causes which affect the phenomenon in all cases, and in considerable degree; while others which affect it in some cases only, or, if in all, only in a slight degree, have not been sufficiently ascertained and studied to enable us to lay down their laws, still less to deduce the completed law of the phenomenon, by compounding the effects of the greater with those of the minor causes. (1843, bk. VI, ch. 3, §1)

The example Mill gives is the science of tides. Physicists know the laws of the greater causes, the gravitational pull of the sun and the moon, but are ignorant of the laws of the minor causes like the configuration of the ocean bottom. The model Mill has in mind when he speaks of "compounding the effects" of causes is the vector addition of forces in mechanics. The notion that economists know and employ only the "laws" of the "greater causes" seems compelling. The "other things" which theorists hold equal are the lesser causes.

The intuitive picture is that many causes influence economic phenomena. Economists focus on a few factors which they believe to be major or distinctive causes. Since economists consider only some of the causes, their generalizations need *ceteris paribus* qualifications; otherwise the omitted causes would sometimes lead to disconfirmations. The claims of economics are true only under special (and not fully specified) conditions. One can regard economic generalizations with their qualifications as laws whenever one has reason to believe that these "laws" truly capture independently functioning or "greater" causes within some domain.

We need more than such an intuitive picture to assess general equilibrium theories of capital and interest intelligently. What precisely is a *ceteris paribus* clause? How are sentences with such clauses to be interpreted? How can they be true?

The same sentence can say different things in different contexts. Following Stalnaker (1972:380–97), let us distinguish the meaning of a sentence, the context-invariant interpretation, from the content of a sentence (or the proposition expressed by a sentence) which may change from context to context. "I hate my economics class" has a single meaning, but its content varies depending on who utters it when. Stalnaker suggests that one should regard the meaning of a sentence as a function from contexts (which can be characterized as sets of a certain kind) to contents or propositions (which can also be given a set-theoretic characterization). The meaning of a sentence determines a content in a given context.

Adapting this terminology, I suggest that *ceteris paribus* clauses have one *meaning*, "other things being equal," which in different contexts picks out different predicates (not propositions). It is the context, the economist's background understanding, that fixes what the "other things" are and what it is for them to be "equal." Although the phrase, "*ceteris paribus*", has an invariant meaning, its content, the *predicate* it picks out, varies greatly from context to context.

The phrase "*ceteris paribus*" does not determine a predicate in every context. Sometimes in uttering a sentence containing such a clause one fails to express a proposition. An example was my writing above that *ceteris paribus*, all ravens are pink.[4] The phrase "*ceteris paribus*" may pick out no predicate here. The predicates *ceteris paribus* clauses pick out in different uses vary greatly in clarity and precision. Coulomb's law, for example, says that in the absence of other forces, or holding other forces equal, any two like charged bodies will repel one another with a force directly proportional to the product of their charges and inversely proportional to the distance between them.

The phrases "in the absence of other forces" or "holding other forces equal" are refined *ceteris paribus* clauses. They have a more precise meaning than do the words, "*ceteris paribus*" in an assertion like "Heavy bodies will, *ceteris paribus*, fall when dropped." The qualification on Coulomb's law picks out relatively precise (though always open-ended) predicates. The law of diminishing returns with its "holding other inputs constant" clause is similar, although it is usually interpreted as carrying a vague qualification as well. Even the predicates determined by these "refined" *ceteris paribus* clauses do not have precise extensions. Although there are formal difficulties with vague predicates, such predicates abound in both science and ordinary language. We cannot now do without them.

What proposition does a qualified law express? Suppose the law is formulated as "*Ceteris paribus* everything which is an *F* is a *G*." (Not all the "laws" of equilibrium theory have such a simple form, but I shall ignore these complications.) Consider first the unqualified generalization, "Everything which is an *F* is a *G*." Modern logicians interpret sentences with this form to mean that there is nothing in the extension of the predicate *F* which is not in the extension of the predicate *G*. The extension of a predicate is the set of all things of which the predicate is true. Provided that the extensions are non-empty, one

[4] Sentences with *ceteris paribus* clauses may be false. In the particular case (and context) I believe that the clause does not pick out any predicate and that no proposition is expressed.

can represent what "Everything which is an *F* is a *G*" asserts in the accompanying set diagram (fig. 7.1)

The box denotes the domain or universe. The interior of the larger circle represents the set of all things which are *G*. The interior of the smaller circle represents the set of all things which are *F*. Since the latter is contained in the former, we can see that all *F*'s are *G*'s. Notice that there is nothing in the diagram which distinguishes generalizations like "All humans are mortal" from generalizations like "All red roses are red" or "All coins in my pocket are nickels."

In the case of qualified generalizations like "*Ceteris paribus* everything which is an *F* is a *G*," some things which belong to the extension of *F* do not belong to the extension of *G*—otherwise one would not need the qualification. In my view "*Ceteris paribus* everything which is an *F* is a *G*" is a true universal statement if and only if the *ceteris paribus* clause picks out a predicate, *C*, and everything which is both *C* and *F* is *G* (fig. 7.2).

Considering only the interior of circle *C*, one sees that all of region *F* contained there is also contained in region *G*. In offering a qualified generalization, one is only asserting that, once the qualifications are met, all of region *F* lies within region *G*. The predicate *C* belongs in the antecedent of the law.[5] I have drawn *C* with dotted lines only to suggest that we do not know precisely what the definite extension of the *ceteris paribus* predicate is, and not to suggest that it does not have one.

Thus, in my view, to believe that, *ceteris paribus* all consumer's preferences are transitive is to believe that anything which satisfies the *ceteris paribus* condition and is a consumer has transitive preferences. One need not be disturbed by intransitive preferences caused by, for example, changes in tastes, because such counterexamples to the un-qualified generalization lie outside circle *C*. In my analysis sentences qualified with *ceteris paribus* clauses are sometimes genuine laws. A sentence with the form "*Ceteris paribus* everything which is an *F* is a *G*" is a (nonstatistical) law, just in case the *ceteris paribus* clause determines in the given context a predicate, *C*, and everything which is *C* and *F* is also *G*.

When someone asserts "*Ceteris paribus* things which are *F* are also

---

[5] Sometimes it seems clumsy to regard *ceteris paribus* clauses as determining predi-cates in antecedents of laws. When economists say, for example, that "*ceteris paribus* businessmen attempt to maximize profits," the qualification appears to be an adverbial phrase rather than a predicate true or false of things which are businessmen. This element of awkwardness is not serious. Regarding *ceteris paribus* clauses as determining pred-icates in the antecedents of laws remains the simplest formal option.

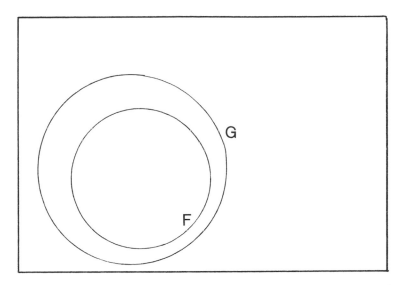

Figure 7.1

G," he or she does not *always* intend to assert that everything which is *F* and *C* is also *G*. When people believe that, other things being equal, aspirin cures headaches, they need not believe that there is any set of conditions they can add to the taking of aspirin which are sufficient for headache cures. They might believe simply that the frequency of cures is high among people who take aspirin and satisfy the *ceteris paribus* clause. That is, in terms of the conditions of figure 7.2 one might believe that inside circle *C* a small portion of region *F* does not lie within region *G*. Imagine shifting circle *C* slightly to the left.

Indeed sometimes scientists may believe that the true law will not involve the predicates "*F*" or "*G*" at all. One can grant that "*Ceteris paribus* (most) things which are *F* are *G*" has some explanatory and predictive force, yet still expect to supersede this generalization in the course of further inquiry. The true law which lies behind the generalization that aspirins cure headaches probably involves chemical or neurological predicates. With various qualifications (*C*), however, the generalization is not without explanatory and predictive power. Scientists may hope through further study to discover precise chemical or neurological laws, but that hope gives one no reason to reject generalizations like "Aspirins cure headaches." Even if such hopes are fulfilled, the inexact generalization may be useful for various practical purposes. Such generalizations may still on my analysis be laws.

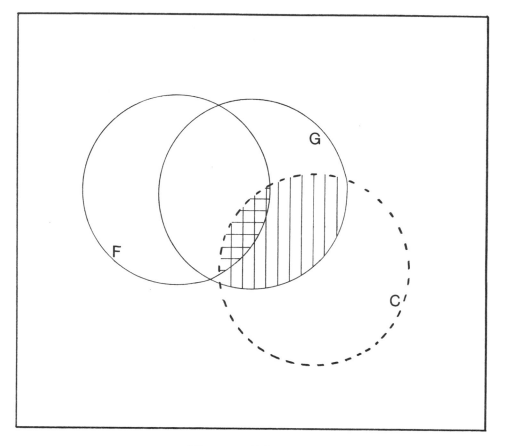

Figure 7.2

Suppose one has two qualified laws: (a) *Ceteris paribus* everything which is an *F* is a *G* and (b) *Ceteris paribus* everything which is an *A* is a *B*. From these two laws one can deduce (c) *Ceteris paribus* everything that is *A* and *F* is *B* and *G*. Although the phrase *"ceteris paribus"* occurs in all three generalizations, the predicates picked out need not be the same. The qualification on (c) will in general include all the qualifications on *both* (a) and (b). Matters are, however, more complicated. Consequences like (c) can only be drawn reliably when one has what J. S. Mill calls "mechanical phenomena" (1843, bk III, ch. 6, §1, §2). In mechanical phenomena the effect of two causal factors acting simultaneously is the same as the total effect of each acting separately. Each factor is independent. It continues to "operate" no matter what other causes are operating. The other causes may hide its influence and alter the total effect, but they do not affect its "operation." When one has such "mechanical phenomena" the causal factor captured in the qualified law is responsible for a "tendency" in the phenomena which is present whenever the causal factor is. One can then compound these tendencies or these effects of the independent causes. In classical physics Newton's law of gravitation or Coulomb's law of electrostatic attraction or replusion always specifies one component of the force on any body. Scientists may make mistaken predictions because they failed to consider other forces, but such mistakes show only that other things were not equal. They do not disconfirm the laws.

When one is not dealing with causal factors which are in this way independent or when one simply does not know whether or how various causal factors will interact, one may still use laws qualified with *ceteris paribus* clauses. Qualified laws dealing with nonmechanical phenomena will, however, be more provisional and will have a much more restricted scope. They may apply only when there are *no* interfering factors. Even if the basic generalizations of equilibrium theory are qualified laws, they will not help one to understand real economies with their inevitable interferences and complications, unless economic phenomena are mechanical phenomena. Mill simply asserts that economic phenomena are mechanical, that the basic economic causal factors continue to act as component forces in the total complicated effect (1843, bk, VI, ch. 7, §1). Such a supposition is implicit in most applications of economic models. Its only justification is the success of such applications.

Is my suggestion that we regard inexact or rough generalizations as qualified laws sensible? Since scientists do not know which predicate a *ceteris paribus* clause picks out, why regard it as picking out any predicate at all? Why regard generalizations like the basic "laws" of equilibrium theory as true or false? One can recognize that they may guide research and help economists to interpret data without regarding them as lawlike assertions and assessing their truth. If a theorist believes that in a certain domain the interferences inadequately denoted by the implicit *ceteris paribus* clause are absent, he or she can regard the generalization (in that domain) as a "virtual" law (Morgenbesser 1956, chs. 1, 2). But the theorist need not regard the unrestricted generalization as true or false. To regard inexact "laws" as thus *schematic* is appealing. It emphasizes the elusiveness of *ceteris paribus* clauses, which I have perhaps understated and emphasizes that scientists regard inexact "laws" differently when they use them to give explanations than when they rely on them in doing research.

These qualms about regarding inexact generalizations as laws do not, however, challenge the position I have defended. There is nothing in my account which demands that one judge all sentences which contain *ceteris paribus* clauses to be true or false. Sometimes one finds that in certain domains the justification conditions (to be discussed below) are satisfied, while in others they are not. In such cases it may be best to regard the unrestricted "law" as schematic rather than as false. If forced to judge the truth of the general lawlike statement that, *ceteris paribus*, *all* agents choose that option which brings them the largest bundle of commodities, one would, I think, have to decide that it is false. In restricted domains like those consisting of market behavior, one might be justified in regarding versions of it as laws. It is best in this case not to regard the completely general claim as fully specified and not to judge its truth. In completely general form, non-satiation should be regarded as an assumption only. Theorists do, on the other hand, use basic economic "laws" to try to explain economic phenomena. In doing so they are no longer regarding these sentences as mere assumptions, but as expressing some truth, however rough it may be. Otherwise, their attempt to explain would be incomprehensible. In discussing laws and explanation here and in §6 below, I am concerned with applications of models, with qualified generalizations which in specified domains can be regarded as laws.

Countenancing qualified laws forthrightly, one is no longer forced to make invidious comparisons between the natural sciences which possess laws and provide adequate explanations and the social sciences which possess at best virtual laws and whose explanations are unsatisfactory. We have instead gradations of inexactness. Scientists strive for exactness, but possessing, as they often do, only qualified generalizations, they nevertheless have achieved some knowledge of a particular subject matter and are able to explain some of the phenomena in the domain.

Generalizations whose scope is not restricted are often best regarded as assumptions in models, not as assertions which are true or false. In making this last assertion I am not denying that one important goal of science is to explain nor that purely theoretical assertions can be true or false. I am only pointing out that sometimes it is unhelpful to assess the truth of unrestricted theoretical sentences—that they are sometimes better regarded as schemata than as statements. I am also not asserting that one must assess each applied theory separately and cannot reasonably accept the claims of some applied theories after testing others in related domains.

It is not enough to provide an interpretation of qualified generalizations which enable us to understand how they can be laws. We must discover when one has reason to believe that a qualified generalization is a law. Standard theories of confirmation provide little guidance, since scientists do not know precisely what the extension of the *ceteris paribus* predicate is (what the size and location of circle *C* is). When is one justified in regarding a statement with a *ceteris paribus* clause as a law?

I would like to suggest four necessary conditions. First the statement must be *lawlike*. It must be the sort of statement which, if true, would be a law. Philosophers do not agree on any analysis of lawlikeness, but scientists and laymen are able to distinguish lawlike from non-lawlike claims. People recognize a difference between accidental generalizations like "There are no poodles in Nebraska" and lawlike generalizations like "Copper conducts electricity." No matter how lawlike statements are to be analyzed, they are not accidental and they support counterfactual or subjunctive claims.

Second, the qualified statement must be *reliable*. In some class of cases, after ignoring the *ceteris paribus* clause or allowing for specific interferences, the scientist should rarely need to explain away apparent disconfirmations. The class of cases considered must be specified in some independent way. "All roses are yellow" turns out to be highly reliable if tested in the class of yellow roses or in the class of roses my mother likes best. The reliability condition is a statistical condition. One takes samples from the independently specified domain of interest. A generalization like "Everything which is an *F* is a *G*" is reliable only if (after making allowances for specific interferences[6]) almost all *F*'s sampled are *G*'s.

Third, one does not have good reason to regard a qualified claim as a law unless it is *refinable*. If scientists add specific qualifications, the generalization should become more reliable or reliable in a larger domain. Theorists may not be interested in actually refining the generalization. The uncomplicated original claim may be more convenient. Refinability only demands that scientists be *able* to make the generalization more reliable. Note that the refinability condition does not demand that theorists can completely replace the *ceteris paribus* qualification with specific provisos.

Finally, no one is justified in regarding a statement with a *ceteris paribus* clause as a law unless it is *excusable*. Intuitively, one should

---

[6] In speaking of "greater causes" in the quotation above, Mill has in mind principally the case in which one can simply ignore the interferences and still have a reliable generalization. Sometimes, however, scientists need to and are able to make specific allowances for known interferences.

not invoke the *ceteris paribus* clause blindly. One should know which are the important interferences and should be able in most cases to justify relying on the *ceteris paribus* clause as an excuse. The excusability condition demands that, with only rare exceptions, which are puzzles demanding further research, scientists be able to point out the interferences and explain away failures of the unqualified generalization.[7] The excusability condition differs from both the reliability and refinability conditions, because it does not demand good statistical results. Unlike the refinability condition it is also unconcerned with amending generalizations. Instead, the excusability condition demands that after scientists have done their tests and have identified those cases in which the generalization is not reliable, they be able to cite the interfering factor in all except possibly a few anomalous cases. It should not seem a miracle that the generalization "works" sometimes and fails others.

One may regard a generalization that would face disconfirmation, if it were not qualified, as a *law* only if it is lawlike, reliable, refinable, and excusable. These conditions are schematic, since I am offering no account of lawlikeness, of theory assessment in general, or of how to specify in an "independent" way a domain of application. Since some degree of inexactness infects general statements in all sciences, it might be better to incorporate such justification conditions into a general account of theory assessment. Since I know of no good general philosophical model of theory assessment, I cannot offer such an integrated account.

The lawlikeness, reliability, refinability, and excusability conditions themselves help to assess general equilibrium theories of capital, interest, and exchange values. They are, I believe, plausible and sensible. Not only are they a reasonable formulation of the implicit criteria by which scientists and laymen assess the legitimacy of invoking *ceteris paribus* clauses to explain away apparent disconfirmation; they are rational as well. Since one does not know precisely which predicate C the *ceteris paribus* clause expresses, one cannot test directly the explicit lawlike statement, "Everything which is C and F is G." One should not believe that there is such a law until one finds a class of cases in which there is a reliable connection between F and G. If scientists could not explain away cases in which something is both F and not G they would not believe that they have a law. If scientists cannot find any qualifications which would lead them to find a more reliable connection between F and G they would once again deny that

---

[7] Rescher (1970:172) asserts a stricter form of this condition.

they have a law. Unless these four conditions are met, one cannot reasonably regard vaguely qualified generalizations as laws. Notice that these conditions are necessary, not sufficient. I am not asserting that one is necessarily justified in regarding any statement which satisfies them as a qualified law.

3. Inexact Laws in Economics

Economists have long recognized that their claims must be qualified. It should therefore seem natural to them to conceive of rough or inexact lawlike statements as qualified with *ceteris paribus* clauses. To assert that people's preferences are transitive is to make a qualified claim. This assertion is not falsified by a change in tastes; such changes are ruled out by an implicit *ceteris paribus* clause. For the same reason, this assertion is not disconfirmed by panic behavior or by the efforts of an experimental subject to make a fool out of economists. Economists describe how agents behave against a fixed background or in the absence of various complications. Equilibrium models are intended to analyze the distinctive "causes" that operate in economic life, although these are modified and sometimes counteracted by other factors. Apparent failures are not falsifications, since economists have the implicit qualifications to invoke as excuses. *Ceteris paribus* qualifications will, in my view, never be eliminable in economics. Social phenomena are so interdependent and subject to so many influences, that it is futile to hope that economics can ever be an exact science. If one included all the "lesser" causes of economic phenomena, economics would merge with the other social sciences.

Ceteris paribus qualifications are powerful excuses, which must not be invoked too often; nor may they be invoked blindly. Is one justified in regarding the nine basic generalizations of equilibrium theory as qualified laws? Although they appear to be lawlike and refinable, they may not satisfy the reliability and the excusability conditions.

In sufficiently restricted domains generalizations of equilibrium theories are reliable: In agriculture there are diminishing returns to larger applications of fertilizers; people are for the most part less excited with their second television than with their first. It would be foolish to deny that the generalizations of equilibrium theory are ever reliable. But what can we say of general equilibrium theories of capital and interest? If we had to directly assess theoretical hypotheses which employ intertemporal general equilibrium models to derive conclusions concerning capital and interest, we would be forced to negative conclusions. Real economies are not approximately in intertemporal general equilibrium. Theoretical hypotheses which assert otherwise are false. Yet one can assess implications of such theoretical hypotheses indirectly. Some of the implications may be true even if the theoretical hypothesis is false. The economic agents referred to in applied general equilibrium theories are the same agents referred to in microeconomic theories. Since qualified generalizations concerning preferences and motivation are reliable in many microeconomic applications, one has good reason to rely on these generalizations in general equilibrium theories as well. I think economists have reasonable indirect grounds to regard most of the basic lawlike assertions of general equilibrium theories of capital and interest as reliable.[8]

Most of the basic assertions of equilibrium theory fail, however, to satisfy the excusability condition. To see why, consider the following generalization: "Heavy bodies will fall when dropped." This assertion seems as rough as any of the "laws" of economics. Without a *ceteris paribus* clause (supposed to rule out cases where the heavy body is tied with a rope, possesses its own rocket engine, is made of iron and subjected to a strong magnetic force, etc.) the assertion is obviously false. The *ceteris paribus* qualification is vague and ineliminable. But note what would happen if someone dropped a brick and it did not fall. If there were no ropes attached or rockets firing or iron bars built in, something surprising would have happened. Scientists might have more important things to do than to find out what the interference was, but they would want to. If scientists had the time and resources, they would investigate the strange brick that did not fall when dropped. Although the *ceteris paribus* clause cannot be replaced with a list of specific qualifications, unknown interferences create puzzles. "Heavy bodies will, *ceteris paribus*, fall when dropped" satisfies the excusability condition.

We may say the same for some of the basic "laws" of equilibrium theory. If someone found an input from which returns never diminished (holding other inputs constant), theorists would be as puzzled as if confronted with a brick that did not fall. If, on the other hand, an economist finds a businessman who does not attempt to maximize profits or a consumer with intransitive preferences and does not find any of the well-known interferences, he or she will generally not be puzzled. Economists do not spend time trying to find out what the

---

[8] The generalization that equilibrium is reached is not reliable. I also have my doubts about the generalizations that businessmen attempt to maximize profits or that there are constant returns to scale.

interferences in such cases might be. They expect their generalizations to fail from time to time. With effort and ingenuity interfering factors might always be identified, but economists do not make such efforts. They do not make such efforts because they do not regard apparent disconfirmations as the result of specific interferences. The "laws" of equilibrium theory do not satisfy the excusability condition.

Since most of the lawlike claims of equilibrium theorists do not satisfy the excusability condition, one cannot regard them as qualified universal laws. Perhaps the basic assertions of equilibrium theory should be regarded as both implicitly qualified, and statistical. Perhaps one should regard economists as asserting only that, *ceteris paribus* consumer preferences are *usually* transitive.

Is such an interpretation justifiable? Economists provide no statistics to support their basic generalizations. All we are told is that, with qualifications, the "laws" are reliable in some domains. If economists can say no more, one might as well concede that these generalizations are false. Until economists specify what statistical claims they are making or philosophers show how false generalizations can be explanatory, one seems driven to conclude that the basic "laws" of equilibrium theory have little explanatory power. I find this conclusion unpalatable. In at least some applications equilibrium models seem to have explanatory worth. I see no philosophical way to support this appearance. My own attempts to develop a philosophical model of explanation employing false generalizations (Hausman, 1979a) have not been convincing. As I argued above in discussing roughness, I do not find the project promising. It thus seems to me that the responsibility lies with economists to develop those basic assertions which do not satisfy the excusability condition as explicitly statistical qualified laws.

In my view all the basic generalizations of equilibrium theory should be regarded as qualified with *ceteris paribus* clauses. In some cases the qualified generalizations satisfy the four justification conditions. One can, I think, regard diminishing returns to a variable input and diminishing marginal utility as qualified laws. The other basic general statements of equilibrium theory cannot be regarded as qualified universal laws. Perhaps one can regard them as qualified statistical laws. Since the statistics are unstated, one should not be satisfied with these generalizations, although we need not deny that they have some value.

The problems with justifying economic "laws" are serious and unresolved. At least the "laws" of general equilibrium theories of capital and interest face no further problems than do the "laws" of more familiar and less abstract equilibrium theories. If the only dubious feature of general equilbrium theories of capital and interest was that they employed the fundamental "laws," I am not sure whether one might regard these theories as explanatory. At least one would have no grounds to compare such theories unfavorably with microeconomic theories of consumer choice or of the effects of rationing. We cannot, however, make even this relative assessment of general equilibrium theories of capital and interest until we consider the other assumptions in general equilibrium models.

As I mentioned before, many economists agree that their "laws" are rough and at best "close to the truth." In the above analysis I have made this view precise and have considered to what extent it may be regarded as a defense of the explanatory worth of equilibrium theory. To clarify the view of economic generalizations I have developed, I shall briefly show how it differs from some influential recent accounts with which it might be confused.

Philosophers and economists have attempted to analyze the inexactness of economic generalizations in many different ways. Fritz Machlup denies that these generalizations are false. He seeks in two different ways to show how they are insulated from apparent disconfirmations. Sometimes he denies that these generalizations say what they appear to (1960:559, 577–79). According to Machlup, they do not describe how consumers or businessmen behave. Instead they are theoretical statements about theoretical entities misleadingly called "consumers" or "businessmen." These terms are in fact only interpreted partially by the econometrician who tests significant implications of the theory as a whole. One has reason to believe that the general statements of an equilibrium theory are true if the theory is well-confirmed. This view of Machlup's is implausible (see Rosenberg 1976b:139–52). Not only does it misapply the efforts of twentieth-century philosophers of science to understand how sentences apparently referring to unobservable items can be testable, but econometric testing has, in fact, provided little confirmation for equilibrium theories. The view I have defended adds *ceteris paribus* qualifications to the general statements of equilibrium theory and considers some of them to be statistical claims, but otherwise interprets them literally.

Machlup sometimes denies that the general statements of equilibrium theories are either true or false (1955:9–11). This view also seems both unreasonable and unsuccessful as a defense of the purported laws of equilibrium theory against the objection that they are false. If one is sensibly to deny that theoretical statements are true or false, as the "noncognitivist" instrumentalist does (Morgenbesser 1969:202), one must be able to distinguish terms denoting observational entities from theoretical terms (here equated with terms denoting nonobservational entities). Otherwise one has no basis to distinguish observational sentences which can be true or false from theoretical sentences which supposedly cannot be regarded as true or false. But if terms like "consumer" or "firm" or "price" are supposed to lie on the theoretical side of the divide, what (except for "here bluish now," or other such phenomenalist grunting) is supposed to lie on the observational side? Furthermore, regardless of its shortcomings, it is hard to see how such an instrumentalist position helps. If one conceives of the purported laws of equilibrium theory as rules for making inferences or as instruments for making predictions, one still faces the problem that the rules or instruments are often unreliable.

In his extremely influential essay "The Methodology of Positive Economics" (1953:3–42), Milton Friedman offers a quite different justification of the basic generalizations of equilibrium theory. Friedman concedes that the general statements of equilibrium theory are false (or inapplicable because their antecedents are not true of any real economic situation). At least this is how I understand his view of them as one kind of "unrealistic assumption." Friedman simply and boldly denies that their falsity matters. If a theory is well-confirmed (is a good "predictor") in the class of cases in which economists are interested, it is a good theory; otherwise not (1953:14). Even assertions as abruptly counterfactual as the attribution of consciousness to tree leaves are perfectly acceptable in theories of the distribution of leaves on the branches of trees. All that matters is how successfully the actual distribution of leaves is "predicted" (1953:19–20).

Friedman's position is a special kind of instrumentalism, which must be distinguished from the noncognitivist kind that Machlup has sometimes espoused. Friedman does not deny that theoretical statements are true or false. In fact the distinction between theoretical and observation statements is irrelevant to his views. What he does deny is that the truth of any fundamental statement ("assumption" in Friedman's terminology) matters. All that counts is whether the theory makes correct predictions concerning the limited phenomena of interest. While many philosophers would agree that we should value a theory which "works" even for a very limited range of phenomena, few would be willing to discount completely the importance of the truth and falsity of consequences that happen not to be of practical concern (Bronfenbrenner 1966:12f).

Friedman's methodological article has nevertheless been popular and influential among economists. Friedman has been so influential partly because he has been misunderstood. Economists often read him as contending merely that one should assess theories by testing their implications. This view is, of course, no defense at all against the criticism that the basic generalizations of equilibrium theory are false and thus have some disconfirmed consequences. What is more responsible for the popularity of "The Methodology of Positive Economics" than such misunderstanding is that Friedman recognizes that the generalizations of equilibrium theory are false as stated, yet defends them anyway. Economists do not believe that businessmen always seek to maximize their profits. To say that businessmen behave this way is to oversimplify reality. The simplification is useful. It so happens that models which employ this and other falsehoods are reliable and useful tools for understanding some economic problems. Friedman defends the usefulness and legitimacy of such models.

Yet the defense is extravagant. According to Friedman, when an implication of a theory is false, one should conclude only that the theory does not apply to the particular phenomenon. Friedman concedes that scientists prefer theories which apply broadly, when theories with such a broad scope are as simple and easy to use as theories which only apply to restricted domains. Whether a given model suits an economist's specific predictive purpose(s) remains, however, the crucial question for Friedman. The truth of the "assumptions" does not matter. We can, of course, agree that a theory full of apparently false assertions may be good enough for certain limited predictive purposes. Such a theory can, however, hardly meet demands for explanation and scientific understanding. The truth of generalizations must count.

Friedman's views have also appealed to economists, because he rejects, as I did, a global or an absolute demand for truth. If one finds that individuals do not behave as self-interested utility maximizers in dealing with their children, one has discovered no major flaw in economic theory. It would be nice to have a general theory of human behavior, but there is nothing illegitimate or misconceived in trying to account for only some ranges of human behavior, for considering only the "major causes" in certain circumstances. The limited generalization that in their market behavior people are utility maximizers will serve just as well. Indeed, such limitations are implicit in the way economists employ their fundamental "laws." Friedman, however, agains goes too far. He believes that even within the limited range of phenomena which economists study, they should be concerned only about whether the particular predictions they make are true. Whether other implications of the theory are true is of no importance. Not only can economists be unconcerned about the discovery that, when on vacation, entrepreneurs do not act like profit maximizers, but, according to Friedman, economists can discount as irrelevant all investigations into the motivation of businessmen. If one has any interest in understanding economies, this view is unacceptable. Some investigations of motivations may be of little interest: they may reveal only that other things are not always equal or that actual behavior does not match any simple motivational generalization perfectly. Theorists can offer some explicit qualifications to take these results into account. Economists can, however, hardly announce, as Friedman does (1953:22, 31), that investigations into how entrepreneurs behave are irrelevant to assessing theories which make assertions about how entrepreneurs behave.

Inexactness is not a mortal sin. Economists can reasonably qualify their generalizations and limit the domain to which they are supposed to apply. The proof of the whole pudding is ultimately in the application and testing. Such is one moral of this chapter. On these points Friedman is right and economists are wise to follow him. But Friedman does not stop with these truths, and his methodological writings become, I believe, apologetics. If accepted, Friedman's views would insulate neoclassical theory from legitimate criticism. The difficulties with the basic "laws" of equilibrium theory are serious. One can reasonably question their explanatory worth.

I have argued that it is legitimate to regard a generalization which is not true without vague *ceteris paribus* qualification as an explanatory law, but only if the generalization is lawlike, reliable, refinable and excusable. It seems to me that generalizations in the sciences nearly always carry such qualifications. The "laws" of equilibrium theory are disquieting, because their inexactness is neither a simple matter of implicit qualification, statistics, nor margin of error. Whether these "laws" can justifiably be regarded as laws in any given application is an open empirical question. The many confirmations of microeconomic equilibrium theories give one some indirect reason to accept the "laws" of general equilibrium theories of interest and prices. We cannot, however, yet offer even a relative assessment of general equilibrium models and theories. We must first consider the other assumptions of general equilibrium models, and we must consider whether the emphasis on economic *models* should in any way affect our assessment.

4. Simplifications and the Application of Equilibrium Models.

In assessing explanatory arguments, "laws," simplifications, and specifications must be carefully distinguished. Economists often think of the basic statements in their models as "assumptions" only.[9] Many are unaccustomed to distinguishing between lawlike and simplifying assumptions. Some are uncomfortable speaking of "laws" at all, because they recognize that the "laws" of economics are qualified, statistical, and limited in scope. In discussing equilibrium theory and equilibrium models in chapter 6, I introduced and defended the distinction between lawlike and simplifying assumptions. The "laws" I listed, unlike such simplifications as perfect information, can be regarded as discovered by or asserted by economic theorists. Finding disconfirmation of the "laws," once these are qualified and limited in scope, creates a problem for the economic theorist. Finding that some commodities, like a Mercedes, come in large indivisible units reveals at most limits to the applicability of economic models.

In assessing possible explanatory arguments in economics, we need to refine and clarify the distinctions among the kinds of statements employed. My distinction between lawlike and simplifying *assumptions* (chapter 6) is not adequate, since in explanations scientists employ not only theoretical hypotheses, but other specifications and simplifications as well. Since there is among philosophers no standard systematic treatment of the differences among kinds of statements employed in explanatory arguments, it seems least confusing to employ *simplification* and *specification* as new technical terms. The distinction between them corresponds only very roughly to the more usual contrast philosophers draw between statements of initial conditions and auxiliary assumptions. The term *specification* avoids the misleading temporal reference of "initial conditions." I count as a specification any non-lawlike claim employed in explanation (or prediction or testing) which one has good reason to believe is true. I count as a simplification any non-lawlike claim employed in explanation (or prediction or testing) which one has no reason to believe is true (and which one may often have reason to believe is false). The assertion that other things are equal, that there are no unspecified interferences, is always at least a tacit premise in an explanatory argument. I place the *ceteris paribus* stipulation in a category by itself and regard it as neither a specification nor a simplification. The distinction between specifications and simplifications is entirely epistemic. One has good evidence for specifications. One does not have good evidence for simplifications. In fact

---

[9] Milton Friedman and others have sometimes called antecedents of conditional statements and even predicates "assumptions" as well. For a taxonomic guide to the controversy concerning unrealistic assumptions in economics see Brunner (1969:501–25) and Hausman (1978:202–6).

scientists are often quite confident that their simplifications are false. Those claims which philosophers often call "statements of initial conditions" will usually be what I call "specifications." Those claims which philosophers call "auxiliary assumptions" or "auxiliary hypotheses" (which are not assertions that there are no unspecified interferences and which are not lawlike) will usually be what I call "simplifications." Many auxiliary assumptions are not what I call "simplifications," but are instead lawlike claims which are independent of the particular theory which carries the major explanatory burden. In explaining the motion of a planet, for example, one may rely on the laws of optics as auxiliary assumptions which justify using data obtained by means of a telescope. Such auxiliary assumptions are not simplifications.

I have distinguished between simplifications and specifications because only the latter seem at first glance permissible in deductive-nomological explanations. As true statements, specifications are (along with laws) just the sort of statements which Hempel expects to find in scientific explanations. Simplifications, on the other hand, often state falsehoods, even impossibilities. Even in those cases in which they may be true, one has no reason to believe they are true and thus no reason, on Hempel's model, to accept purported explanations which employ them. Yet simplifications seem largely unavoidable in explanatory arguments. Human abilities to specify initial conditions (like the precise degree of divisibility of each commodity) are limited. Human mathematical abilities to employ such specifications, even if they are available, are also limited. Economists, like scientists generally, compensate for these limitations by substituting convenient simplifications for unavailable or inconvenient specifications. In the derivation of the ideal gas law, physicists use as a premise the claim that gas molecules are point particles. In relying on simplifications to derive important results, economists are proceeding in the way in which all scientists must.

Simplifications which appear extreme, even outrageous, are common in highly respected science. Idealizations, which I shall discuss in the next section, are usually such extreme simplifications. The prevalence of simplifications, however, neither proves that they are desirable nor justifies relying on particular simplifications in particular cases. Simplifications may be legitimately included in explanatory arguments only if they satisfy certain conditions. Friedman has the barest account of these conditions. For him there is only one. A simplification is legitimate if and only if the predictions one is interested in are correct (1953:p.17). For Friedman, a model of free fall in a vacuum would be an adequate model of the fall of a steel ball in a vat of molasses in a strong magnetic field if the distance the ball falls is proportional to the time squared. Friedman is right that one necessary condition is a confirmation condition, but wrong to believe that it is sufficient. In my view a simplification is legitimate—one is justified in employing it in an explanatory argument—only if

1. *Confirmation condition.* One needs the simplification not only to derive the statement of what is to be explained, but to derive other testable consequences, most of which are confirmed.
2. *No-accident condition.* One can understand why, even though one has no reason to believe the simplification is true, one can use it in explanations and predictions and meet the confirmation condition.
3. *Sensitivity condition.* If one replaces the simplification with a specification or with another simplification which is more realistic or a better approximation, one is able to explain more phenomena or is able to explain the given phenomena under a more refined description or within a smaller margin of error.
4. *Convergence condition.* In those circumstances in which the simplification is a better approximation, one is able to explain the phenomena under a more refined description or within a smaller margin of error.

Like the lawlikeness, reliability, refinability, and excusability conditions discussed above, these four conditions are justification conditions. The conditions discussed earlier must be satisfied before one can be justified in regarding a statement as an inexact law. The four conditions just listed must be satisfied before one is justified in employing a simplification in an explanation—that is, before one is justified in regarding a simplification as "legitimate." The conditions in the two sets are related to one another, although the correspondence is rough.

There is nothing mysterious in either the relations or the lack of precise correspondence. An explanatory argument, like a law, exhibits some nonaccidental connection between phenomena. Indeed, if one rewrites a valid explanatory argument as a conditional statement with the non-lawlike constituents of the explanation in the antecedent and the description of what is to be explained in the consequent, one can regard that statement as a highly specific law. If such a conditional statement can be regarded as a law, the simplifications it contains must be legitimate. The confirmation and no-accident conditions are thus variants of the reliability and lawlikeness condition, once we correct for the fact that in an explanation one is concerned with a single phenomenon or with a much more limited range of phenomena than in enunciating a law. The lawlike statement into which an explanatory argument can be translated will be refinable only if the simplifications in the explanation satisfy the sensitivity condition. The lawlike statement into which one can convert an explanatory argument will be excusable only if the simplifications in the explanation satisfy the convergence condition.

These justification criteria are implicit in the assessments scientists and laymen make of explanatory arguments. The derivation of the ideal gas law from kinetic theory, for example, satisfies these conditions. The simplifications employed are legitimate. The ideal gas law is testable. For certain gases and for certain ranges of temperatures and pressure it is well confirmed. Indeed, one can use the ideal gas law to make reliable gas thermometers. The no-accident condition is also satisfied, since scientists have independent reasons to believe that gases are made up of small particles which in some cases exert only very weak attractive forces on one another. Without any reason to believe in the existence of such particles or to accept the laws of motion these particles supposedly follow, the derivation of the ideal gas law from kinetic theory would not be explanatory. The convergence condition is also satisfied. Scientists know that gas molecules are not point particles and that molecules attract one another. Scientists have independent ways to estimate the size of the particles and the strength of the attractive forces. They find that the ideal gas law is more accurate for gases with smaller molecules that exert weaker attractive forces on one another. Finally the sensitivity condition is satisfied. When one takes into account the size of gas molecules and the attractive forces between them, one is able to derive a more accurate law relating volume, temperature, and pressure of gases.

But *why* do scientists tacitly demand that the simplifications used in explanations satisfy the confirmation, no-accident, sensitivity, and convergence conditions? I have suggested that unless a simplification satisfies these conditions, one should not judge it to be legitimate. But what is it for a simplification to be legitimate? What property must it have in order to *be* (not merely to be considered as) part of an explanation? For the presence of what property is one testing by checking whether the simplification satisfies the four justification conditions? Not only is this question itself important, but we must answer it to evaluate the reasonableness of my proposed criteria of justification. Regardless of how prevalent or plausible those criteria are, we cannot rationally decide whether scientists should employ them until we know what scientists are testing for.

A simplification is legitimate, I think, if and only if it is approximately true.[10] Simplifications are approximately true only if either they are true within a margin of error, or they are statistical or probabilistic statements which are true or true only within a margin of error. In an explanatory argument one is showing the connection between the factors cited in the argument and the phenomena to be explained. The factors one cites must actually be present and must actually be responsible for the phenomena; otherwise, one has not explained anything. If the simplifications one employs were not close to the truth, one would not be showing a real connection and would not be explaining.

The four justification conditions are in fact reasonable criteria for judging whether a claim used in an explanatory argument is true within a margin of error. The confirmation condition tests whether things are as if the simplification were true. The no-accident condition demands that to the best of one's knowledge there actually be a connection between what the simplifications assert and the phenomena being explained—which could not be the case if there were no truth to the simplifications. The convergence condition looks for more accurate consequences in those cases in which the error in the simplification is smaller. The sensitivity condition does the same by revising the simplification itself rather than by considering more restricted cases. Scientists thus do, I suggest, demand that a simplification employed in an explanatory argument be approximately true. They check to see whether a simplification is thus legitimate by seeing whether it satisfies the confirmation, no-accident, convergence, and sensitivity conditions.

If we assess attempts to employ current general equilibrium models to explain the phenomena concerning capital, interest, and exchange values, we are forced to negative conclusions. When the simplifying assumptions those models include are closed and taken as statements, they do not meet all of the above four conditions. The models contain illegitimate simplifying assumptions. Theoretical hypotheses employing intertemporal general equilibrium models or temporary equilibrium models cannot be confirmed.

There is thus no good way to tell whether the simplifications in such general equilibrium theories satisfy the sensitivity or convergence con-

---

[10] This claim is probably too restrictive. Simplifications may perhaps be legitimate if they are replaceable in an explanatory argument by a true statement, even though scientists do not yet know how to carry out the replacement. There may be other possibilities as well. Confining my discussion to the simplest kind of legitimacy does not, I believe, bias my conclusions.

ditions. One can, however, argue that applications of intertemporal equilibrium models like the one in chapter 5 will contain simplifications that fail to satisfy the convergence condition. Suppose one could somehow measure on a single scale the accuracy and extent of an individual's information about current and future economic data. Can one say that as individuals move up the scale (within the attainable range) that the values of the economic variables approach those calculable from intertemporal equilibrium theory? There are good grounds for doubt. Better knowledge *within the attainable range* might lead to disastrous decisions. Lipsey and Lancaster's work on the theory of the second best (1956–57:11–32) establishes an analogous result. These considerations do not prove that simplifications like perfect information will not satisfy the convergence condition, but they give one good reason to doubt. More practical general equilibrium theories, like input-output analyses, are not so entirely without explanatory merit. There is, however, a tradeoff. As general equilibrium theories come closer to being explanatory, they come to have fewer implications concerning capital and interest. Recall that making even the small move from intertemporal equilibrium models to temporary equilibrium models means that one can no longer (in theory) say anything about the real rate of return on investments.

Can anybody devise a general equilibrium model that is both explanatory and that has significant implications concerning capital and interest? I do not know. I have argued only that current abstract general equilibrium models, which contemporary economists regard as fundamental for the understanding of economics, are not explanatory, while more practical general equilibrium models do not answer any of the interesting questions concerning capital and interest. Who knows what theorists may be able to accomplish in the future? At present, however, neoclassical economists cannot justifiably claim to be able to explain the major phenomena of capital and interest.

From this conclusion one might be tempted to jump to the more radical conclusion that abstract general equilibrium models are worthless. That jump would be unjustified. In §7 I shall argue that such models are extremely valuable. Once one ceases to regard them as explanatory, one can see much more clearly what their role and importance is. Before turning to these issues, however, we need to consider some questions concerning economic theorizing which the discussion has so far left hanging. We have not yet considered carefully the nature or significance of idealizations in economics nor the importance of the economist's reliance on models.

5. Models and Idealizations in Economics

Many economists, as I have noted, regard their models and theories as idealizations. It is not always clear, however, whether the view that economic theories involve idealizations is regarded as opposed to or as complementing the view that economic theories are approximations. Economists have generally been unclear about what idealizations are, what role they are supposed to play, and what significance their presence has. Until recently, economists have not had much help on these questions from philosophers. Even a philosopher as eminent and sensible as Ernest Nagel conflates idealizations and theoretical terms (1961:160; 1971:49). After interpreting talk of idealizations in economics as sympathetically as I can, I shall argue that it has little to contribute to understanding the apparent inexactness of economic theories and is of no help in defending their explanatory worth.

An ideal entity or property is one which one knows cannot be real. The knowledge that there are no perfectly rigid bodies or point particles is supplied by scientific theories (Shapere 1969:131–49). No scientific theory reveals that there are no complete futures markets or that individuals do not have perfect information concerning the economic future. It would, however, be a mistake to deny, as Alexander Rosenberg does (1976b:133), that these claims are idealizations. Well-developed scientific theories are not the only sources of knowledge. Notice that none of the fundamental generalizations discussed in chapter 6 themselves appear to be ideal. People's preferences are not always transitive, but during any given time interval, they might be. Entrepreneurs do not always attempt to maximize profits, but they might.

Economics employs simplifications that are idealizations. In this it resembles the natural sciences. But what can we conclude from the resemblance? Unconditional ideal assertions are always false. Why should one regard the fact that a theory makes ideal claims as a defense rather than as a criticism? Even if the "laws" of equilibrium theory were ideal, which they are not, merely calling attention to that fact would not provide a clear interpretation of them. Nor do we learn much about simplifications when we are told, correctly, that some of them are idealizations.

In fact it seems to me that although economists often use the words "ideal" or "idealization," they are not really interested in idealizations, at least as I defined them above. Instead they wish to interpret their models as making unrealistic claims (hence the use of the term "ideal") about how things *would be*, were various complications absent. I shall call this view of economic models the "modal model" view, since it interprets models as making *modal* claims about how things would be. According to the modal model view, sentences like "Entrepreneurs attempt to maximize profits" do not merely define predicates in models and make inexact claims in theories. Rather they state truths about certain *possible* economies. The assumptions of economic models not only appear to concern highly simplified and in some cases ideal circumstances, but they are in fact about unreal entities and properties.

The modal model view does not necessarily demand different justification conditions than those discussed in the previous two sections. The modal model view, as baldly stated above, says nothing about justification. The theorist who regards the assumptions of economic models as counterfactual is questioning instead whether one should interpret the purported laws of economics as making qualified claims about actual economies. The modal model view is in some ways stronger and in other ways weaker than the qualified empirical assertion view. If one grants the scientific legitimacy of talking about how things would be, one will be able to deduce counterfactual claims from qualified non-counterfactual claims. If it is the case that, given certain qualifications, businessmen attempt to maximize profits, then it is the case that they would do so were the qualifications unnecessary. The converse does not always hold. From the claim that businessmen would all attempt to maximize profits in certain hypothetical circumstances, it may not follow that one can make any qualified claims about what businessmen actually do. The modal model view thus appears (once we grant the legitimacy of talk of possible economies) more circumspect than the qualified assertion view. Yet the modal model view is, of course, committed to a more ambitious metaphysics. Someone who regards the purported laws of economics as making qualified and statistical claims may never need to refer to any hypothetical circumstances.

Many economists have regarded their theories as making claims about how things would be were various complications absent. I do not see any way of arguing that this view of economic models and theories is incorrect. I have, however, two qualms. First I am disposed toward metaphysical modesty. If one can thoroughly and sensibly understand economic theory without making reference to any merely possible economies, so much the better. Second I think that the modal model view tempts economists to take applied theories seriously even when the claims of such theories do not satisfy the eight justification conditions discussed in §2 and §4. In cases in which there is no way to apply or test the equilibrium models in question, economists still insist that the models provide a guide to which concepts are most important and a significant framework for making comparisons or contrasts (see, for example, Bliss 1975:301 or Weber 1949:90–91).

The modal model view leads one to take assumptions of models *themselves* seriously and to blur the distinction between assumptions and statements. Nothing real belongs to the exact extension of predicates defined by many economic models. The modal modelist, unhappy with empty or fuzzy extensions finds possible economies or economic sectors which the predicates denote. This "finding" is not automatic. Not all models define predicates which denote possible economies. Definitions must satisfy some conditions before one can see in them accounts of possible economies. These conditions may be identical to those discussed in the last two sections. Such talk of possible economies is, in my view, of value only to the extent that it helps one understand (real) economies. Taking the assumptions of economic models themselves seriously as providing information about possible economies, theorists are distracted from assessing the various resultant theories and are more likely to be sloppy about questions of justification.

If I am right that the modal model view tempts economists to take the claims of their models themselves seriously and to be sloppy about justification, then it certainly does matter whether one adopts this view or the view I have defended which regards economic theories as inexact. Many economists tend, I think, rather lightly to regard comparisons and contrasts of real and hypothetical economies as significant. Were they to heed the justification conditions discussed in §2 and §4 (or to propose rational alternatives), their manipulations of models might be more informative and less questionable. Those assertions of economics which help explain economic phenomena provide information about actual economies.

6. Inexact Explanation in Principle

A great many actual scientific explanations are inexact explanations in principle. In the nonstatistical case, one explains an event or state of affairs by deducing a description of it from a set of statements which include qualified laws, specifications, legitimate simplifications, and the assertion that other things are equal, that there are no unspecified interferences. In the statistical version the set of statements must make the description of what is to be explained highly probable. Explanations need not include statements from all four categories, although they must always contain laws.

If the above account of inexact explanation in principle is correct, we can see that such explanations are never literally deductive-nom-ological explanations or inductive-statistical explanations, since the simplifications they contain are by definition false. This conclusion is, however, pedantic. If we allow a little rephrasing, we can regard many inexact explanations in principle as deductive-nomological or induc-tive-statistical. Qualified laws on my analysis are genuine laws. Spec-ifications are true statements. Since simplifications are approximately true, one can rephrase them as less specific but literally true assertions. (In doing so the description under which one explains the phenomenon also becomes less specific.) The stipulation that other things are equal is vague, but it may nevertheless be true. Inexact explanations in principle, charitably interpreted, often satisfy Hempel's conditions[11] (*pace* Rescher 1970:176).

Two factors led me previously to challenge the deductive-nomolog-ical model (Hausman 1981). In part I failed to distinguish carefully between the conditions an argument must satisfy it it is to *be* an ex-planation and those it must satisfy before one can regard it as an explanation. After discovering the difficulties involved in knowing that the statements in explanations are true and in some cases laws, I looked to justification conditions for an alternative model of explanation that could be more easily used to evaluate purported explanations. The justification conditions were also attractive as an alternative model, since I recognized (as has Cartwright 1980) that the statements in scientific explanations are often not literally true.

It now seems to me a mistake to challenge the deductive-nomological model of explanatory arguments on either of these grounds. Scientists demand that the statements in their explanatory arguments be true. Without truth, there is no explanation and no rationale for the justi-fication conditions I have presented. We can better study the criteria

---

[11] They need not always do so. Sometimes the simplifications are not approximately true. Instead one believes that they are replaceable in the explanation by true statements, which scientists cannot yet provide. The explanatory argument thus contains false state-ments which cannot now be replaced with true ones. Such arguments are thus not deductive-nomological or inductive-statistical explanations. We have two choices. We can continue to regard such arguments as explanatory and change Hempel's models, or we can conclude in these cases that one does not yet have an adequate explanation. I see nothing to be gained in changing the model of explanation. We can account for the apparent explanatory power of inexact explanations in principle which are neither de-ductive-nomological nor inductive-statistical by pointing out how close such inexact explanations in principle come to satisfying the conditions of Hempel's models. Despite the many complications involved in actual scientific explanations, the deductive-nom-ological model seems to provide reasonable necessary conditions for nonstatistical ex-planatory arguments.

scientists employ in assessing explanations if we distinguish these criteria from the necessary conditions something must satisfy in order to be an explanation. The two need not always be different. Sometimes it is helpful directly to ask, for example, whether the statements in a purported explanation are true. Yet, as we have seen, scientists must often settle for statements that are not, as stated, true, but that have some truth in them. Doing so does not force one to reject the deductive-nomological model of explanation, but only to recognize that literally false statements may, with reinterpretation, express truths. In assessing an inexact explanation in principle, one cannot judge directly whether it consists of a set of true statements, some of them laws, which entail a description of the phenomenon to be explained. Instead one must consider whether its lawlike statements satisfy the reliability, refinability, and excusability conditions and whether its simplifications satisfy the confirmation, no-accident, sensitivity, and convergence conditions.

Applying these conditions, we reach the same judgment concerning general equilibrium explanations of the phenomena of capital and interest as does the naïve critic who notes that such explanations contain apparently false statements. Yet our judgment has not been summary or naïve. I have not merely applied abstract philosophical dicta, but have considered directly whether the peculiarities of general equilibrium models conflict with the demands of explanation. For the "laws" of equilibrium theory, I could make at least a partial apology. General equilibrium explanations of the phenomena of capital and interest are no worse off on account of the laws they employ than are many persuasive microeconomic explanations. For the simplifications employed, on the other hand, I could make no apology at all. General equilibrium models do not enable economists to explain the phenomena of capital, interest, or exchange values.

7. The Merits of General Equilibrium Models

If we must conclude, as I have argued, that abstract general equilibrium theories do not explain the characteristics of real economies, what worth do they have? Is the work of the abstract general equilibrium theorists more than some pretty mathematics? Can abstract general equilibrium models be of value if they say nothing about real economies?

These are difficult questions upon which leading theorists disagree. Some, like Debreu (1959:ix), mistakenly believe that general equilibrium models can be used to explain prices. Malinvaud (1972:242) argues that intertemporal models like the one presented in chapter 5 "must be considered to be aimed at the analysis of one aspect of reality, namely that concerning the intervention of prices and interest rates." My argument here shows that no current general equilibrium models achieve that aim. C. J. Bliss is more cautious:

> Of course, that model does not serve to represent reality and that is not its purpose. Where the simple model of an intertemporal economy with all the forward markets functioning can prove useful is as a point of departure, as a guide to which concepts are central and fundamental and which peripheral, and as a reminder that time and capital make an important difference precisely because and only because the system of forward markets . . . are [*sic*] not in fact extant. (1975:301)[12]

Why should one believe that the simple model in question is a good "point of departure" or a good "guide to which concepts are central and fundamental and which peripheral" or a valid "reminder that time and capital make an important difference precisely *because*" the forward markets postulated in the model do not exist? In my view one has no good reason when one is unable to apply the model (or similar models) and confirm some of its implications. Economic models can only help one understand economics if they meet conditions of §2 and §4. Economists are fond of saying that their models only provide some sort of logic of economic phenomena or that they are merely tools one can use when convenient. These claims have reasonable interpretations, but as I argued in §5, they do not provide any way around the demands of §2 and §4.

There is, however, something more in Bliss' attitude. General equilibrium models may be of great heuristic value.[13] One can show that general equilibrium models have been of heuristic value merely by showing that they have in fact helped in developing valuable empirical economic theories. General equilibrium models have in fact been valuable as the source of conceptual and mathematical devices which have been employed in other, less abstract, models. Although some of these devices, such as dated and spatially located commodities,

---

[12] Bliss does not always speak so generously of intertemporal models. "If, therefore, we reinterpret the basic equilibrium model of the atemporal economy by supposing that goods have been labelled according to the date at which they become available, . . . we would place an impossible strain upon the assumption of perfect knowledge. Thus the appropriateness for an economy that persists through time of a model that is formally analogous to the perfect knowledge atemporal model is to be doubted" (1975:44).

[13] Conversations with Edward Green helped me to appreciate this point.

facilitate proving the existence of equilibrium, their heuristic value is independent of the proofs these models provide.

Are general equilibrium models only of heuristic value? Frank Hahn has argued at some length that general equilibrium models, although not explanatory, are of great value. In response to Kornai's extended critique of general equilibrium theory (1971), Hahn emphatically denies that general equilibrium theories are descriptive or explanatory. "It does not occur to him [Kornai] that the most obvious explanation why one studies this theory, which is known to conflict with the facts, is that one is not engaged in description at all" (1973:323). "It is Kornai's besetting sin that he writes as if such a lunatic claim had ever been entertained" (1973:329).

Hahn goes on to defend emphatically the worth of abstract general equilibrium models. First, he argues that such models are *reductio ad absurdum* arguments against the claim that competitive economies are optimal or efficient:

> Someone proposes an explanation of the origin of the earth, say that it was sucked out of the sun. There is no way in which the event itself can now be observed. A theoretical physicist calculates the angular momentum of the earth if the explanation were true. In doing so, he provides a way in which the theory can be falsified. When the claim is made—and the claim is as old as Adam Smith—that a myriad of self-seeking agents left to themselves will lead to a coherent and efficient disposition of economic resources, Arrow and Debreu show what the world would have to look like if the claim is to be true. In doing this they provide the most potent avenue of falsification of the claims. (1973:323–24)

Let us call the old claim of Adam Smith's "the invisible hand postulate." Hahn is suggesting that general equilibrium models "provide the most potent avenue of falsification" for the invisible hand postulate. They show us how *infeasible* a certain sort of social ideal is.

It seems to me, however, that neither economists nor laymen need general equilibrium models to show that any real (and thus at most semi-competitive) market economy does not regularly achieve full employment or optimal allocation of resources. If general equilibrium models were needed for the purpose, they would not help anyway, since the existence proofs the models present do not show what conditions are necessary, but only what conditions are sufficient for competitive equilibrium.

Hahn also argues that general equilibrium models have a more practical use. He writes, "When it is claimed that foreign aid is unnecessary *because* only investment profitable to private investors can be beneficial, we know at once that the speaker or writer does not know the findings of GE [general equilibrium theories]. Anyone who has this knowledge will have no difficulty in pointing to those features of the actual situation which are at variance with what would have to be true if such a claim were to be true" (1973:324). General equilibrium models are thus supposed to be a palliative against practical recommendations based on inadequate theory. General equilibrium theories lack predictive power and do not solve practical problems, but they can reveal that conclusions of previous theories depend on implicit assumptions which are not true of actual economic situations. This benefit from general equilibrium models is real, but should not be exaggerated. Earlier economic theory did not show that only investment profitable to private investors can be beneficial. The public demands a great deal of economists. They must often make recommendations which they realize are not based on solid theoretical foundations. It is unclear whether general equilibrium models ought to or will make economists more cautious in their predictions or recommendations.

Neither of these assertions on behalf of general equilibrium models shows that they are of any great worth. One can understand their merits better when one focuses on the relations between general equilibrium models and other neoclassical economic models. Hahn argues that "The student of GE believes that he has a starting point from which it is possible to advance towards a descriptive theory" (1973:324). "General equilibrium theory" according to Hahn should not be identified with theorems in Debreu's *Theory of Value*. It is instead nothing but the attempt "to study rigorously the interactions of many economic agents" (1973:324). There is no reason why one cannot attempt to study change and development in this way. General equilibrium theory, according to Hahn, involves only a *kind* of model or a *program* for developing adequate economic models. It must not be identified with any of the current and inadequate models.

This defense of general equilibrium theory is not fully consistent with the previous two, since equilibrium theories appear to involve the same invisible hand postulate (that equilibrium will be reached) which, according to the first defense, general equilibrium models help to falsify. Nor is this defense, as thus far stated compelling. We need to see more precisely *how* general equilibrium models help economists advance toward an adequate economic theory.

One can appreciate better what general equilibrium models offer when one accepts my conclusion that general equilibrium models are not themselves the foundation of modern neoclassical economics, but special augmentations of equilibrium theory. Once one realizes what

general equilibrium models are, one can ask "what is such an augmentation for?" Although Arrow and Hahn do not explicitly pose this,
the crucial question, they do sketch the answer as follows:

> The immediate "common sense" answer to the question "What will an
> economy motivated by individual greed and controlled by a very large
> number of different agents look like?" is probably: There will be chaos.
> That quite a different answer has long been claimed true and has indeed
> permeated the economic thinking of a large number of people who are in
> no way economists is itself sufficient grounds for investigating it seriously.
> The proposition having been put forward and very seriously entertained,
> it is important to know not only whether it is true, but also whether it
> could be true. (Arrow and Hahn 1971:vii)

Since the eighteenth century many economists have believed that,
given reasonably favorable conditions, self-interested voluntary exchanges lead to coherent and efficient economic organization. Yet the
theories which economists have possessed have not enabled them to
explain how this order in fact comes about nor even to show how it
is possible that such order could come about. Economic theorists might
thus reasonably be in doubt concerning both whether their theoretical
framework captures the crucial features of the economy and whether
it is likely to lead them to an adequate theory. The curiosity that
motivates the general equilibrium theorist is thus much like the curiosity that motivates the cosmologist. In developing equilibrium models,
will one ever be able to explain how self-interested individual action
within certain institutional constraints can lead to coherent economic
order? Does one really have a grip on the most important and central
economic regularities? Will one ever be able to understand whether
the results of individual actions are truly efficient and whether they
lead to the achievement of other economic goals?

 Clearly there is no way to show in advance that equilibrium models,
when refined and developed, will enable theorists to explain (inexactly
in principle) detailed as well as overall characteristics of economies or
of economic events. The successes of partial equilibrium models or of
practical general equilibrium models give one some reason for hope.
Furthermore, both as a way of working toward such an adequate theory
and as a way of testing the promise and power of equilibrium theory,
it is sensible and important to investigate the explanatory possibilities
of equilibrium models. If one augments the generalizations of equilibrium theory with various simplifications, can one explain the existence
of any sort of economic equilibrium, even if it is only imaginary? If
theorists can use such augmentations of equilibrium theory to show

how economic order can result from independent self-interested individual actions, they have reason to believe that they have captured
the fundamental elements of economic life and that the neoclassical
approach may succeed.

In proving the existence of equilibria under various conditions, the
abstract general equilibrium theorists formulate models one can use
to assess the potentiality of equilibrium theory. Such models show that
equilibrium theory is capable of explaining at least some sorts of complicated economic equilibria, and thus they give theorists reason to
believe that they are on the track of an adequate general economic
theory. Economists thus do have some uses for talk of possibilities
(although no need for the more extravagant views of the modal modelist). This sort of an investigation of the possibility of an explanation
needs to be distinguished both from the above discussion of the *fea-
sibility* of economic equilibria and from philosophical discussions of
explaining how possibly.[14] General equilibrium theorists ask whether
it is possible to use equilibrium theory to explain complicated economic
phenomena.

The abstract general equilibrium theorists have shown that, were
the world very much simpler than it is or will ever be, economists
could use their "laws" to explain in principle how economies work.
Theorists thus have reason to believe that they are on the right track.
The existence proofs provide this theoretical reassurance. They are
not explanations. These abstract general equilibrium models may also
help improve current explanatory theories. By weakening and com-
plicating the stipulations needed to demonstrate the existence of more
complex equilibria, theorists can come closer to being able to apply
the models to real economies.

There is, however, only so much that mathematical work can do.
The fundamental generalizations of equilibrium theory need improvement. Much difficult work remains to be done in characterizing the
sort of economic order (and disorder) there actually is that needs explaining. Economists disagree about whether equilibrium models can
ever adequately account for certain aggregate economic phenomena.
The mathematical efforts of the abstract general equilibrium theorists
cannot resolve these problems, although they can help. They can, for
example, show economists how to make do with weaker formulations
of the "laws" of equilibrium theory and may even suggest replace-

---

[14] Hempel 1965:428–30; Dray 1957:158f. In explaining how possibly, one is concerned
with the case in which something happens contrary to one's expectations which needs
explaining away. Economists are not, of course, trying to explain away the existence
of some sort of competitive equilibrium.

ments. The existence proofs offer economists some reassurance that equilibrium models will eventually do the trick.

Perhaps equilibrium models will someday enable economists to explain the phenomena of capital and interest. Meanwhile, neoclassical economists remain unable to do so. Perhaps some alternative to equilibrium theory might enable economists to do better. Let us turn to Sraffa's work and examine the possibility of such an alternative.

CHAPTER EIGHT
Sraffa and Neo-Ricardian Value Theory

In Chapters 2 through 5 we traced neo-classical views of capital and interest and exchange values from their intuitive roots to their precise formulation in abstract general equilibrium models. The final product is logically rigorous and avoids the difficulties faced by capital theories like Clark's or the Austrians'. Yet, if the arguments and analyses of Chapters 6 and 7 are correct, that theoretical achievement cannot be regarded as an adequate theory of capital and interest or of exchange values. No existing general equilibrium theory explains even the principal phenomena of capital and interest. To reach this conclusion, we required both the economics and the philosophy of the previous chapters. We return now to the classical approach to problems of capital and interest, as revived and modified by Piero Sraffa. Perhaps the refurbished older approach will be better able to account for the relations between capital, interest, and prices. In examining Sraffa's work we shall also be probing more deeply into the Cambridge criticisms of chapter 4.

Sraffa's work is intriguing. His economics is strikingly different from neoclassical economics. Juxtaposing Sraffa's work and Marx's suggests the outlines of an alternative to the vision of economic life as the reconciling of the plans of self-interested individuals who only interact through exchange. In analyzing Sraffa's work and reactions to it, we shall uncover further philosophical assumptions underlying the commitment of most economists to general equilibrium models. Sraffa's achievement is modest, however. His work is interesting not for what it shows, but for the vision of economic theorizing that guides it.

1. Sraffa's System

Sraffa regards his work as a continuation and a development of the thought of the classical political economists, particularly Ricardo. He presents a system of "physical cost" or production equations from which prices may be calculated as soon as the distribution of income is given. In this sense he presents what I called a physical cost cum distribution theory of exchange values. An easy example will be adequate for the purposes of this investigation. Although mathematical complexities are involved in its justification, Sraffa's equation system is quite simple. For reasons which I will discuss later, I am uneasy calling Sraffa's work a theory.

Sraffa's system relies upon a much more compact set of assumptions than do intertemporal general equilibrium models. The assumptions may be listed as follows:[1]

D1. There is no excess demand.
D6. Total expenditure equals total income.
New Givens:
E1: The size and composition of output.
E2: The technology used to produce that output—that is, exactly how much of which inputs were combined to produce each output.
E3. The economy is in a stationary state: prices, output, and technology are not changing.
E4. There are no joint products, no fixed capital, and no original factors of production except homogeneous labor.
E5. All commodities enter directly or indirectly into the production of all commodities.
E6. Wages are paid at the end of the production period.
F1. Economic generalization: The rate of profit in all productive activities is equal.

Assumptions E4, 5, and 6 are dispensable, although dispensing with

[1] My presentation of Sraffa's system involves a good deal of interpretation. Sraffa says nothing about demand or excess demand. Alessandro Roncaglia denies that Sraffa makes any assumptions concerning the clearing of markets or the existence of equilibrium. "There is no reason to suppose that prices of production should equate the quantity demanded with the quantity supplied for any commodity. . . . It is then incumbent to try to understand the sense in which 'prices of production' represent a point of reference that increases the understanding of economic reality" (1978:16–17). "Sraffa has undertaken an examination of prices of production on the basis of an assumption of a uniform rate of profits in the various sectors of production. His book thus confronts a different problem from the marginalist problem of finding the 'equilibrium prices' which guarantee the equality between supply and demand" (1978:118). On Roncaglia's view, the "values" Sraffa discusses are almost entirely disconnected from equilibrium prices. The text probably supports Roncaglia's interpretation at least as well as mine. The problem is that if Sraffa's values are not connected to equilibrium prices, then it is unclear what "point of reference" they are supposed to represent. On Roncaglia's interpretation I do not see any but a purely mathematical point to Sraffa's work. On my interpretation Sraffa's work may help explain exchange values.

6 destroys the linear relationship between wages and the rate of profit Sraffa derives for the "standard system." Assumption 4 is made by Sraffa only in part I of *The Production of Commodities by Means of Commodities*. Sraffa does not make assumption 5 at all (except briefly in his chapter 1); but it simplifies the exposition to add it. Some economists misinterpret Sraffa as assuming constant returns to scale and only one primary factor of production.[2] In fact in part II of *The Production of Commodities*, Sraffa explicitly considers land rent. Not only does he deny in the introduction that he is assuming constant returns to scale, but he never makes any reference to changes in the scale of any productive activity. The manipulations by which Sraffa derives the standard system do not involve changing the scale of any productive activity.

In Sraffa's work F1, the assumption that there is an equal rate of profit in all productive activities, is primitive. Sraffa is not concerned with the institutional arrangements and psychological characteristics which explain why rates of profit will be equalized. One is trading depth of theoretical analysis for directness and possible applicability. It is, however, worth noting which of the assumptions of intertemporal equilibrium models are needed to prove that the rate of profit in all productive activities will be equal. These are:

B2. Entrepreneurs or firms seek to maximize their profits.
D1. There is no excess demand.
D2. No one is able to influence the prices of what he or she buys or sells.
D3. There is free mobility of labor and all commodity inputs.
D4. All parties on the market have complete and accurate information concerning all available commodities, the going prices, and all technological possibilities.

D2 is needed in standard proofs that rates of profit will be strictly equal. Yet Sraffa's work need not presuppose such perfect competition. The rate of profit may be nearly equal with highly imperfect competition. From the perspective of an equilibrium theorist who insists that axioms of an economic model be "primitive," F1 should be replaced by B2 and D1–D4. If the axioms of an economic model need not themselves be beyond further economic analysis, then there seems no

---

[2] See for example Bliss (1975:251n). It is an appealing move to make, because having made it, one can invoke the nonsubstitution theorem (see Pasinetti 1977) to show that exchange values are independent of demand. With constant returns to scale Sraffa need not require stationary equilibrium (E3), but can permit steady state growth as well.

pressing reason to replace F1 with D1–4 and B2. In any event, Sraffa's system, like neoclassical models, relies on simplifications and "unrealistic assumptions," although the list of those Sraffa needs is shorter.

Given these assumptions Sraffa can write down a set of production equations. In what follows I shall assume that there are only two commodities, x and m, wood and axes. L is labor, w wages, r the rate of profits. The superscripts will indicate, as before, the productive activity in which the input is used.

$$(8.1) \qquad (x^x p_x + m^x p_m)(1 + r) + L^x w = x p_x$$

$$(8.2) \qquad (x^m p_x + m^m p_m)(1 + r) + L^m w = m p_m$$

Interest is not paid on wages, because they are paid at the end of the production period. x^x, x^m, x, m^x, m^m, m, L^x, and L^m are all known. There are only four unknowns: p_x, p_m, r, and w. Since one can take one price as a numeraire or otherwise fix a numeraire, there is one degree of freedom both in this simple example and in general. Sraffa accomplishes two things. First he systematically presents a relationship between prices and distribution. Second, he demonstrates that when r is fixed and less than some maximum value, a unique all-positive set of prices and a unique positive wage can be calculated.

If one substitutes some value for r in (8.1) and (8.2) and takes one price as numeraire, one has two linear equations in two unknowns and it seems, speaking unrigorously, that there should be no difficulty in solving them. To prove that a unique solution exists and that, if r is less than some maximum value, the other price and the wage are positive is a subtle but now well understood mathematical task. To give such a proof as well as to show more systematically how prices and distribution are interrelated, Sraffa presents what he calls the standard system. I am concerned here with what Sraffa's system has to say about the relations between interest and exchange values.

Since one knows the vector of inputs: $a = (x^x + x^m, m^x + m^m)$ and the output $b = (x, m)$, one also knows the net output, $y = [x - (x^x + x^m), m - (m^x + m^m)]$. Suppose it were the case that $y_x/a_x = y_m/a_m$ or equivalently that $b_x/a_x = b_m/a_m$, where the subscript x indicates the first, x, component of the respective vectors and the subscript m indicates the second component. If it were the case that $b_x/a_x = b_m/a_m$, then, entirely independent of the prices of x and m, one could calculate the ratio of surplus product to inputs or the maximum rate of profit. Let R be this maximum rate of profit. When $r = R$, all net product goes to profits and wages are zero. To simplify, Sraffa treats the entire wage as variable. There is no minimum "subsistence" wage. Consumption goods which enter into the wage are thus in general "non-basics" (see §2). A more plausible treatment of the wage, which Sraffa outlines, but does not adopt, is to divide it into two components, a subsistence and a surplus wage. The subsistence wage could be incorporated into the production equations. One might, for example, add inputs like bread, shirts, or Christmas cards to one's specifications of the technology employed for making steel. The surplus wage would then be treated in the way Sraffa treats the whole of the wage (1960:9–10).

If $b_x/a_x = b_m/a_m$ and R is the maximum rate of profit, one has the following relations:

$$(8.3) \qquad (x^x p_x + m^x p_m)(1 + R) = x p_x$$

$$(8.4) \qquad (x^m p_x + m^m p_m)(1 + R) = m p_m$$

$$(8.5) \quad (1 + R) = \frac{x p_x + m p_m}{x^x p_x + m^x p_m + x^m p_x + m^m p_m} \left(= \frac{p \cdot b}{p \cdot a} \right)$$

$$(8.6) \quad (1 + R) = \frac{\dfrac{x}{x^x + x^m}(x^x + x^m)p_x + \dfrac{m}{m^x + m^m}(m^x + m^m)p_m}{(x^x + x^m)p_x + (m^x + m^m)p_m}$$

If $x/(x^x + x^m) = m/(m^x + m^m) = b_x/a_x = b_m/a_m$, then this ratio is equal to $(1 + R)$ and $y_x/a_x = y_m/a_m = R$.

In general, of course, the ratio of the output of any commodity to the inputs of that commodity will not be the same for all commodities. But one can "notionally" change the scale of the productive activities until this condition is met. One is *not* actually changing the scale of production. What production would actually be if the scale were changed is entirely irrelevant; one is merely making use of a technique to find the maximum rate of profit and an interesting numeraire.

To change the scale of production in this notional way, one applies positive multipliers c_1 to (8.1) and c_2 to (8.2). These multipliers transform the actual system into the standard system only if, for $w = 0$, b_x/a_x now equals b_m/a_m. In attempting the transformation one derives the following two equations in three unknowns:

$$(8.7) \qquad (c_1 x^x + c_2 x^m)(1 + R) = c_1 x$$

$$(8.8) \qquad (c_1 m^x + c_2 m^m)(1 + R) = c_2 m$$

Since only the ratio of the multipliers is significant, Sraffa sets the scale of the standard system by stipulating

$$(8.9) \qquad c_1 L^x + c_2 L^m = L^x + L^m = 1$$

It can be proven that such positive multipliers can always be found.[3]

Applying non-zero multipliers to equations does not change their solutions, so whatever values of the unknowns one finds in the standard system are the actual values.

Sraffa now selects the following numeraire:

$$(8.10) \qquad p \cdot y^* = 1.$$

where the asterisk denotes values in the standard system and p is the (row) price vector. Since the standard net product, y^*, is made the numeraire, prices will measure proportions of standard net product. Since $L^{x*} + L^{m*} = 1$, w $(= w^*)$ is the proportion of the standard net product going to labor. Thus in terms of this numeraire, when $w = 1$, $r = 0$. By the definition of the rate of profit

$$(8.11) \qquad r = \frac{1 - w}{p \cdot a^*}$$

But $R = [(p \cdot b^*)/(p \cdot a^*)] - 1$ from (8.5). Thus $R = (p \cdot y^*)/(p \cdot a^*)$ $= 1/(p \cdot a^*)$. From (8.11), one can thus conclude that

$$(8.12) \qquad r = R(1 - w)$$

In terms of the chosen numeraire, there is thus a particularly simple wage profit line (Fig. 8.1).

What corresponds to "capital" (ch. 4, §2), the slope of the wage-profit line, $1/R$ $(= p \cdot a^*)$, is the value of all commodity inputs to the standard system in terms of the standard net product. From (8.12) one can, for any value of r $(\leq R)$ find w and vice versa. Substituting into (8.1) and (8.2), one can solve for p_x and p_m which are provably positive and unique. (Sraffa 1960:26–29; Newman 1962:64–66; Schwartz 1961:17–27; Burmeister 1968:83–87). All ratios are the same in the actual economy as in the standard system, although after the calcu-

---

[3] Sraffa states this proposition on pp. 23–24 and offers a peculiar informal proof on pp. 26–27. Newman (1962:68–70) states this claim more formally and relies on proofs in Gantmacher (1959, chapter 3). An excellent formal treatment of systems like Sraffa's is provided by Schwartz (1961, part A). See also Blakeley and Gossling (1967:427–31).

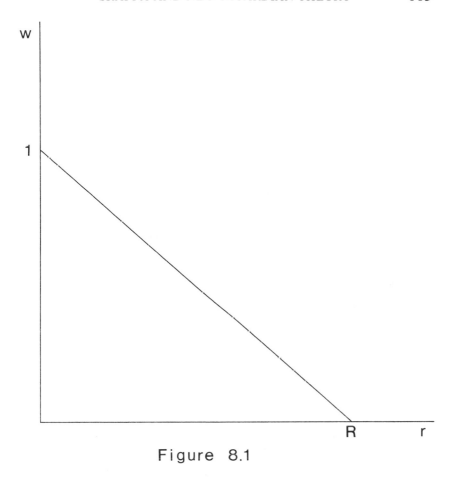

Figure 8.1

lations are complete, one might well want to pick a new numeraire. The simple straight-line relation between wages and profits does not survive a change of numeraire, but Sraffa does prove that, provided there are no joint products, w is smaller relative to the price of every commodity whenever r is larger (1960:38–39, 61–62).

2. Sraffa and the Critique of Neoclassical Theory

Sraffa subtitled his book, *A Prelude to a Critique of Economic Theory*. The economic theory is neoclassical or "marginalist" economics. Some of the Cambridge economists regard the criticisms based on Sraffa's work as showing that the whole neoclassical approach to economic theory is a mistake (Garegnani 1970:427f; Eatwell 1975c). Distribution is not even ideally determined by voluntary exchanges. The theory of value should be separated from the theory of output or distribution. Profits are determined by macroeconomic considerations, including class struggle.

Two questions concerning Sraffa's work are crucial: Has he provided the foundation or the materials for some serious criticism of established economic theory? Has he pointed the way to any attractive alternative to equilibrium theory? Many economists believe that the answers to both questions are yes.

Some economists believe that Sraffa's work strikes at the very heart of neoclassical theory, since it reveals that demand has no role to play in the determination of exchange values! John Eatwell, for example, writes, "Since the determination of the real wage is related to social and historical phenomena, and has nothing to do with the relation of supply with demand, and the structure of production may be taken as a datum, then the 'forces' of supply and demand have no role to play in the general analysis of value" (1974:288). Eatwell does not explicitly assert that "the 'forces' of supply and demand" do not affect exchange values, only that they have no role "in the general analysis of value." Alfredo Medio is more explicit. "Sraffa's and Schwartz's solutions have moreover the specific merit of showing that demand plays no role in determining the rate of profit and relative prices undermining the neoclassical theory of value and distribution based on the concept of demand and supply of commodities and of 'factors of production'" (1972:325). Medio has since changed his mind (1977:392), but like Eatwell and, apparently Robinson (1965:31), was tempted to conclude that Sraffa had shown that demand has no role to play in determining exchange values.

Consider the rather different conclusions Maurice Dobb draws from Sraffa's work:

> Let me emphasize that what we are confronted with here is . . . the much more general problem of the relativity of all price relations to income distribution: i. e. to the wage-profit relation. The latter cannot, therefore, be determined within the sphere of price-relations (what Marx called the sphere of circulation); for its determination one has to look beyond and outside it (or if you like, beneath it). This is "back to Marx" with a vengeance. (1970:350)

Dobb believes that Sraffa's work shows that, contrary to the sketch in chapter 1 above and to the orthodox theory erected upon it, the wage-profit relation *cannot* be determined within the sphere of exchange. The rate of profit is not determined (causally) by individual exchanges constrained by technology and the availability of unproduced factors of production.

Dobb draws on another of Sraffa's results to reinforce this conclusion. Sraffa shows that production processes for commodities that do not enter directly or indirectly into the production of all commodities have no influence on the wage rate, the rate of profit or prices (except of their own outputs). Sraffa calls such goods "nonbasics." Complications arise when several nonbasics are interconnected (1960:7–8). Unproduced resources like land are also nonbasic and introduce further difficulties. The precise specification of a nonbasic, once joint products and land are introduced, becomes quite complex (1960:47–52). Nonbasics are excluded from the simple cases I am considering by E5 above.

Following von Bortkievicz (1906–7), Dobb argues that the irrelevance of nonbasics to the rate of profit shows that profits must originate in the relation of wage-labor to capital, not in the ability of capital to increase production (1970:358). Dobb is implicitly arguing as follows. Since the productivity of capital does not influence the general rate of profit or prices, when that capital is employed in producing nonbasics, the productivity of capital cannot be responsible for profits. The origin of profits must lie in the relation between wage-labor and capital, because capital only has an influence on profits or interest when it is employed in producing basic commodities. The size of the wage compared to the price of wage goods is, of course, affected by the productivity of inputs employed in producing wage goods, regardless of whether wage goods are basics or not. The rate of profit is, however, independent of the methods employed in producing nonbasics. Strictly speaking, in Sraffa's system wage goods are nonbasic, but with the minor emendation discussed in §1, they become basic.

According to Edward Nell, Sraffa's work and the criticisms of capital theories based on it show us that "the payments to capital are dispositions of a surplus and do not involve any kind of exchange" (1967:17–18). He continues

> But in the market for factors, income is paid out to those who have property rights in the productive process, in accordance with the nature and extent of their property. Of course, . . . both capital and labor will shift in response to differentials in earnings between industries. But such movement does not imply that any *exchange* takes place between the recipient of net income and the source of income. The only service the owner of capital renders to industry is the service of permitting it to be

owned by him. Labor receives wages in exchange for work, but the level of wages, which cannot fall below a basic cost of living, is determined by bargaining power and not, as in the case of ordinary commodities, by a relationship between cost of production and value of product. (1967:21)

The rate of profits is not determined by exchanges and not related to the productivity of capital. Furthermore, the interactions which result in a payment of profits are not exchanges at all. Nell draws the last conclusion because he believes that capitalists supply no commodity or service in return for the profits they receive.

What Nell may mean by this strong and puzzling claim is not clear. He may intend several or all of the following:

(1) Capital is not a commodity or service.
(2) Capital is not productive.
(3) The long-term interest elasticity of investment is near zero and not uniformly negative (in the long run investment is not sensitive to the rate of interest).
(4) The rate of profit is not causally determined through voluntary market exchanges of commodities, but through the general relation between wage-labor and capital.
(5) It is unjust that capitalists receive profits.

The Cambridge criticisms may be regarded as supporting (1). Since Sraffa's system never mentions "capital," one might regard it as supporting (2), although the arguments the Cambridge critics use seem to *refute* (2). Recall that equations (4.8) and (4.1) suggest that an increase in capital increases output. Although the second clause of (3) gains some support from the capital reversing phenomenon, (3) appears to be a straightforward empirical claim which is potentially testable. If true, (3) would give one reason to regard profits as similar to rents and might provide some reason to accept (5). (3) is not a serious criticism of equilibrium economics. (4) is Dobb's claim. It is consistent with (1)–(3), but not supported by them nor supportive of them. (5) finally is an important normative thesis that lurks in the background of much of the argument concerning capital and interest. It belongs to a different, but not completely unrelated sphere of discourse.

With the exception of the normative claim, it seems to me that the conclusions critical of neoclassical theory which economists have drawn from Sraffa's work are the following four:

(I) Capital is not a commodity or service, and interest is not the price of capital.

(II) Exchange values are determined by costs of production; demand has little or no role to play.

(III) The rate of profit is not causally determined by individual exchanges as constrained by technology and the availability of factors of production.

(IV) The distribution of income is determined by the relations between workers and capitalists including possibly their relative bargaining power.

The two questions I am concerned with are whether Sraffa provides the basis for a serious critique of neoclassical economics and whether he provides the elements of a reasonable alternative approach. As shown in chapter 5, conclusion (I) does not pose any challenge to *fundamental* neoclassical theory. Conclusions (II)–(IV) are serious challenges. Their assessment is rather complicated. I shall argue that Sraffa's work *alone* does not support them.

3. Sraffa's System and Equilibrium Models

What has Sraffa accomplished? He forged critical tools which the Cambridge critics have used to attack simplified aggregative capital theories. To show that, given D1, D6, E1–E6 and F1, a unique all positive price vector can be calculated [once r ($\leq R$) is given] is a substantial result, as is the demonstration of an inverse relation between r and w and of a maximum rate of profit. Like general equilibrium models, Sraffa's avoids aggregation, but unlike them, demand has no explicit role and the rate of profit is not endogenously determined. The maximum rate of profit is related to purely technological characteristics of the system.

Do these results show that demand has no role in value determination, that individual exchanges do not determine the rate of profit, or that the distribution of income is determined by the relations between workers and capitalists? Do these results enable one to erect an alternative to equilibrium theory? From the perspective of fundamental and rigorous equilibrium models, Sraffa's work appears to present no challenge or criticism whatsoever. Everything Sraffa shows is consistent with a suitably restricted general equilibrium model. Indeed, Sraffa's production equations appear to be a fragment *of* a general equilibrium model.

Suppose one adds E3–E6 to the assumptions of the model in chapter 5. D9 (that the wage is paid at the beginning of the period) must be deleted. Doing so is not a serious change. Since one is changing to stationary equilibrium analysis, the time subscripts disappear. If one knew the utility and production functions and the various initial conditions, one could solve for equilibrium outputs, prices, consumption, inputs, wage, and rate of profit. Since all own rates of return are equal ($p_{x,1} = \bar{p}_{x,2} = p_x$ and similarly for p_m), and since wages are paid at the end of the period of production, (5.15) and (5.16) become (8.1) and (8.2). Given the equilibrium solution one can fill in the values of x, x^x, x^m, m, m^x, m^m, L^x, L^m and we have Sraffa's production equations.

Sraffa can then, if he likes, perform his manipulations on these equations and find R, the maximum rate of profit, and determine the standard system. For any given value of r, he can solve for all relative prices. Since the general equilibrium system satisfies all of the assumptions of E and F, and since the system is formally valid, the quadruple (r^e, w^e, p_x^e, p_m^e) must be solutions to Sraffa's production equations, where e denotes the general equilibrium value. Moreover, from the perspective of intertemporal equilibrium theory, a solution to Sraffa's production equations (r, w, p_x, p_m) has economic meaning *only* if it is an equilibrium solution. All other solutions would set in motion economic changes and violate the assumption of a stationary state, as well as the assumption of market clearing and no excess demand.

Once one recognizes the intimate and intricate relations between Sraffa's system and equilibrium models, one should realize that Sraffa's work does not establish conclusions II, III or IV of §2. It does not show that demand has no role in determining exchange value, that the rate of profit is not determined through exchanges, nor that the distribution of income is determined by the relations between capitalists and workers. To take size and composition of output and market clearing as given is to take demand as given. It is then hardly surprising that one can calculate prices without any explicit mention of demand. Whatever else Sraffa may show, he does not demonstrate that demand is irrelevant to price determination.

That the rate of profit is not determined through voluntary exchanges is also not supported by Sraffa's work. Appearances to the contrary, one cannot take technology and size and composition of output as given, arbitrarily fix the distribution of income, and expect the calculated prices to bear any relation to the actual exchange values that would prevail in the given economy. As Sraffa himself notes (1960:81f), not all of any wage-profit line can be taken seriously. Robinson puts the point nicely. "Some readers have interpreted the calculation of the movement up and down of the rate of profit and the share of wages as a story about class war. But that is a complete misunderstanding. . . . the movement is only the movement of the eye running up and down a curve on the blackboard'' (1977:58). If a wage-profit pair is chosen that is not on the wage-profit *frontier*, changes in which technology is employed will be induced. Since the economy will not be in a stationary state, one will not be able to calculate net output by subtracting inputs in any given year from outputs in that year. The whole Sraffa apparatus breaks down. It provides no information about the results.

Furthermore, demand is sensitive to the distribution of income. Demand disrupts the relationship between p and r, because even small changes in the distribution of income will generally affect aggregate amounts demanded. Since prices change, the quantities demanded change. The size and composition of output must, however, match demand. Otherwise there will be market imbalances, shifting of resources and changes in production, or changes in technology employed. In any of these three cases the initial conditions for the application of Sraffa's apparatus are not satisfied and his apparatus is mute. Furthermore, capitalists and workers have different tastes. Changes in the distribution of income will shift the aggregate demand curves. Indeed, one might value Sraffa's apparatus because it allows one to see how sensitive prices, output, and the structure of production are to changes in distribution.[4] In general, if r changes, one needs an entirely new set of givens. The rate of profit is exogenous in Sraffa's system only in the sense that one cannot calculate what it is from the information that Sraffa considers. To leap to the conclusion that the rate of profit is not calculable from any information relevant to exchanges and thus not determined by any features of constrained voluntary exchange is without justification.

Dobb's conclusion that the rate of profit must be determined by the relations between workers and capitalists, since the productivity of capital in producing nonbasics does not affect wages, profits, or distribution, also does not follow. Consider the production equation for a nonbasic luxury good, v ("velvets"):

$$(8.13) \qquad p \cdot c(1 + r) + wl = vp_v.$$

As before, p is a row vector of prices, c is the vector of all of the inputs needed to produce velvets, w is the wage, l the amount of labor needed,

---

[4] If we add the assumption of constant returns to scale and consider constant proportional growth economies, we have the additional difficulty that changes in distribution will affect the aggregate propensity to save. See Hicks (1965, Part II).

v the quantity of velvets produced and p_v the price of velvets. Suppose that the technique for producing velvets changes so that (8.13) becomes

$$(8.14) \qquad\qquad p \cdot c(1 + r) + wl = 2vp_v'.$$

Sraffa shows that p_v' must equal $\frac{1}{2}p_v$. Profits and wages are thus undisturbed. Of course, this result depends on certain axioms—including D1, that there is no excess demand. The new quantity of velvets produced, $2v$, must be sold at $\frac{1}{2}p_v$. The market *may* clear at this price. In general, however, after the change in technique, market and equilibrium price will not be the same and some inputs will have to be transferred to restore an equilibrium. If there are constant returns to scale in the production of basics, it *may* be possible to transfer inputs without disturbing the rate of profits or the wage.

Thus a change in technique (and therefore of the "productivity of capital") in producing a nonbasic will fail to affect wages or profits only in special circumstances. But this is only a partial response to Dobb. His argument can be revised in two ways. First, it remains *possible* that with a change in "the productivity of capital" in producing nonbasics, profits and wages will be unchanged. Is not this possibility enough to refute neoclassical views of the rate of interest? Second one might argue that the change in the rate of profit that will normally result is secondary, the result of a demand-induced change in the production of basics, not the direct reaction to a change in the productivity of capital that neoclassical theory demands.

The second argument is unconvincing. We have seen (chapter 2) that marginal productivity theory does not assert that the marginal productivity of an input *causes* (let alone causes directly) its recompense. Both are supposedly determined by the various economic givens in equilibrium models. Although I shall have more to say about the philosophical ramifications of this view (chapter 9), nothing I shall say will salvage this attempt to reinterpret Dobb's argument.

In order to see whether the *possible* irrelevance to profits of the productivity of capital in producing nonbasics refutes any claims of marginal productivity or equilibrium theory, we need to be clear about what neoclassical theory asserts. At first glance it might seem as if neoclassical theory *requires* that the return to a factor of production be larger if its marginal physical product, in any process of production, is larger. But such is not the case. The return to an input must be larger if its marginal physical productivity in producing *itself* (or its own technical interest rate) is larger (see ch. 5, §2). The return to an input need not be larger if its increased marginal physical productivity in a particular process does not imply an increase in its own technical interest rate. This is possible only when the input's marginal physical productivity increases *only* in the production of a nonbasic. The value of the marginal product must remain constant. The increased physical productivity must thus lower the scarcity or marginal utility of the nonbasic output or it must be possible to transfer the input with constant returns to the production of other outputs. These are precisely the cases in which an increase in the productivity of "capital" fails to have an effect on profits. The possibility that a change in the productivity of any commodity in producing a nonbasic will have no effect on profits or wages does not refute neoclassical theory or show that the origin of profit lies in the relations between workers and capitalists.

Sraffa's work thus does not establish that demand does not affect exchange values, that profits are not determined within the process of exchange, or that profits depend on the relations between workers and capitalists. Yet it would be a mistake to conclude that Sraffa's work cannot possibly present an alternative to general equilibrium models or function as part of a criticism of them. The relations between Sraffa's work and general equilibrium models need to be made more precise. In what sense are the two consistent with one another?

This question is not an easy one to answer. If we look at the two theories formally and treat *all* the assumptions of the models in this chapter and in chapter 5 as assertions, then it is clear that the two structures have some inconsistent consequences. Suppose one is comparing stationary general equilibrium states in which the distribution of income differs. Examining one stationary equilibrium, one can use both Sraffa's system and general equilibrium theories to predict prices in the others. These predictions will generally differ, since in Sraffa's system there is no allowance for changes in technology employed. To give another example, one might well find an economy in which, to some degree of approximation, the relationship between distribution and prices Sraffa identifies holds, but in which the claims of general equilibrium theory about prices and interest rates are falsified—perhaps because of some sort of generalized monopolistic competition.

The difficulty with the above observation is that Sraffa's apparatus is misapplied in the first example, and, general equilibrium theory is misapplied in the second. As mentioned above, Sraffa recognizes that with changes in the distribution of income, techniques which are more or less labor intensive will be introduced. He is only analyzing a single stationary state. On the other hand, few general equilibrium models apply to situations involving imperfect competition. The question of the consistency of Sraffa's work and general equilibrium models is not so straightforward as it might appear to be.

I argued that the heart of equilibrium theory consists of the nine "laws" discussed in the second section of chapter 6. We might then plausibly conclude that a theoretical claim is inconsistent with equilibrium theory if and only if it is inconsistent with the conjunction of those nine laws. Sraffa's work by this test is not inconsistent with equilibrium theory. One might wonder what the identity of Sraffa's work turns on. F1 is surely not sufficient. It seems to me that something is a Sraffa model if and only if it includes assumptions D1, D6, E1–E3, and F1. I am not sure how to justify this claim. Fortunately nothing depends on it, since *all* of the assumptions of §1 of this chapter are consistent with the nine "laws" of chapter 6.

Yet Sraffa's work also is consistent with contradictories to the basic assumptions concerning utilities and production, (1)–(7) of Chapter 6, §2. One may thus combine Sraffa's work with further models which are inconsistent with equilibrium theory. Sraffa's work can, through such a combination, have applications which are incompatible with equilibrium theory. There are various possible applications. One might explain why, with a very small change in distribution, goods produced in a labor-intensive way grew cheaper. One might assume fixed proportions and constant returns to scale and offer quantitative predictions. For some interesting (and curious) possibilities see Bose (1975, part II). One might join Sraffa's account of the determination of exchange values to a Marxian theory of profits or exploitation. Through such expansion and development, one may find in Sraffa part of an alternative to equilibrium theory. It is not possible to know whether a physical cost cum distribution theory of exchange value presents an alternative to a constrained balancing of marginal utilities theory of exchange value, until one sees how Sraffa's work combines with other theoretical claims.

At least we can see why so much dispute remains concerning the significance of the Cambridge controversy. In the whole Cambridge enterprise neoclassical theorists see nothing but some peculiar equilibrium models that make vivid some of the unsolved problems posed by capital and interest. The Cambridge critics, on the other hand, see their work as part of or as leading to an alternative kind of economic theory.

This conviction of the critics has not yet been explained. Sraffa shows that if one takes output, the technology employed to produce that output and the distribution of income between wages and profits as given, one can calculate prices. This demonstration does not establish that demand has no effect on exchange values, or that distribution is not determined by individual exchange. Indeed one might question whether Sraffa's work has any interesting economic content at all. That many talented economists find in Sraffa's work the germ of an alternative approach to economics may seem puzzling. I shall now solve this puzzle by emphasizing the contrasts between the method or strategy of equilibrium theorizing and the method or strategy implicit in Sraffa's work.

CHAPTER NINE
Philosophical Assessment of Sraffa's System

In Chapter 8 I presented a simplified Sraffa system. Although more complicated cases demand further apparatus, that system reveals the essentials of Sraffa's work. He shows that one can calculate prices without mention of utility or production functions whenever one is given enough information.

The implications and significance of Sraffa's work are not clear. Some of his interpreters have greatly exaggerated the consequences of Sraffa's formal achievement; his work does not show that exchange values are unaffected by demand, nor does it show that the rate of profit or of interest is not the result of individual exchanges. In addition, it does not show that the distribution of income is determined by the relations between capitalist and workers. Other theories, compatible with Sraffa's work, may enable one to reach these conclusions, but they are not consequences of anything in *The Production of Commodities by Means of Commodities*. One might argue that Sraffa does provide some reason to believe that capital is not a commodity or service and that interest is not the price of capital, but well-informed neoclassical economists do not believe that capital is a single commodity or service.

Sraffa does not provide a theory of capital or of interest. Sraffa's work might be usefully combined with some theory of capital or of interest, but it is not itself a theory of either. Sraffa does say what capital is—the value of the produced means of production—but he says nothing about what determines its quantity or its growth. The rate of interest or of profit is just given exogenously. At most, Sraffa provides a theory of exchange values and of the relations between exchange values and the rate of profit or interest. The extent to which Sraffa's work is not only compatible with equilibrium theory, but *is* a kind of equilibrium model does not preclude the possibility that Sraffa has provided a distinct theory of exchange value. Has Sraffa in fact provided such a theory? As in the assessment of general equilibrium models we face here questions which are as much philosophical as they are economic.

In considering whether Sraffa has provided an alternative account of exchange values or of the relations between interest and exchange values, we shall encounter other interesting questions. Sraffa's approach to theorizing is quite different from the sort which characterizes equilibrium models. The differences need to be clarified and evaluated. Through this clarification we shall come to a better understanding of the foundations of mainstream economics.

1. Does Sraffa Explain Exchange Values?

It is not clear whether Sraffa's work satisfies the conditions a theory must satisfy in order to be regarded as explanatory (chapter 7). At least it comes closer to doing so than do general equilibrium models. Sraffa's work contains only one lawlike generalization, Fl, that the rate of profit is equal in all productive activities. This generalization is, I think, lawlike and in many important domains reliable, refinable, and excusable. There are natural classes of circumstances in which, after one allows for risk and perhaps prestige, the rate of profit in most firms is roughly equal. Adding further qualifications, the generalization can be made more reliable or reliable in more domains. When it fails, economists can usually point to specific interferences to explain why. Whether Fl satisfies the reliability, refinability, and excusability conditions is an empirical question. I suspect that most economists would agree with my belief that Fl does satisfy these conditions. Fl seems at least as reliable as the fundamental general statements of equilibrium theory.

Less clear, however, is whether the simplifications Sraffa employs satisfy the confirmation, no-accident, sensitivity, and convergence conditions. Until empirical work is done there is no way to know whether Sraffa's system satisfies the confirmation condition. Applying Sraffa's work on the scale of a whole economy is beyond our mathematical capabilities, but there is no reason why one could not attempt to apply it to some sub-economy after making adjustments for the openness of any sub-economy. Given how little "theory" there is to Sraffa—given the weakness of Sraffa's assumptions—economists are not in much doubt about the results of such tests. If Sraffa's work can be confirmed, that fact would not seem an accident. Moreover it seems that, when one introduces the complexities of joint products and the like, the results of the calculations should be better confirmed. More dubious is whether Sraffa's work satisfies the convergence condition. Lipsey and Lancaster's results (1956–57) provide possible grounds for doubt. Is it possible that the elimination of a monopoly, for example, might decrease excess demand yet result in prices which are in worse agreement with those calculated from Sraffa's apparatus? In most of the cases in which Lipsey and Lancaster show that eliminating some obstruction to competition brings one further from a competitive equilibrium, one is also moving to situations in which Sraffa's assumptions are *less* well satisfied. Given current knowledge one can, however, compare Sraffa's work favorably here with general equilibrium models. Current abstract general equilibrium models clearly do not satisfy the confirmation and convergence conditions. Sraffa's work *may* satisfy them.

Yet few mainstream economists would concede that Sraffa provides an explanation of exchange values. Remember that the conditions of chapter 7 are only *necessary* conditions. Sraffa's work may satisfy those conditions yet still not be *explanatory*. Economists have, in fact, explicitly challenged the explanatory worth of Sraffa's system for reasons other than its ability to satisfy such conditions. Consider the following comments of Y. K. Ng:

> For example, Sraffa's conclusion that prices are determined by the methods of production leaves unexplained why a particular system of production is being used. Since producers are able to vary input proportions, at least over time, this explanation cannot be advanced without bringing in the preferences of consumers which are completely absent from Sraffa's system. In other words, Sraffa's system of analysis . . . simply ignores the very real role of consumer preferences and hence cannot serve as a relevant explanation of price formation and income distribution. (1974:121–22)

Ng is evidently arguing that Sraffa's work is in some ways inadequate as an explanation of exchange values or "price formation." In what ways does Ng find Sraffa lacking? Is he right to conclude that Sraffa's system "cannot serve as a relevant explanation"?

Ng is criticizing at least the narrowness of the scope of Sraffa's work. It "leaves unexplained why a particular system of production is being used." This criticism is justified. Sraffa's system contains at most one lawlike statement. As a result its explanatory power is limited. Isolated "laws," as compared to theories, have limited scope and provide relatively superficial explanations. Since the evidence upon which theories are based is more diverse and usually less closely related to the particular data to be explained, theories provide better explanations. In addition, one is less certain that unexplained generalizations are laws than that the highly systematized statements of a theory are. As a narrow system with only one lawlike claim, Sraffa's work has little explanatory power.

Second, Ng may feel that Sraffa's work is not explanatory, because it provides no *causal* account of the determination of exchange values. As Sylvain Bromberger points out (1966:71), the derivation of the height of the Empire State Building from some specific data and the principles of geometrical optics satisfies the conditions of the deductive-nomological model just as adequately as the derivation of the length of the shadow. Yet we believe that the latter derivation explains the length of the shadow while the derivation of the height of the Empire State Building does not explain why it has that height. What is the difference? One answer with considerable initial plausibility is that the derivation of the length of the shadow tells a causal story, while the derivation of the height of the building does not. Many scientific explanations are causal explanations. Ng may be questioning whether Sraffa provides a causal explanation.

Sraffa's work is not in any strong sense causal. Consider one simple analysis of causality in economics. H. O. A. Wold argues that those variables which one controls in an experiment should be regarded as "cause variables," while those whose values one then observes are "effect variables" (1954:165). One should, Wold suggests, regard a functional relationship of the form $y = f(x_1, \ldots, x_n)$ as causal "if it is theoretically permissible to regard the variables as involved in a fictive controlled experiment with $x_1, \ldots, x_n$ for cause variables and y for effect variable" (1954:166). This criterion is appealing, but it is not well worked out. Not all the variables which one controls in a real or fictive experiment exert any causal influence on the outcome. Wold fails to elaborate on how judgments about causality depend on the theories one accepts. Whether it is "theoretically permissible to regard the variables as involved in a fictive controlled experiment" depends on prior judgments concerning which relationships are causal. Unless these prior judgments can be justified by actual experiments, which are unavailable for the theories we have been considering, one has only postponed answering the question of whether a given relationship is causal.

Thinking about "fictive" experiments does help us make our intuitive judgments vivid. One might offer the story that, before prices are calculated, capitalists and workers bargain for shares in the net product. Those shares determined, prices then result. Finally people buy what they want. Can one, however, make sense of this producing and bargaining before prices are known? Perhaps production might be determined by tradition, but it is difficult to understand this supposed bargaining for shares in the net product. Sraffa himself does not mention it. How could such bargaining work? It seems quite implausible to believe that Sraffa describes what causes exchange values to be what they are.

To reach this conclusion is not to condemn Sraffa, since in Wold's strong sense of cause, general equilibrium models are not causal either. The hypothetical story of *tâtonnement* (see Arrow and Hahn 1971:264f) is not much more plausible. Can one conceive of all bargaining occurring before any actual production? Perhaps we need a different analysis of causal explanation in economics (see Hicks 1979).

One way of resisting this conclusion and arguing that general equilibrium models, unlike Sraffa's work, meet Wold's vague criterion is question-begging. One might argue that Sraffa provides no causal account of price formation, because economists have already learned from equilibrium theory what the real mechanism of price formation is. Given the acceptance of equilibrium theory it is not "theoretically permissible" to regard Sraffa's variables "as involved in a fictive controlled experiment." Consider the following analogous case. If one knows the prices, the rate of profit, and the actual inputs used to produce each kind of commodity, one can calculate how much of each commodity is produced. Can one regard prices, the rate of profit, and the actual inputs used as cause variables in a fictive experiment with output as the effect variable? From the perspective of any current economic theory, the answer is clearly no. The calculation is not an explanation. In the same way, if one accepts the general account of price determination that equilibrium models provide, Sraffa's apparatus is at most a calculating device. This criticism is persuasive only if one accepts the neoclassical account of price determination.

C. J. Bliss provides an alternative account of causality in economics which may lie behind Ng's criticism of Sraffa. Bliss argues that one may speak of x causally determining y if and only if y is an economic variable, x is a "primitive feature" of an equilibrium system, and y is dependent on x; y is dependent on x if a change in x "might necessitate an alteration" in y (1975:34). x is a "primitive feature" if it is "largely outside the domain of theoretical economics as such" (1975:29). The "givens" to an equilibrium system—utility and production functions and the size and distribution of the initial endowment—are primitive features. Although the factors that determine exchange values in

Sraffa's system are exogenous to that system, they are not primitive, his account thus cannot be causal. All Sraffa shows is how to calculate prices, given other information. An accountant's manual is in this sense an account of how the profit of a firm is determined.

Another way to put this objection is to claim that Sraffa's apparatus overlooks the fact that in general all variables in an interdependent system must be solved for simultaneously. As thinking through Sraffa's own system reveals (see ch. 8, §3), factors like technology or distribution cannot simply be taken as given, but must be determined along with exchange values and cannot be regarded as causal determinants of exchange values.

This objection to Sraffa's work is forceful, but inconclusive. It can be directed against equilibrium theory as well. Although utility functions and production functions are taken simply as givens, as "primitive features" which are neither subject to economic analysis nor dependent on the nature of the economy, everyone recognizes that utility functions are affected by the form production actually takes and that economic factors cause technological innovations. A true simultaneous solution of all the mutually dependent variables would have to include as variables what general equilibrium models take as givens. Sraffa's sins are of the same kind as equilibrium theorists's.

It might be argued that such an *ad hominem* response is not fair, because utility functions, for example, are insensitive to changes in output or prices, while composition of output, a given in Sraffa's apparatus, is extremely sensitive to changes in exchange value. The extent to which utility functions should be regarded as primitive givens is a matter of controversy; but some important difference between taking utility functions or output as given must be conceded. Sraffa *does* leave out of his apparatus important economic relations among his givens and between his givens and the values one solves for.

Does such an "error" render Sraffa's work empty, noncausal, and without explanatory worth? The full answer will have to wait until we consider the contrast between Sraffa's theoretical strategy and the approach implicit in equilibrium models. It is, of course, silly to deny that one feature (an increase in the wages of steel workers) causes another (a steel price increase) on the grounds that the first is not "primitive." If we interpret Bliss charitably, we must understand him to be offering an account of causality within the framework of general equilibrium analysis. Even within such a framework, I do not see why one should want to deny that some economic phenomena affect others, merely because both depend on other relatively primitive features. Sraffa has shown that a functional relationship exists between output, technology, distribution, and prices. I see no reason to deny that this relationship is of *some* causal significance.

Sraffa's apparatus has features that limit its scope, the extent to which the relations it identifies can be regarded as causal and the precision with which it can explain. It is at best a limiting case of a scientific theory; but it may turn out to be the best account of exchange values economists have.

2. Sraffa and the Separate Science of Economics

Equilibrium models share a set of assumptions which, when pruned or augmented in various ways, are supposed to enable economists to account for all major economic phenomena. In a sense mainstream economics rests upon a single theory. If we examine the actual theories economists employ, we can readily see that this claim is not entirely accurate. Macroeconomic theories, for example, are not augmentations of the same fundamental model. Yet the *ambition* remains. Neoclassical economists would like to be able to employ variations on the same fundamental model in accounting for all economic phenomena.

Sraffa cannot share this ambition. The system that he presents cannot be augmented to provide, for example, a model of the role of demand in price determination or of the factors influencing size of firms. Sraffa may have designed his system to serve exclusively critical purposes. He does, after all, subtitle his book, *Prelude to a Critique of Economic Theory*. Yet it seems to me that, regardless of Sraffa's intentions, his work may be considered as part of an alternative project for economic theorizing. Such an alternative project employs an utterly different strategy. This difference in strategy accounts, I believe, for the bewilderment many economists feel when they read Sraffa. Just what can he be up to?

Implicit in the manner in which equilibrium models are conceived and deployed is a conception of economics as a *separate science*. The terminology is John Stuart Mill's and is, I think, useful. Mill writes:

> Notwithstanding the universal *consensus* of the social phenomena, whereby nothing which takes place in any part of the operations of society is without its share of influence on every other part; . . . it is not the less true that different species of social facts are in the main dependent, immediately and in the first resort, on different kinds of causes; and therefore not only may with advantage, but must, be studied apart (1843, book VI, ch. 9, sec. 3).

Mill is not asserting, trivially, that some social phenomena depend principally on a limited number of causal factors. Rather he is suggesting that a few causal factors are sufficient to account for at least the major features of a whole range of social phenomena. A full statement of Mill's view is the following:

> There is, for example, one large class of social phenomena in which the immediately determining causes are principally those which act through the desire of wealth, and in which the psychological law mainly concerned is the familiar one that a greater gain is preferred to a smaller. I mean, of course, that portion of the phenomena of society which emanates from the industrial or productive operations of mankind. . . . By reasoning from that one law of human nature, and from the principal outward circumstances (whether universal or confined to particular states of society) which operate upon the human mind through that law, we may be enabled to explain and predict this portion of the phenomena of society, so far as they depend on that class of circumstances only, overlooking the influence of any other of the circumstances of society. . . . It makes entire abstraction of every other human passion or motive, except those which may be regarded as perpetually antagonising principles to the desire of wealth, namely, aversion to labor, and desire of the present enjoyment of costly indulgences. (1843, book VI, ch. 9, sec. 3)

Like economists today, Mill conceives of this separate science of economics as unified and reductive. Since a single set of causes is "immediately determining" for "one large class of social phenomena," economics will be unified. It is not as if a single theory could serve *all* the explanatory and predictive purposes economists have. Instead a single theory is supposed to account for all the "major" economic phenomena.

Economic theorizing consists not of developing different general theories for different domains in economics, but in adding various assumptions to the basic equilibrium model in order to account for more phenomena. Furthermore, except for details and qualifications, economics is supposed to be complete within its domain. Both Mill and modern theorists believe that no significant explanatory or predictive purposes of economics would be served by fusing economics with any other science. There may be explanations of the fundamental "laws" of equilibrium theory, but those explanations are not part of, and have nothing to contribute to, economics. Since the fundamental "laws" are not to be explained within economics, the discipline is in a sense reductive. In principle one might explain economic phenomena by means of noneconomic laws and specifications of economic initial conditions. If we ignore such a possible reduction, we can recognize the crucial point: all theoretically central parts of economics can be explained and predicted by equilibrium theory alone.

The general idea Mill espouses is relatively clear. If theorists can isolate the principal causal factors, they can develop economics as an inexact science. Economists will then be able inexactly to explain and predict the principal phenomena. Neoclassical economists do not seek to make their fundamental theory increasingly exact. What they want in equilibrium theory is a versatile set of lawlike claims which, with qualifications and allowances, they can employ no matter what economic problem they face. In some of these applications economists should be able to test and confirm the resulting applied theory. Otherwise there would be little reason to take seriously the assumptions of the basic equilibrium model. Provided that this condition (and the others mentioned in chapter 7) is satisfied, neoclassical economists can then employ the basic theoretical apparatus as an all around guide to the understanding of economic phenomena.

Neoclassical economics thus has a distinctive theoretical strategy. Because economists have not been able to do better, and because they want to keep the fundamental theory versatile, economists work with a loose and highly inexact basic set of assumptions. Applying them to provide empirical theories of different sorts of economic phenomena is quite difficult. Numerous revisions and additions are always necessary. Sometimes the problems of augmentation and revision remain unresolved for a long time, as is the case in the theory of capital and interest. Yet the basic assumptions provide guidance and confidence that problems like those concerning capital and interest are soluble— even where there are no immediate prospects of solving them.

This theoretical strategy might easily be assimilated to some of Kuhn's views concerning paradigms (1970) or to Lakatos' views concerning research programs (1970; see also Latsis 1976b). Kuhn says so many ambiguous things about paradigms that one can interpret him as arguing that scientific communities employ paradigms in just the way that I have suggested that economists employ equilibrium theory. I do not believe, however, that reading these views into Kuhn's suggestive but unclear discussion contributes to an accurate appreciation of equilibrium theorizing.

On my interpretation, equilibrium theory should not be regarded as what Lakatos calls a research program. I thus believe that the interest of a number of economists in Lakatos' work (see Latsis 1976b) is misplaced. According to Lakatos, in a research program one has a series of related theories. Later theories in the series have more content than earlier ones (unless the research program is degenerating) and are more exact. Consider Lakatos' discussion of Bohr's theory of the atom (1970:140–54). The research program is not identical to any of the specific theories; it is defined by the related series. What relates the theories in the series is a certain "hard core" of theoretical assumptions and a general methodological approach. Although this characterization of research programs overlaps to some extent with my comments concerning the development of equilibrium models, it differs fundamentally. The goal of equilibrium theorists is not an increasingly precise general economic theory. Equilibrium theorists do not devote their major efforts toward developing better general theories. The hard core *is* the theory. The task is mainly to apply it. One does not find a series of improving theories like the successive versions of Bohr's model of the atom. Equilibrium theory, apart from a few details, has been fixed for nearly a century. The efforts of economists are devoted mainly to its application and its mathematical elaboration. In neoclassical economics, we find a (highly inexact) theory variously employed, not a "hard core" to a series of theories with increasing content.[1]

Sraffa's work implicitly defines an economic methodology and a conception of the relationship between economics and other social theories unlike the neoclassical approach. Sraffa himself has not written on these methodological questions. I have no specific grounds upon which to assert that he would agree with my comments, except that the conception of economics and its relationship to other social sciences sketched in this section seems to me not only consistent with Sraffa's work, but to make that work more intelligible.

Sraffa does not take economics to be a separate science with its own distinctive laws and causes. It is to be distinguished roughly from other social studies by its concern with production, distribution, exchange and consumption of commodities and services, and with social phenomena closely connected with these. Its laws are not necessarily individualistic or psychological, although some may be. In seeking to explain given economic phenomena one should draw freely upon the results of other social studies. No special set of causal factors is predominantly responsible for all major economic phenomena. In each given problem situation, the economist must isolate the major causal factors by empirical investigation and theoretical ingenuity. Occasionally these may coincide with the factors equilibrium theorists pick out as primitives. Often there will be no such coincidence. Economists should seek many different (but mutually consistent) explanations at

---

[1] Utility theory, for example, has had a *decreasing* content.

different levels of detail. Examples of such work are macroeconomic theories and some of Marxian economics.

Sraffa does not base his account of exchange values on factors that can be taken as givens for all economic analyses. Nor is his work either individualistic or psychologistic. In fact, the motivational forces and the individual actions that are responsible for the equalization of the rate of profit and the congruence of market prices and exchange values are concealed. These elements are undeniably important, but Sraffa apparently believes that they can be relegated to the background in his account of exchange values. If one's conception of the enterprise of theoretical economics is that of an equilibrium theorist, these aspects of Sraffa's work will seem bizarre. If, on the other hand, one envisions economic theory proceeding in a piecemeal way, Sraffa's efforts are completely intelligible.

Is there anything wrong with piecemeal theorizing? Are there any methodological grounds upon which to dismiss Sraffa's work? I think not. I can see no justification for the requirement that explanation in economics be unitary. Equilibrium theorists may object that Sraffa's work senselessly chops up an interdependent system (of which neo-classical economists possess the outlines of a unified theory). Defenders of Sraffa can reply that Sraffa disputes that theory and repudiates the methodological ideal of a separate science of economics. Of course, for all I have said, it may be that economists can learn nothing at all from further piecemeal theorizing compatible with Sraffa's work. I see, however, no general methodological reason to believe that such is the case.

3. What Sraffa Has To Offer

Sraffa's work thus withstands, I believe, philosophical criticism. It is not yet clear, however, what, if anything, one can learn from it. Sraffa's work does not support the strong conclusions (discussed in chapter 8) that Dobb and others have drawn. Is it anything more than mathematical analysis of functional relations between certain variables and parameters? Apart from its contribution to the Cambridge criticisms of aggregate simplified capital theory, does Sraffa's work have any general interest and importance?

It might be argued that no account of exchange values in terms of physical costs is possible. Not only are values dependent on distribution, but recall Samuelson's objection (1959:21f) mentioned in chapter 1 (see also Findlay 1974:6). Both Ricardo's and Marx's theories of rents make the margin of cultivation and thus the labor necessary to produce agricultural products depend on demand for agricultural products. Samuelson argues that for this reason price cannot be determined by the cost of production or by the labor inputs.

Is the dependence of labor values on demand that Samuelson points out a refutation of the labor theory of value? Why can one not claim that exchange values are determined by labor value (or physical cost cum distribution) but that labor value or physical cost are themselves affected by demand? Robinson appears to make just such a claim:

> When we are provided with a set of technical equations for production and a real wage rate which is uniform throughout the economy, there is no room for demand equations in the determination of equilibrium prices. (When we take down our protective fence, and allow that changes in distribution affect the composition of output, we shall need a fresh set of equations, but that is quite another matter.) (1961:57)

The passage is not entirely clear. Robinson may be making the mistaken claim that demand is irrelevant to exchange value. On the other hand, she may be suggesting that we can accept a physical cost cum distribution theory of pricing despite the dependence of "physical costs" on demand. Garegnani expresses this point more explicitly. He relates the views of the classical economists (as he interprets them) to his own views as follows:

> Since they regarded these "necessaries" as determined by social as much as physiological conditions, we may see them as recognizing that distribution is governed by social forces, the investigation of which falls largely outside the domain of the pure theory of value. The proper object of value theory was seen to be the study of the *relations* between the wage, the rate of profits and the system of relative prices. . . .
>
> Thus, the separation of the pure theory of value from the study of the circumstances governing changes in the outputs of commodities does not seem to meet any essential difficulty. On the contrary, it may open the way for a more satisfactory treatment of the relations between outputs and the technical conditions of production. Moreover, by freeing the theory of value from the assumption of consumers' tastes given from outside the economic system, this separation may favor a better understanding of consumption and its dependence on the rest of the system. (1970:427–28)

Garegnani would thus like to adopt a physical cost cum distribution theory of exchange value while conceding that physical costs are not primitives, but are sensitive to other economic factors, including demand. Sraffa's work makes such a position possible. Assuming that Sraffa's system can satisfy the conditions of chapter 7, it shows how a physical cost cum distribution explanation of exchange values is possible. Sraffa thus shows how the theory of distribution might be separated from the theory of value. He shows that one need not believe that the rate of profit is established through exchanges. Neither Sraffa nor his followers can explain in detail why prices are what they are. The economies they study are, after all, not in stationary equilibrium. Even if there were stationary equilibria, economists do not now and will never possess enough data for such detailed explanations. Recognizing this fact should not, however, blind us to the value of explanations in principle of the sort Sraffa helps provide.

Sraffa thus gives a new shape to theorizing about competitive economies. If one regards the theory of exchange value as the fundamental economic theory, then Sraffa's work is certainly inadequate. His account of value cannot serve as a foundation from which theories of demand, technology, distribution, or whatever could be deduced or developed, for the simple reason that his account of value takes so much as given. Instead of being basic, the theory of value turns out to be derivative, perhaps even superficial. Sraffa is saying in effect, "Look, this is all there is to exchange values. The neoclassical (and classical) preoccupation with exchange values is a mistake. Now let's get down to the real problems." It is in this way that I would reconstruct Garegnani's comments quoted above. If Garegnani is correct that Sraffa "opens the way for a more satisfactory treatment of the relations between outputs and the technical conditions of production" or favors, "a better understanding of consumption and its dependence on the rest of the system," Sraffa does so by minimizing the role of the theory of value. Such a step is not without dangers. Economists may be lost in a maze of special theories without any adequate means of knowing whether they are even consistent.

Such a view of the theory of value is, of course, in sharp contrast to the general vision of economic theory that has dominated mainstream economic theorizing. Whether such a demotion of the theory of value is tenable depends on whether one needs a unified equilibrium theory to theorize adequately about population growth, technological change, demand, the nature of firms or of financial institutions, and so forth. Some general account of how commodities and thus the various activities of people are related is a crucial part of economic theorizing, but must that account be a fundamental and unified theory of exchange? Sraffa answers negatively.

4. Marx and Sraffa

The relationship between Sraffa's work and Marx's work is controversial. Some Marxian economists have applied Marx's criticisms of Ricardo in *Theories of Surplus Value* to Sraffa's work. In Volume 2 of *Theories of Surplus Value* Marx repeatedly chastises Ricardo for confusing value and average price (by which Marx means exchange value) and for not theorizing in terms of labor values (1968, esp. p. 106). Since both Ricardo and Marx recognized that in equilibrium goods will not exchange according to the ratio of the labor embodied in them, what is the disagreement? Perhaps it is only some Hegelian baggage that Marx was never able to discard. Marx insists on the distinction between value and average price because the former is "prior" and the latter must be "derived" from it. Consider a passage like the following: Ricardo "does not realise at all that in order to *create* the general rate of profit value must first be transformed into cost-prices." (1968:434; Marx's emphasis). Marx's criticism seems obscure and, in a pejorative sense, "philosophical."

There are two ways in which this criticism might be clarified. Medio (1972:320–21, 326) and Rowthorn (1974:77) argue that by focusing on exchange values or average prices, Sraffa diverts our attention from the central task of analyzing the formation of the surplus under capitalism. They object to Sraffa's abstraction from the social relations involved in capitalism. Labor values, unlike Sraffa's prices, supposedly provide a key to understanding capitalist social relations. Second, one might interpret Marx as criticizing Ricardo for using the wrong theoretical construct for analyzing production and distribution under capitalism. Some reference to prices of production or exchange values is unavoidable. Marxian values must be related to prices. Yet for basic theoretical investigations even of purely economic aspects of capitalist production and distribution, values, not prices of production are the more fruitful theoretical terms.[2]

Rowthorn (1974:81) and Roosevelt (1975, esp. pp. 8, 19) have offered one further related objection to Sraffa's work. They argue that Sraffa isolates production from distribution in an artificial and misleading way. He focuses on the effects of different distributions of income, as if the actual relations of production did not already determine the distribution of income. Sraffa's work might in this way be linked to "vulgar" socialists whose principal complaint against capitalism concerns inequalities in distribution.

---

[2] I am indebted to Mr. Jake Shearer for this interpretation of Marx.

I do not find these criticisms fair. Sraffa does not say that production and distribution are unconnected; he just does not give any theory of what those connections are. Sraffa is not saying that in order to understand capitalist production or the origin of a surplus under capitalism one need consider only technological facts. He gives no theory of production at all. He is not challenging the claim that labor values may sometimes be a useful theoretical construct. Sraffa's task and achievement are narrow. The relevant question for Marxian economists is whether that achievement may be of any assistance. Some believe that it is (see Hollis and Nell 1975, ch. 7; Eatwell 1974, 1975b:550–55; Steedman 1977; Roncaglia 1978, ch. 8).

Although intended as the foundation for a general social theory, the theory of value is as central in Marx's work as in any of the classical political economists. Sraffa's demotion of the theory of value is thus unappealing to those who would stick to the letter of Marx's economics. Indeed, Sraffa's work can be employed in a critique of the labor theory of value and of the so-called "transformation problem" (Steedman 1977, ch. 1–4). Yet much of Marx's achievement, despite the centrality of the labor theory of value, can be reformulated using Sraffa's work. Crucial components like the theory of exploitation are actually more solidly grounded when they are divorced from the labor theory of value (Cohen 1979). In my view Marx simply did not know how to develop an account of values like Sraffa's. He had to work with a scalar index, with single numbers that would reflect the technological givens.

I believe Sraffa's work can be useful to Marxian economists. That it supersedes the labor theory of value is its virtue, not its defect. Consider how easily it may be meshed with the following simplified version of Marx's theory of profits. Let us abstract from land and other scarce resources that earn rents. In that case the actual total product is divided between workers and capitalists. Partly because of the discipline imposed by the capitalists, more goods are produced than are needed to replace the means of production and provide everybody with the means of subsistence. There is thus a social surplus that is divided between workers and capitalists. Given specific institutional constraints, the control capitalists hold over the means of production enables them to appropriate a portion of the surplus. Profits are nothing but a part of that surplus, specially distributed. Marx believed that capitalists usually appropriate the whole of the surplus. It now seems that they only get part; and some recent Marxian economists believe that the size of that portion is determined by direct and indirect struggle between organized capital and organized labor (Ferguson and Nell 1972:450; Robinson 1965:33–34).

One can only invest in productive capital goods if one owns "capital," and most people own little or no capital. This fact itself needs explaining: how could capitalism get started? According to Marx, the key event was the creation by expropriation of the free laborer. The greater productivity of capitalist enterprise perpetuates and expands the system, while the greater productivity of larger scale enterprise leads to a concentration of capitals.

In order for the ownership of capital to become exclusive and remain so, society must have special features. First, it is crucial that the legal system permit private ownership and free transfer of wealth. It must be legal to employ wage labor and to earn a profit. Second there must either be no state administration of wages, prices, or profits, or that administration must directly insure the existence of profits. In a competitive economy, the existence of profits is only threatened when, as a result of capital accumulation, labor becomes scarce enough that wages rise sharply. Scarcity of labor is not generally a problem, since a rising wage induces investment in labor-saving technology, which insures the existence of a pool of the unemployed. The actual theory is developed by Marx in great sociological detail. Moreover, he calls attention to the role of ideological factors in social reproduction. The peculiarities of profits as a particular form of the social surplus are discussed at considerable length.

Although I have stated some of the major features of Marx's theory of profits without mentioning the labor theory of value, there are some value theories with which Marx's theory of profits cannot be combined. Neoclassical price theory, for example, leaves no room for any story concerning class struggle over the surplus. Sraffa's apparatus, in my view, provides Marx with the theory of exchange value that he needs. It shows how the results of production manage to get sold with an equalized rate of profit. Whether it is legitimate to discuss the basic features of production, distribution, and accumulation, as Marx does in Volume 1 of *Capital,* in terms of labor values is a separate question, which I am leaving open.

5. Normative Factors

As other writers on capital theory have noted, normative issues lurk behind analytic ones (Bliss 1975:345–52; Blaug 1975:75–78). To analyze what is lurking and to begin to assess its significance is a difficult and subtle undertaking. I shall offer only some brief comments, sketching one way in which the acceptance of Sraffa's work along with the rejection of general equilibrium models can have normative implications.

As mentioned in chapter 8, many economists take Sraffa's work to support some strong conclusions. Recall in particular (III) The rate of profit is not causally determined by individual exchanges as constrained by technology and the availability of unproduced factors of production. Sraffa's work does not support III. It says nothing about what determines the distribution of income. In equilibrium models, on the other hand, III is false. III is only defensible if one denies that general equilibrium models can be used to explain the rate of interest. Sraffa's work, on the other hand, is consistent with III. It provides some reason to believe that an alternative to equilibrium theories is possible. Sraffa's work also helps make Marx's theories tenable.

III is a causal claim. How can it be of any normative importance? Consider J. B. Clark's views. He regarded his theory of the distribution of income as crucial to an assessment of the justice of the earning of profits by capitalists. He writes, "If they [the workers] create a small amount of wealth and get the whole of it, they may not seek to revolutionize society; but if it were to appear that they produce an ample amount and get only a part of it, many of them would become revolutionists and all would have the right to do so" (1902:4). Clark seems to be relying on some sort of quasi-Lockean theory of justice that says that individuals have a right to the product of their labor. On such a theory it is important to know whether III is true. Suppose it is false, and that profits are the result of voluntary exchanges related, as general equilibrium theory shows, to the productivity of capital goods and the general impatience of people to consume. According to the theory of justice Clark relies on, workers would then have no right to complain about the existence of profits. If, on the other hand, III is true, one needs some other explanation of what determines the distribution of income. If it is some sort of coercive power that the capitalists possess, then, on Clark's view of justice, workers may have a right to the profits the capitalists are earning. With more sophisticated theories of distributive justice and more specific economic analysis, the relations are no longer this simple; but this example illustrates how the propositions of capital and interest theory may affect our assessment of capitalism.

CHAPTER TEN
Conclusions

We have considered carefully three theories relating capital and interest to exchange values, and have investigated thoroughly the interconnected economic and philosophical issues the three theories raise. Here now are some general conclusions concerning capital and interest and their relations to exchange values.

My principal conclusion is negative. Economists possess no good theory of capital or interest, or of their relations to equilibrium prices. Certainly, they possess elegant models and are able to prove many theorems. Unfortunately, these models and theorems do not enable one to explain real phenomena of capital and interest; and I know of no theory undiscussed here which avoids the difficulties faced by those I have considered. The kinds of problems which the Austrian theory, general equilibrium theories, and Sraffa are unable to avoid or solve defeat all theories of capital and interest and their relations to exchange values that I know of. Economists do not understand the phenomena of capital and interest. They do not understand why the rate of interest is generally positive (and thus how it is that capitalism can work). They do not know how large-scale technological changes will affect wages and interest or how changes in the rate of profits will affect innovation. Of course, economists are not totally ignorant about any of these problems. There is some large scale historical evidence. Various theoretical tools may be of help in special limiting cases. Yet our ignorance remains vast. Recognizing this fact is not necessarily to condemn the efforts of economists. Even the most brilliant and sensible work does not always succeed. One should honor the efforts of economic theorists not by exaggerating their achievements, but by attempting to understand them correctly and to build upon them.

1. Assessing the Specific Theories

Although the general negative conclusion possesses some drama, the specific points established along the way toward it are more important. The Austrian theory of capital, general equilibrium theories and Sraffa's work are all three unable to answer the questions concerning the phenomena of capital and interest, but each fails in a different way. The problem with the Austrian theory of capital is that it is unfounded. It is not a minor application of the basic equilibrium model, but adds substantive but unsubstantiated claims. Böhm-Bawerk's law of roundaboutness is nicely illustrated by aging wine or by Lange's wood and ax model, but economists have no reason to believe that it is generally reliable. The Cambridge critics' models are no less plausible than are Wicksell's and Lange's. Until theorists possess empirical evidence to show that more roundabout processes are reliably more productive and that the rate of interest is inversely related to the degree of roundaboutness, theorists have no good reason to accept the Austrian theory. Examining general equilibrium models should further incline one to be skeptical of the possibility of representing the role of capital goods in production by some single index like the degree of roundaboutness or the quantity of "waiting."

General equilibrium theories, unlike the Austrian theory, do not add new "laws" to the basic equilibrium model. The extent to which equilibrium models have been successfully applied to various specific economic problems provides general equilibrium theories with a good deal of initial credibility. After all, they are merely a more general application of the same basic model. Yet general equilibrium theories which are sufficiently unrestricted that they have implications concerning the phenomena of capital and interest are currently untestable and thus unconfirmed. The confirmation of the "laws" of such theories in certain restricted domains does not provide sufficient reason to accept these theories as explaining the phenomena of capital and interest.

The inadequacies of Sraffa's work, like those of general equilibrium theories, are methodological. Sraffa's work is not necessarily inapplicable or untestable, but its scope is simply too limited for it to be regarded as a good explanation of the relations between interest and exchange values. Sraffa provides, of course, no theory of capital or interest at all. His work might be combined with theories of capital or interest, but none of the known candidates is well supported. Furthermore, the "law" that Sraffa relies on, that the rate of profit will be equal throughout the economy, although useful and well confirmed in certain limited domains may well not be true of whole modern economies (even with qualifications to some margin of error).

For these rather different reasons, neither Sraffa nor general equilibrium theories nor Austrian theories resolve the puzzles of capital and interest. It thus seems to me unhelpful to think in terms of *choosing* among these options. Indeed, the three theoretical ventures are not necessarily opposed to one another. One is not in any position now to decide what is the truth. Yet economists must decide how to do their work. Which (if any) of these approaches should theoretical economists devote their efforts to? Which of these approaches should economists employ in attempting to answer pressing practical questions addressed to them by government or industry or labor? All three of the approaches provide tools for solving problems. These tools may be seriously defective, but without alternatives or a demonstration that they do more harm than good, they will be used anyway.

Once one recognizes that neither Sraffa's work nor general equilibrium models provide answers to questions like "How much of the growth of the productivity of labor is due to capital accumulation?" I see no reason why theorists should not attempt to make use of simplified accounts of capital and interest like Clark's or Böhm-Bawerk's. The Cambridge criticisms have not refuted these aggregate capital theories, but at most emphasized the risks of employing them. In employing these theories, not only does one face normal inductive risks, but one is also gambling that Clark's or Böhm-Bawerk's, rather than the Cambridge models apply in the given situation. One should be cautious and skeptical about applying aggregate capital models. It might turn out that one can learn nothing at all from them. Yet at least they are well fashioned tools. Economists do the best they can with them and hope for fruitful results. Should one spurn the use of such tools merely because one has little reason to believe that they will work and few ways of telling if they have? It all depends on how pressing our needs are, how dangerous the mistakes might be and what alternatives are available.

Much the same is true in applying models of the other kinds. In employing Cambridge-style models or less abstract limited general equilibrium models, one again runs many risks. If economists must employ models in unjustified ways, I suppose it is best that they have as broad a range of such models to pick from as is practical. Although current reliance on Cambridge models or on practical constrained general equilibrium models is on a par with reliance on Austrian models, Cambridge and general equilibrium theorists have grander ambitions. The Cambridge theorists hope to develop an interlocking set of models whose applications can be tested and which will provide a general grasp of economic phenomena. The general equilibrium theorists hope to be able to refine their models sufficiently to make good the claims of mainstream theorists to have found *the* fundamental theory of economics. Austrian theorists might also strive for a distinctive vision of economics as a whole. Their account of capital and interest, however, is clearly only one way of simplifying the story the general equilibrium theorists hope to tell correctly. If one cannot develop the fundamental theory for which general equilibrium theorists strive, one may never have models any better than those of the Austrians. Yet if theorists cannot fulfill the ambitions of all those who have regarded economics as a separate science, the Austrian theory seems an incongruous stopping point. If theorists cannot employ the basic equilibrium model to understand all the major economic phenomena, surely they should endeavor more diligently to develop nonunified, interdisciplinary, broader-ranging theories of specific economic phenomena. When one shifts from the practical question, "Which approach should I use to answer this specific question," to the theoretical question, "To which approach should I devote my efforts as an economic theorist?" the Austrian theory largely drops out of the running.

2. Strategies of Economic Theorizing and Their Implications

Equilibrium theories possess many virtues. With very few fundamental predicates they enable one to provide remarkably uniform accounts of extremely diverse economic phenomena. In these ways they are simple. The fundamental equilibrium model is extremely flexible, yet simultaneously provides detailed and precise instructions for dealing with new problems. Equilibrium models possess the sort of mathematical sophistication and elegance that are characteristic of advanced theories in the natural sciences. The basic equilibrium model is highly systematized and its scope is supposed to extend to the entire domain. Next to this body of theory Sraffa's work is pale and puny indeed. The most one can say for it is that it offers a new challenge. It is certainly not a well-developed competitor.

The many virtues of equilibrium theories help explain the monotheoretic strategy of mainstream economics. Yet these virtues are certainly in part the *result* of that strategy. It would be quite surprising if the basic assumptions of equilibrium models could not be elegantly formulated by now. After all, they have been formulated and reformulated by a century of economic theorists. If these assumptions were not, when first specified, fairly flexible, they would not have found their way into the foundations of neoclassical theory. Yet much of the flexibility is due to the efforts of later theorists. Consider, for example, how the device of dated commodities increases the potential applicability of the basic "laws" of equilibrium theory.

The power of equilibrium theorizing is great and has grown. It is easy to give rational reasons for the allegiance of so many economists to the same basic model and the same strategy for solving problems. Once one fully appreciates the distinctiveness of the strategy of mainstream economic theorizing, one can better understand some of the general methodological controversies mentioned in the Introduction and chapter 1. Once one appreciates some of the abuses or exaggerations which result from allegiance to this theoretical strategy, one can see how some of these controversies should be settled.

A. Definition of Economics

As I mentioned in chapter 1, economists have long disputed the definition of economics. Until the last century economics was regarded as the science of the production, exchange, distribution, and consumption of those goods and services that contribute to material well-being. In contrast to this "substantive" definition of economics, most economics now accept a "formal" definition. In Lionel Robbins' classic formulation, economics is "the science which studies human behavior as a relationship between ends and scarce means which have alternative uses" (1932:15). I suggest that this formal definition essentially defines economics as equilibrium theorizing.

To see why, one needs to understand what Robbins and other neoclassical economists mean by "scarcity." Robbins lays great stress on the notion of scarcity:

> Scarcity of means to satisfy given ends is an almost ubiquitous condition of human behavior.
>   Here, then, is the unity of the subject of Economic Science, the forms assumed by human behavior in disposing of scarce means. (1932:15)

> On the analytical side Economics proves to be a series of deductions from the fundamental concept of scarcity of time and materials.
>   . . . Unless it is made quite clear that in the marginal analysis we possess the basis for a completely unitary Economic Theory, it is safe to say that the inner significance of that analysis has not been recognized at all. (1932:77)

Like Walras, Robbins links the notion of scarcity to that of marginal utility. This is as it should be, since a good or service or resource is scarce in the neoclassical sense of "scarce" if and only if it possesses a marginal utility to somebody. We can thus see that Robbins is defining economics to be marginal analysis. The "unity" of the subject lies in constrained maximization of utility. In economics, according to Robbins, one seeks and obtains "a completely unitary Economic Theory."

Given that marginal concepts are derivative and that neither marginal utility nor marginal productivity is supposed to have any causal role in a full equilibrium theory, the notion of scarcity ought also to be regarded as secondary or as derivative, at least by equilibrium theorists. In the spirit of Robbins' devotion to neoclassical theory, we should interpret him as defining economics not as marginal utility theory (which is not fundamental), but as equilibrium theory.

Once we have thus clarified the formal definition of economics and have recognized that it is equivalent to deciding by definitional *fiat* that equilibrium theory is all of economics, it is easy to see how unreasonable that definition is. The debate over the definition of economics has contemporary echo in general philosophy of science. Wolfgang Stegmueller maintains that scientific theories determine which phenomena they apply to (1976:93, 176–77). We can see that Robbins agrees. While it is certainly true that the way that one classifies phenomena is strongly influenced by the theories one accepts, both Robbins and Stemueller err in denying that scientists possess any way of determining domains independent of the specific theories they are considering. The substantive definition of economics I gave above is crude, but in its crude way it picks out the phenomena with which economic theories must contend. The vogue enjoyed by the formal definition is merely one of those excesses which results from the strategy of equilibrium theorizing. It may turn out that equilibrium theory is indeed the fundamental theory of all economic phenomena. It is not such a theory by definition.

B. General Laws

Behind the dispute concerning whether economics possesses general laws lies the same peculiarity of equilibrium theorizing. One plausible way of interpreting both Marx's and Veblen's criticisms of general laws in economics is to regard both as denying that mainstream theory is the basis for a separate science of economics. Marx and Veblen were, of course, objecting to different theories, but, as we have seen, the ambition of dealing with all major economic phenomena in a single unified theory antedates the development of marginal utility theory and explicit general equilibrium theories.

Consider what questions one might be asking when one considers whether economics does, can or should possess general laws. Many theorems of both classical and neoclassical theory are clearly parochial. Outward circumstances, even the very existence of markets, vary from society to society. On the other hand there are obviously some generalizations which are true of all economies. As Marx noted (1973:85) all production requires some sort of instrument of production. The controversy concerning whether economics should seek or currently possesses general laws is best understood as a controversy concerning the proper strategy of economic theorizing. In its quest for a set of assumptions which can be applied to manipulate and analyze all significant economic phenomena, mainstream theorizing bases economics on a set of general laws. While not denying the existence (or even necessarily the utility) of such general laws, both Marxian and institutionalist economists have argued that there is more to be learned by focusing on the distinctive features of the phenomena studied. According to Marx and Veblen, economists can most profitably employ laws which are not general and best explain phenomena by citing factors which are not primitives in some equilibrium theory. Of course, they may be mistaken. For all that I have said, it may be that one will always learn more through developing equilibrium theories. There is, however, no warrant for attempting to rule out *a priori* piecemeal approaches like the one suggested by Sraffa's work.

   How one defines economics and how one regards the laws of economics are thus crucial to how one conceives of the relations between economics and the other social sciences. From the perspective of equilibrium theory, economics stands apart. Lionel Robbins, for example, vehemently denies that economics "rests upon any particular psychological doctrines."

> If, therefore, Economics rests upon particular psychological doctrines, there is no task more ready to hand for the intellectually sterile, than every five years or so to write sharp polemics showing that, since psychology has changed its fashion, Economics needs "rewriting from the foundations upwards" . . . and the lay public, ever anxious to escape the necessity of recognising the implications of choice in a world of scarcity, has allowed itself to be bamboozled into believing that matters, which are in fact as little dependent on the truth of fashionable psychology as the multiplication table, are still open questions on which the enlightened man, who, of course, is nothing if not a psychologist, must be willing to suspend judgment. (1932:84)

At first glance this scathing attack on those who regard economics as resting on psychological foundations might appear puzzling. After all, the basic laws of utility theory are, in a perfectly ordinary sense of the term, psychological. The puzzlement fades, however, when we recognize that Robbins is here espousing the vision of economics as a separate science. Economists do not seek more refined psychological laws which will, for example, help explain panic behavior in certain markets. Such an investigation, in Robbins' view, is scarcely a part of economics. Economists have their basic model. Their tasks are to refine and apply it. Economics is complete unto itself. Although some Marxian theorists even more vehemently deny the importance of psychology, Marxian, institutionalist, and Sraffian theorists have no such prior commitment to rejecting the findings and tools of the other social sciences.

C. Methodological individualism:[1]

It is often said that equilibrium theory is individualistic, that it is not sufficiently holistic. The charge is ambiguous. Equilibrium theory is anti-holist, since it treats economic phenomena as isolable, at least for purposes of analysis and control, from more general social influences. It is also individualistic, since the bulk of its fundamental generalizations concern psychological features of individuals. Yet in one important regard it is holist. Although one may disregard certain interconnections among economic phenomena for practical purposes, true equilibrium is general equilibrium, a simultaneous and mutual determination of properties of the whole economy.

A certain measure of individualism seems to me sane and sensible. Virtually all significant social scientists, including *in practice* Marx and Durkheim, insist that the "laws" one invokes in explaining social phenomena concern features of individuals or themselves be explainable in terms of other individualistic laws. Such a view is not reductionist, in at least one sense of "reductionism." One is only insisting that the *laws* be individualistic or psychological. The specifications and simplifications may mention groups, institutions, etc. Except in so far as one is criticizing neoclassical economics for its overly restrictive theoretical strategy, I do not think it is reasonable to object to its methodological individualism.

---

[1] See O'Neill (1973), Ryan (1973), and Morgenbesser (1967a) for some of the main contributions to the extensive and often confused debate concerning methodological individualism.

D. Naturalism:

All of the economic theories I have considered are in most ways naturalistic. The debate over social scientific naturalism which has occupied philosophers is extremely messy, because there are a number of different questions involved. Social scientific naturalists argue that the social sciences are in certain important respects similar to or at one with the natural sciences. Antinaturalists argue that the social and the natural sciences differ. Until one is more specific about the comparisons and contrasts involved, one knows little about the debate (see Morgenbesser 1970). Naturalists have argued that, at a certain level of generality, the goals, conceptual structures, and methods of social sciences are the same as those of the natural sciences. They have also sometimes argued that the social sciences can ultimately be reduced to the natural sciences. Anti-naturalists have argued for differences along one of these dimensions.

I began my investigation of theories of capital and interest and their relations to exchange values presupposing that the general goals, methods, and logical structure of economic theories were the same as those of the natural sciences. Whenever I found economic theories lacking, I needed to consider whether the naturalistic presupposition with which I began had led me to apply an incorrect standard. I found little reason to reject that presupposition.

One well-known complication demands some attention. The concepts economists employ differ from those of the natural sciences in one noteworthy way. When economists explain the behavior of an individual, they do so in terms of the agent's beliefs and desires. Desires are, of course, dressed up as utility functions, while beliefs are made transparent by the assumption of perfect information. Both belief and desire are intentional concepts. As many have noted (Quine 1960, chs. 4, 6; Chisholm 1957, ch. 11), verbs like "believes" or "desires" possess logical peculiarities.[2] These logical peculiarities are weeded out of

---

[2] Let me note three of these peculiarities (Chisholm 1957:170–71). From a non-intentional sentence like *(1) Samuelson teaches at MIT* one can infer that both Samuelson and MIT exist. From *(2) Consumers prefer noncarcinogenic artificial sweeteners* one *cannot* infer that there are any noncarcinogenic artificial sweeteners. From intentional sentences, one cannot infer whether the referents of the terms exist.

Second, from an ordinary noncompound sentence which contains a propositional clause, one can infer whether the proposition embedded in the clause is true or false. From *(3) The big cars American manufacturers built sold well* one can infer *(4) American manufacturers built big cars.* But *(5) Ford Motor Company hoped the Edsel would sell well* is entirely consistent with the sad truth *(6) The Edsel did not sell well.*

Finally, the truth or falsity of nonintentional sentences is unaffected when one subeconomic theory by the assumptions of perfect information and complete and transitive preferences. Those cases in which the intentionality of belief and desire matter violate economists' *ceteris paribus* conditions.

The fact remains that economists explain individual behavior in terms of the beliefs and desires of agents. Economists are not greatly concerned with the behavior of the individual; but their theory depends upon individual choice and action. In explaining behavior in terms of beliefs and desires, economists are explaining behavior in terms of the agent's *reasons*. In ordinary speech, an agent's reasons for performing an action *may* differ from the causes of the action. An agent may cite as his or her *reason* for closing a window the "fact" that it was drafty. The draft (if there was one—there need not have been) is not necessarily (although it might have been) what *causes* the agent to close the window. Perhaps the agent was given a post hypnotic suggestion or possessed an unconscious aversion to the smell of the roses outside the window. Can there be scientific laws relating reasons and actions or concerning the components of reasons themselves? Can reasons for actions be causes as well?

These are large questions and have been often discussed. I shall rely on the arguments offered by Davidson (1963), Rosenberg (1976b, ch. 5) and Goldman (1970, ch. 5). Like these authors I believe that reasons can be causes.

I should say a bit more about one argument which many anti-naturalists have found compelling, since in the writings of economists like Lionel Robbins it connects to the monotheoretic strategy of neoclass-

---

stitutes for any of its terms another term that refers to or denotes the same object(s). From *(7) Ford Motor Company made Pintos* and *(8) Pintos are cars which are likely to explode* one can infer *(9) Ford Motor Company made cars which are likely to explode.* But (8) and *(10) George believed that Pintos are safer than Japanese cars* are consistent with *(11) George believed that Japanese cars are safer than are cars which are likely to explode.*

Given these peculiarities one might argue that any discipline which makes intentional assertions must differ significantly from the natural sciences, in which only nonintentional statements are made. Intentionality seems to require a different logic. Whatever the merits of this general suggestion, neoclassical economics circumvents it. Given perfect information, sentences containing the verb "believes" are no longer intentional. Given perfect information and the completeness and transitivity of preferences, neither are sentences stating preferences. In the real world belief and preference are, of course, intentional. People will have beliefs and preferences concerning nonexistent objects. Their beliefs and preferences will sometimes be inconsistent and indeed incoherent because of various inadequacies in their knowledge. In all of these cases, the economist notes that "other things" are not equal and that the theory does not apply.

ical economics. Economists sometimes argue that the "laws" of utility theory ((1)–(5) ch. 6, §2) and possibly the claim that entrepreneurs are profit maximizers are not generalizations about the behavior of people. Instead, they prescribe how *rational* agents behave or how *rational economic* agents behave. What I have identified as fundamental "laws" of equilibrium theory are often regarded as definitions of a rational agent or of a rational economic agent. Moreover, economists and philosophers have urged that since these statements articulate what rationality is, one has good reason to accept them (Rosenberg 1976b: 106–7, 129, 137–38). According to these authors, one should not assess such claims the same way one assesses purported laws in the natural sciences.

These views are confused. The basic "laws" of equilibrium theory do not define "rationality." There is nothing irrational about being satiated or having some increasing marginal utilities or changing one's tastes. One can, if one wants, treat the basic claims about individuals as defining "a rational economic agent"—that is, as assumptions in a model. But definitions are not enough. Once theoretical hypotheses are offered, closures of the assumptions about individuals are recovered as empirical generalizations. Nor should one or can one apply economic theory only to rational agents. Economists have no specification of what it is to be rational other than that given (inadequately) by the fundamental "laws" of equilibrium theory. To say that equilibrium theory applies only to rational agents is thus to say that it applies only to what it applies to. At best one is rehearsing the excuses one may want to give when the theory fails. Although everyday experience, as well as introspection, provides some evidence for economists' claims, there is nothing privileged, a priori, or intuitively evident about the basic model they employ. Behavior of the sort assumed in the model is in some ways rational, but that gives one no reason to cling to the model or to believe, without testing, that it applies in any particular domain.

Nowhere in this book have I offered any proof that anti-naturalists are mistaken. I have instead done my best to present a coherent and compelling naturalist construal of economics. The anti-naturalist is correct in asserting that economists make use of intentional verbs like "believes" and "prefers" and explain individual behavior in terms of the reasons for that behavior. Yet I do not believe that these facts establish an anti-naturalist case. The intentionality of beliefs and desires is neutralized by the assumptions economists make. Explaining individual action in terms of reasons for the actions, especially within the confines of perfect information, does not imply that economics cannot share the goals, the methods and the logical structure of natural scientific theories.

Interesting loose ends remain. How serious are the complications of intentionality once one admits uncertainty? Economic theories achieve their straightforward logical structures by using *ceteris paribus* clauses and simplifications to rule out the complexities that beliefs and desires can introduce. If these complications, from which the theories abstract, are not themselves subject to scientific analysis and explanation, can one still claim to have a naturalistic science of economics? The arguments here are quite unclear (see Davidson 1976 and Knight 1956:245–46).

Compared with the best the natural sciences have to offer, theories of capital and interest are inadequate; but that comparison is not the relevant one to make, if one wants to know whether economics is a scientific discipline. The principal difficulties confronting theories of capital, interest, and value are in isolating and testing the regularities they point to. I have given no arguments for social scientific naturalism; but I have found little reason to regard the difficulties that economic theories face as refutations of social scientific naturalism.

3. Philosophical Theses and Puzzles

In the course of this inquiry, philosophical theses, arguments and conclusions have played an important part. I have avoided addressing philosophical issues in a completely general way. Instead I have considered only those issues important for understanding theories of capital and interest and have only attempted to defend the validity of my philosophical conclusions for the particular economic subject matter I have addressed. Yet many of the questions I considered are of general importance and interest. In considering theories of capital and interest, I have addressed six sets of philosophical issues. I shall briefly sketch here for each set the general questions, the suggested solutions and the problems remaining for further investigation.

A. Models and Theories (ch 3, §2, §3; ch 6, §2, §3; ch. 7, §1, §5)

Crucial to any philosophical discussion of economics or of any science is a careful construal of the structure of the discipline's theories. Economists think and write in terms of models, which consist of assumptions. I attempted to analyze theoretical work concerning capital and interest in these terms. Models in theoretical economics can be construed in the way that Suppes, Snead, Stegmueller, and Giere have analyzed scientific theories—as predicates or as definitions of predicates. Theoretical hypotheses assert that these predicates are true of something. Theories are sets of related statements. These statements are implied by theoretical hypotheses. The assumptions of models become, when closed or applied, the statements of theories. Special case models are those which are employed to illustrate, teach, develop, or criticize more general models or, when (hypothetically) closed, to confirm more general theories.

This conception of models and theories enables one to analyze the work of economic theorists as simply as any other conception and to employ the terms which economists themselves use. I could have employed other analyses of scientific theories without substantially changing my conclusions (see Hausman 1978). Doing so would, however, have complicated the exposition. One's choice of a conception of scientific theories should be based on which conception is easiest to use and which enables one to describe the efforts of the given scientists most intelligibly. I have risked confusing my readers by using "*model*" to mean what Suppes, Snead, Stegmueller, and Giere mean by "*theory*", and by then using "*theory*" in a more traditional way. Perhaps my terminological change and the compromise that results will be useful in other work in the philosophy of science. I suspect that what is most substantial and interesting about the structure of scientific theories depends heavily on the particular domain.

B. Explanatory Arguments (ch 7, §1, §6)

In assessing economic theories one must face the question of how arguments full of apparently false premises can be explanatory. Although this question is particularly vivid in the case of economics, it is quite general. I argued that one should not attempt to answer it by searching for a new model of scientific explanation. There is nothing to be gained in developing a model of "messy" explanation. In fact I endorsed the standard deductive-nomological model of nonstatistical explanatory arguments. In doing so, I did not intend to ignore or conceal the roughness of the fit between the model and the arguments which scientists consider to be explanatory. Once one recognizes that literally false sentences can make true assertions (and that there is a large and diverse category of "near explanations"), one can capture the judgments of scientists concerning which nonstatistical arguments are explanatory without surrendering the deductive-nomological model. Proceeding in this way, one can acknowledge the complexity and messiness of actual scientific explanation without one's own analysis becoming messy or unwieldy.

Many loose ends and open questions remain. Statistical explanations, particularly the sloppy ones given by economists, create additional complications, which I have avoided. Much further work on causality in economics is needed before one can reach a balanced assessment of economic explanations. Questions about the completeness and generality of my analysis of nondeductive explanatory arguments remain as well. Does the analysis apply in other social sciences which lack the mathematical (deductive) structure of economics? Am I right to discount the importance of *Verstehen* (subjective understanding) in economic explanations?

C. Simplications and Idealizations (ch. 7, §4, §5)

A simplification is a statement in a theory or explanation or other application which a scientist makes use of, although he or she has no reason to believe it is true. Often one has good reason to believe that simplications are false. In many cases simplifications are idealizations—statements which must be false. The presence of simplifications in apparent explanations is problematic. If one knows the simplification to be false, one knows that the apparent explanation does not, as stated, satisfy the conditions of the deductive-nomological model. If one has no reason to believe the simplification to be true, one has no reason to accept the purported explanation.

There is no mystery about the prevalence of such simplifications in explanatory arguments. Scientists often cannot specify accurately the initial conditions and could not deduce the consequences if they did know all the initial conditions. Substituting simplifications, they offer what I call "explanations in principle." The puzzle comes in understanding how explanations in principle can be explanations. How can one accept an explanation which contains false statements? I have considered one solution to the puzzle.[3] Sometimes, after reinterpreting

---

[3] In other cases, not discussed in the text, there may be no way to interpret the simplification as a true statement. Instead scientists believe it can be replaced by a true statement without appreciably affecting the explanation. In this case, one does not strictly possess an explanation, but one possesses a near-explanation or is close to being able to explain. Such near-explanations are considerable scientific achievements and can greatly help us understand, even though they do not fully satisfy the necessary conditions on scientific explanations.

the simplification as a statistical claim or with a margin of error, one can regard it as a less specific but nevertheless true statement. The argument may then be interpreted as an explanatory argument, although the description of what is to be explained can no longer be *deduced* or must itself be made less specific.

To conceive of explanations in principle in this way raises questions of justification. When does one possess good reason to believe that simplifications are thus legitimate? I have suggested four necessary conditions, which in outline are:

1. Confirmation condition. By employing the simplification, one can derive testable consequences and confirm many of them.
2. No-accident condition. One can understand why the confirmation condition is satisfied.
3. Sensitivity condition. If one replaces the simplification with a more realistic alternative, one's explanation becomes more accurate.
4. Convergence condition. In those circumstances in which the simplification is a better approximation, one's explanation is more accurate.

These conditions seem consistent with the judgments scientists make. We can also understand why it is rational to demand that a simplification satisfy these conditions before one employs it in an explanation.

On this analysis explanations in principle employ simplifications which are approximate. One is justified in accepting an explanation in principle only if its simplifications satisfy the four conditions. The most important question this analysis raises is one of generality. How well does my schema stand up to the evidence provided by the history of various sciences? Are there other kinds of explanations in principle which I have overlooked? How useful are my justification conditions in understanding and assessing the work of scientists in other domains?

D. Inexact Laws (ch. 7, §2, §3, §5)

Actual explanatory arguments in the sciences are messy not only because they include simplifications. The "laws" such arguments invoke are usually, as stated, not quite true. This problem is particularly striking in the case of economics; the inaccuracies in the basic "laws" are glaring.

There are a variety of ways in which one can regard generalizations that face apparent disconfirmations as laws nevertheless. One might regard them as statistical, rather than as deterministic laws—although without better specification of the statistics involved, this interpretation seems a mere rechristening. One might regard such generalizations as approximate laws—laws which are true with a margin of error. Loosening the statement of the generalization, the disconfirmations may disappear. Third, one might regard the true law as a modal claim. The law asserts what would happen were certain conditions met. Since actual circumstances differ from the hypothetical circumstances, things do not always turn out as a nonmodal reading of the law would require. The disconfirmations are, however, only apparent. In each case the antecedent of the law is unsatisfied. Finally, one might regard generalizations which face disconfirmations as qualified laws. Implicit in the law is a *ceteris paribus* clause. Apparent disconfirmations of the unqualified generalization occur when the *ceteris paribus* clause, which may be regarded as determining a predicate in the antecedent of the law, is unsatisfied.

Without any constraints one could use these devices (especially the last two) to interpret any generalization as a law. Yet merely incanting the words "*ceteris paribus*" or the words "how things would be, were . . . " does not transform a false generalization into a law. If a nonstatistical generalization appears to be false, even given a margin of error, one cannot justifiably regard it as a law unless certain conditions are met. I have proposed the following four necessary conditions:

(1) Lawlikeness.
(2) Reliability. In some independently specified class of cases with no qualifications or with specific qualifications only, the generalization must be disconfirmed only rarely and confirmed often.
(3) Refinability. Adding further qualifications to the generalization should increase the frequency of confirmations and decrease the frequency of disconfirmations.
(4) Excusability. Scientists should almost always be able to discover the interfering factor responsible for an apparent disconfirmation.

I have argued that one is justified in regarding a generalization that faces apparent counterexamples as a qualified law only if these four conditions are met. These conditions must, I think, also be met before one can regard inexact generalizations as modal laws. I have not, however, considered the justification of modal claims in any detail. Spurred by metaphysical modesty and trepidations about the temptations of counterfactual talk, I prefer to interpret economic "laws" (and scientific laws generally) as qualified rather than modal claims.

Laws which are statistical, approximate, qualified, or modal can all be employed in explanatory arguments, although in each case one must modify the argument slightly. Qualified laws fit into the deductive-nomological model easily. All one needs is the additional premise that other things are equal. On my analysis such premises may well be true. Questions remain concerning when we are justified in believing that such premises are true. The conditions above provide materials for an answer.

Loose ends remain. Philosophers have often noted, but have rarely carefully analyzed the inexactness of scientific laws. Which laws, if any, are true as stated without qualification or modal reinterpretation? Is it correct to interpret such phrases as "in the absence of other forces" as more specific *ceteris paribus* clauses? How does the presence of *ceteris paribus* clauses limit scientists' ability to deduce new laws from a number of known laws? Are there kinds of inexactness other than those I have discussed? Should one attempt to interpret explanatory rough generalizations, as I did, as laws at all? Might it not be better to change one's model of explanation to permit explanation without laws? How adequately do my justification conditions agree with the judgments good scientists already make? How useful are they in philosophical investigations of scientific explanations?

E. Causal Judgments (ch. 9, §1)

The deductive-nomological model only provides necessary conditions which explanatory arguments must satisfy. Not all deductive-nomological arguments are explanatory, nor are all arguments which satisfy the eight justification conditions of chapter 7 deductive-nomological or explanatory. When economists deny that the marginal productivity of labor explains the wage or that Sraffa's derivation of prices explains prices, they are not usually denying that the arguments are deductive-nomological. Instead they question whether the purported explanation is causal. Economists deny that the marginal product of labor explains the wage, because they deny that the marginal product of labor *causes* the wage to be of a certain size. They deny that Sraffa's derivation of prices from the size and composition of output, the technology employed, and the rate of profit explains prices, because they deny that these factors *cause* the prices.

Yet when we look more carefully, we see that economists lack rational principles upon which to make such judgments. The principles economists like Bliss or Wold explicitly invoke are inadequate and implausible. The problem of distinguishing causal relations among economic variables is largely open. Much further research is needed. The philosophical question, "What further conditions must arguments satisfy to be explanatory?'' is an important practical question for economists.

F. Theory, Domain, Method and Strategy (ch. 6, §2, §3; ch. 9, §2, §3; ch. 10, §2)

In analyzing theories of capital and interest, we faced a number of connected questions concerning the relations between neoclassical theories and the general project of neoclassical theorizing. The issues which arose overlap with those discussed by philosophers like Kuhn (1970), Lakatos (1970), Laudan (1977) and Shapere (1977). I did not, however, attempt to relate the questions considered to such philosophical discussions of larger structures in scientific theorizing. Rather than seeing in economics the general importance of paradigms or research programs or research traditions, I observed a strategy of research and application that grows out of the specific dominant theory. If the program for economic theorizing suggested by Sraffa's work were dominant, one could, no doubt, still identify some sort of paradigm or research program, but the differences between that program and the one which dominates orthodox theory are much more significant and interesting than are the similarities.

Equilibrium theory is a grand theory. Given principles governing individual choices and constraints on production, one seeks those prices which will coordinate and harmonize the plans of individuals. Ideally one solves simultaneously for prices, quantities produced, actual technology employed, incomes, and actual consumption. The theory of how individuals exchange under constraints appears from this point of view virtually to exhaust the subject matter of economics. Economics is redefined as the science which studies the applications of equilibrium theory. The many important questions which equilibrium theory cannot answer are, when possible, regarded as questions for some other discipline. The circle never completely closes, however. Equilibrium theory remains subject to challenges and criticisms since, at least through its policy implications, economics is continually (although quite indiscriminately) tested. Applications of equilibrium theory must work. When they fail, excuses, of course, abound. Given the extent of the failures, economists should, however, be eager to explore alternatives.

In fact, despite the limited success of equilibrium theories, there is little support for alternatives and, indeed, great resistance to entertaining any. There are many reasons for such fervent adherence to equilibrium theory, the most important of which is that equilibrium theory provides economists with so much guidance. Regardless of its empirical adequacy, equilibrium theory remains an incredibly flexible tool. Faced with almost any problem recognized as economic (problems of national income and aggregate demand being the main exceptions), equilibrium theory provides virtually mechanical rules for analyzing and solving it. None of the competitors, particularly not the piecemeal theorizing of the Cambridge economists, offers the possibility of such a systematic grasp of the subject matter. Given the enormous complexities involved in any general testing, this essentially heuristic virtue becomes paramount. There are also, to be sure, less rational causes for the allegiance of economists to equilibrium theory. The force of habit is appreciable. Equilibrium theory is more acceptable on ideological grounds to business and government than are most of its competitors. Those who possess great economic power would certainly prefer that everyone conceive of competitive economics as great cooperative ventures. I see no grounds for the allegation that the allegiance of economists to equilibrium theory rests mainly on habit and ideological grounds. Neither do I see any grounds for denying that these nonrational influences are important.

Regardless of its causes, a rich nexus of connections between equilibrium theory, what counts as an "economic" phenomenon, and the method of equilibrium theorizing remains. This nexus is too complex and too dependent on the peculiarities of the given theory to fit into a general philosophical vision of the larger structures of scientific theorizing. The characteristics of the neoclassical enterprise could, however, be highlighted by detailed comparison with such philosophical visions. Detailed comparisons of the strategy of equilibrium theorizing with the development of other theories in the natural and social sciences might also be enlightening. There is room for much further research.

These, then, are the main philosophical issues which I have touched on in this book. None are digressions. To analyze and assess theories of capital and interest these issues had to be faced. Nor should these issues have been faced in a purely philosophical context, with only the results figuring in this inquiry into capital theory. For it is principally in contexts like this inquiry that such issues must be decided.

4. Ideological Criticisms

Two kinds of comments can be made about the ideological relevance of theories of capital and interest. In this section I shall outline what an *ideological critique* is and discuss ideological criticisms of aspects of equilibrium theorizing. To offer an ideological critique is (1) to show that the assertions in question are false, and moreover, given the evidence available to the author and the author's methodological commitments, that they ought not to have been made, and (2) to explain the mistake in terms of the author's social role. There must be a mistake; conscious deception is not ideology.

One can offer ideological criticisms of applications of equilibrium theory and of methodological dicta designed to condemn all alternatives. The following comments of Irving Fisher's exemplify a common kind of ideological misapplication of equilibrium theory (including here a theory of capital and interest):

> It is true, as the socialist maintains, that inequality is due to social arrangements, but these arrangements are not, as he assumes, primarily such as take away the chance to rise in the economic scale; they are, on the contrary, arrangements which facilitate both rising and falling, according to the choices made by the individual. The improvident sink like lead to the bottom. . . .
> But the great masses, once they get near the bottom, are likely to remain there. Their high rates of impatience manifested through generations have brought many if not most of them to poverty. . . . They are a self-selected group of those impatient by nature or habit or both. They tend to spend rather than to save. (1930:339–40)

These comments are glib and unjustified by the laws of equilibrium theory. They are not the sound conclusions of rigorous argument. That they are false does not require, I think, serious argument; although similar claims emanate from politicians whenever questions of welfare policy are publicly debated. They may also be explained (very roughly) by Fisher's social role (he was an economist respected by the business community).

Social and natural scientific theories are often misapplied. One has not shown that there is anything wrong with equilibrium theory when one points out that it has been misused (See Sidgwick 1885:30). More seriously, one can criticize the methodological *demand*, enunciated by Robbins and others, that economics be devoted to the application of equilibrium models. This demand dismisses or regards as dubious theorizing like Sraffa's. It excludes from economics, or treats as secondary, all questions concerning the dependence of individual motivations or technology on the state and development of the economy. In certain economic theories, such an exclusion is justifiable. To theorize, on the other hand, about large scale economic growth and development by applying an equilibrium model seems unjustifiable. This error might be explained by pointing out that economists have long had the job of portraying capitalist economic organization (although not necessarily all its details) as optimal and in some sense the result of voluntary individual choices or of regrettable perturbations. Mainstream economists have avoided the question of how the broader economic system reproduces itself (and how it brings about its own transformation). This ideological criticism is only addressed to the pretense that equilibrium theory is, in outline, the whole of economics and that its challengers are *ipso facto* mistaken. I have offered no ideological criticism of equilibrium theory itself. I see no way to do so, because I see no obviously avoidable mistakes in equilibrium theory.

5. Capital Theory and Liberal Ideology

Instead of seeking ideological criticisms, one might discuss the relations between theories of capital and interest and systematic bodies of attitudes called "ideologies." In giving an ideological critique, one need never refer to an ideology. In speaking of ideologies one need not engage in ideological criticism. The two enterprises are distinct. By an "ideology" I mean a short description or theory of society and of human beings about which a large number of people in a certain society have two beliefs. First that this theory provides the best short description available, that it captures the essential features of society; second that it is a description of a *good* society or of a society that must and can be transformed into a good society. As a result, this description serves as the relevant standard for assessing individual conduct and social policy. Different varieties of Marxism and of liberalism have been ideologies in this sense. I shall deal with one question to which talk of ideologies sometimes gives rise. The basic equilibrium model is a refinement of the theoretical vision sketched in chapter 1. That vision is related to some forms of liberal ideology. What is that relation and how does it help one to understand theories of capital and exchange value?

Marxist or liberal *ideologies* are not sophisticated philosophical doctrines, but popular creeds. They thus resist any precise definition. Nevertheless, I hope the reader will grant that the basic vision of a competitive economy is a recognizable part of classical liberal views of society. Such a view is less prevalent today than it was a century ago, although it may be making a comeback.

The sort of liberalism expressed in the popular agitation against the

Corn Laws, for instance, not only accepted the vision of economic life expressed by the three claims of chapter 1, §3, but regarded that vision as a sort of practical ideal. Liberal ideology thus links economic and moral theorizing. Economic and moral *theories* should not, be regarded as part of any ideology, although they may be inspired by or support an ideology. Sophisticated theories rarely fit perfectly into any ideology; they always rely upon evidence and traditions that transcend ideologies, and they are, in any case, far too complex to permit mass understanding or to command mass allegiance. To point out the relationships between moral and economic theories and ideologies is not in my view to criticize those theories. The claims ideologies make are not necessarily false. Those who are influenced by an ideology can perfectly well do conscientious and rigorous theoretical work.

The vision of the market as reconciling efficiently the plans of self-interested individuals through their voluntary exchanges is a crucial part of liberal ideologies. That vision is central to general equilibrium models. Indeed one might point to equilibrium theory as a scientific success to which an ideology has led. Not all economists who employ equilibrium models accept any version of a liberal ideology, but the historical and heuristic connections are clear. If the discussion in chapter 1 is correct, accepting a liberal view of economic life commits one to regarding the theory of exchange value as the fundamental economic theory. The liberal vision of economic life thus leads to the conception of economics as a separate science. If the properties of economies result from voluntary exchanges between rational self-interested individuals, one ought to be able to explain economic phenomena entirely in terms of the principles regulating individual behavior and the constraints on exchanges. Economists should be able to achieve a unified theory, since all major economic features of a competitive economy result from voluntary exchange behavior. Obviously this is an oversimplification; but ideologies are oversimplifications. Mill's and Robbins' methodological positions, although congruent with the vision presented, are more sophisticated.

We can thus see another link between the method Sraffa uses and his demotion of the theory of exchange value from its central position. Given a liberal vision of the functioning of competitive economies, Sraffa's work makes little sense in either regard. Such a vision is, however, neither unchallengeable nor unchallenged. Sraffa's work is methodologically legitimate. So are neo-Marxian efforts to make use of Sraffa's work. When a dispute about the details of an esoteric subject has such broad ideological ramifications as the capital controversies have, obscure argument, methodological disagreement and difficulties in testing are only to be expected.

Mill's comments, with which I began this book were a suitable prologue; many differences of opinion in capital theory are caused by different "conceptions of the philosophic method of the sciences." Yet the choice of a methodology is not the spontaneous act of a free will. Different "conceptions of the philosophic method of the sciences" may originate in different views concerning what society is and what it ought to be. The philosophy of science leads one in thinking through capital theory, to the study of ideology.

The relations between capital, profits, and prices remain perplexing. Economists have offered plausible hypotheses, but they are still unable to understand the phenomena. Their efforts have been subtle and intelligent, but they have not yet succeeded. Why not? Are the questions just too difficult? Does this failure reveal some fundamental inadequacy in the dominant theory, perhaps due to the influence of ideology? We know that people feel strongly about profits and the economic power that capital brings. We know that most economists rigidly cling to a theory whose "laws" are dubious and whose simplifications border on the outlandish. Yet neoclassical theory also has immense heuristic power and is unchallenged by any evidently superior alternative. With these doubts and a plea for methodological tolerance I close this book, but not this inquiry. There is too much still to learn.

Methodological Postscript

My arguments and conclusions concerning theories of capital and interest are complete. I shall now return to some questions concerning my methodology, and explain in general terms what a philosophical inquiry into an economic theory is, why such inquiries are worth undertaking, and what place such work should have in the philosophy of science.

Although philosophers of science have always been interested in the actual work of scientists, there was a strong turn, especially in the 1960s and 1970s away from prescribing how science ought ideally to proceed and toward studying more carefully how science has proceeded.[1] In part this turn has been a reaction to previous work in philosophy of science, which to many seemed misguided and largely irrelevant to the sciences. In part this change reflects a general skepticism about the possibility of doing traditional foundationalist epistemology. Such skepticism is itself a reaction to the failure of the foundationalist program of the logical empiricists. The contemporary turn toward careful empirical study of the sciences constitutes a new program for the philosophy of science, which I shall call "empirical philosophy of science" or "the empirical approach to the philosophy of science."

1. Empirical Philosophy of Science

The credo of the empirical approach may be stated trenchantly and simplistically as follows:

The philosophy of science is itself an empirical science. All conclusions about the scientific enterprise that the philosopher of science

---

[1] See Asquith and Kyburg (1979), Kuhn (1970), Lakatos and Musgrave (1970), Laudan (1977), Shapere (1969) and Suppe (1977).

draws are, or should be, scientific conclusions and must be defended in the same way or ways that the results of the sciences are defended. Pronouncements by the philosopher of science about the goals of science, the bases upon which scientists accept various theories, or any other feature of science, should be regarded as scientific claims. One should assess them as one would assess the various assertions the sciences make.

The empirical approach denies that epistemology can be distinct from empirical study of the human cognitive faculties, the history of the human search for knowledge, and the general progress of the sciences. In Quine's terminology (1969), epistemology is "naturalized." It aims no longer to justify kinds of knowledge claims in terms of an epistemologically prior (self-evident or indubitable) foundation. In justification one must always take for granted scientific and every-day knowledge. "Justifying" an assertion consists solely of showing that it is supported by evidence in the way or ways that scientific claims generally are. When claims to know are challenged, the best one can do is to explain scientifically how one knows (or can know) what one does. As empiricists, philosophers, scientists, and laypersons accept these explanations ultimately because they help organize, and are supported by, experience. There is no other ultimate warrant. The goal is to construct empirical theories of human knowing which are consistent with theories of other subject matters and which explain how one can know all these theories.

Is such a goal sensible? One might argue that a scientific explanation of the acquisition of knowledge is inconceivable because empirical scientists cannot explain why some methods of acquiring beliefs *justify* beliefs, while others do not. The claim is that determining *standards* for justified belief is not and cannot be the task of any empirical science. I do not find this claim compelling. A psychologist might, for example, by means of sufficiently cunning experiments, be able to show that certain methods of acquiring beliefs are more likely to lead to true beliefs in certain circumstances than are others. Moreover, a psychologist who could show *why* some grounds for believing lead to more reliable beliefs would be in a position to explain how in certain circumstances people acquire knowledge. There are obviously circularities here, but they are benign. I thus see no reason to believe it impossible that philosophers can explain how we know what we do.

The empirical approach to philosophy of science is not purely "descriptive." Although philosophers' claims about the sciences should be defended in part by showing their consistency with scientific practice, empirical philosophers of science can still assess the work of scientists and offer advice and instruction. Philosophers of science can sometimes contribute directly to the scientific disciplines they study. What scholars learn about acquiring scientific knowledge provides the basis for such assessment and advice. Empirical philosophy of science thus does not reduce to history of science. Not all of the history of science is relevant to the questions with which the philosophy of science is concerned. The precise details of how scientific results are reached are only important to philosophers of science when they help them understand how scientists come to know. On the other hand, there are other sources of evidence (for example, from psychology) about how humans acquire knowledge.

2. The Epistemological Circle

In attempting to study science as an empirical philosopher of science, one enters a logical circle with at least four forms or manifestations. Such an "epistemological circle" is, in fact, common to every theory of knowledge. Hegel states the predicament well:

> We ought, says Kant, to become acquainted with the instrument [of cognition], before we undertake the work for which it is to be employed; for if the instrument be insufficient, all our trouble will be spent in vain. The plausibility of this suggestion has won for it general assent and admiration; . . . In the case of other instruments, we can try and criticize them in other ways than by setting about the special work for which they are destined. But the examination of knowledge can only be carried out by an act of knowledge. To examine this so-called instrument is the same thing as to know it. But to seek to know before we know is as absurd as the wise resolution of Scholasticus, not to venture into the water until he had learned to swim. (1830:14)

Some theories of knowledge find their way through these difficulties easily. If one maintains that there are self-warranting truths, for example, then one can easily meet the demand that one know some of the results of epistemology in order to do epistemology. The empirical philosopher of science, on the other hand, has serious problems.

The first form of the epistemological circle is perhaps the most striking. Empirical philosophy of science is itself a science. In doing philosophy of science empirically, one should thus follow scientific method or scientific methods. But one of the goals of the empirical philosophy of science is to find out what scientific methods are. It thus seems that one must already know at least tacitly what one is supposed to find out. If one does not already know how to do science, how can one find out (scientifically) how to do science?

The circularity is not vicious. Empirical philosophers of science disavow seeking any justification for scientific knowledge other than the broadest possible coherence among theories, including various theories of acquiring knowledge, and perceptual beliefs. There is nothing improper in beginning empirical philosophy of science in midstream, believing that one already knows something tacitly or consciously about how to acquire knowledge. Justification, although philosophically interesting, is not the immediate task. Investigating scientific knowledge in accordance with one's initial conception of scientific investigation, one improves and articulates this conception (and revises the procedures for carrying out this improving and articulating) as one proceeds. There is no guarantee that one will not be forced to change one's beliefs and procedures. (My own views concerning, for example, theory structure in economics changed enormously in the course of writing this book.) Although philosophers cannot start learning about the sciences from scratch, they can learn about the sciences. This circle remains disturbing, since many philosophers find it difficult to eschew wholeheartedly searching for justification for knowledge that goes beyond such broad coherence among beliefs. Contemporary philosophers, however, show little enthusiasm for any alternative. The talk of "coherence" here should not be misconstrued. Scientific and philosophical theories must be consistent with perceptual beliefs.

When one questions the philosophical theses upon which the empirical approach is based, the epistemological circle manifests itself in a second way. Suppose some traditional philosopher maintains, as many have, that there is knowledge to be gained in epistemology which is different in kind from the empirical knowledge the sciences provide. Such a philosopher could accuse the empirical philosopher of science of avoiding the real epistemological tasks of assessing and justifying (not merely explaining) scientific knowledge. Such a philosopher would deny that this book is a work of philosophy. In answer to such a challenge, the empirical philosopher of science must either deny that there are any such justificatory tasks or deny that there is any way to tackle them. But on what basis is either of these denials to be made? The grounds must themselves be the results of empirical philosophy of science (or of naturalized epistemology) or an anticipation of those results. But the traditional philosopher of science denies that philosophers ought to rely on (or ought to rely *only* on) such grounds. All empirical philosophers of science can do is to repeat their (scientific) reasons for surrendering the ambitions of traditional foundationalist epistemology. They can, of course, also criticize in detail epistemologies which attempt to do more.

The third way in which the epistemological circle manifests itself is somewhat different. Much of the evidence upon which empirical philosophy of science bases its conclusions comes from the history of science. Unless empirical philosophers of science are content only to describe all cognitive enterprises whatsoever, they must add to the presuppositions of their investigations discriminations between good and bad science, between science and pseudo-science, and between knowledge and conjecture. These initial discriminations are revisable as the inquiry proceeds, but they are indispensable. To contribute to understanding how humans acquire knowledge by investigating theories of capital and interest, I had to assess those theories. To make an informed assessment, I had to do economics—to find out what there is to be learned at present about capital and interest. The philosopher of economics must attempt to be a competent economic theorist. Standards to assess scientific work are also needed. Yet the standards of assessment and the methods to be employed in learning about economics had to be anticipated and could only be clarified in the course of the investigation. In trying to learn more, philosophers need to rely on all the knowledge they think they have, even if some of it is not well-founded and turns out not to have been knowledge at all.

Since empirical philosophers of science must begin by discriminating knowledge from superstition and science from pseudo-science, is not the way open for astrologers, for example, to begin by regarding astrology as the paradigm of a science? Might they not then come up with an empirical philosophy of science which shows how humans can acquire such astrological knowledge? After all, a crucial test, among astrologers, for any philosophical account of science will be whether it successfully shows how people can know astrology. But if astrologers can invent an empirical philosophy of science that "justifies" the claims of astrology, what does more orthodox empirical philosophy of science, which criticizes astrology, accomplish? Are not philosophers merely rationalizing prevailing prejudices?

Once one denies that there is any certain or self-evident foundation for human knowledge, the possibility of consistent and incommensurable knowledge systems cannot be ruled out. The fact that the astrologer (or theologian or paranoid) begins with different beliefs does not, however, itself show that such incommensurable knowledge systems can be constructed. Alternative philosophies of science are not easily created. It is hard enough to come up with one. Astrologers who attempt to develop a naturalized epistemology which coheres with both their purported knowledge of astrology and their nonastrological knowledge of the everyday world will face a difficult task. If they find that epistemology is to be done as a nonastrological science is done, they will discover that their attachment to astrology is irrational. If they develop some other sort of epistemology, they might (in some sense) be able to come up with a coherent body of knowledge. Yet this body of knowledge would have to be drastically different from the body of scientific knowledge. Given this virtual incommensurability, one would not expect that orthodox philosophers could show astrologers that they are in error. Developing an empirical philosophy of science is not a trivial task of rationalization, but an arduous systematic task.

The fourth form of the epistemological circle concerns the relations between empirical philosophy of science and empirical philosophical investigations of particular sciences. The conclusions of empirical philosophy of science rest largely on investigation of the history and structure of actual sciences. To that extent empirical philosophy of science in general depends on empirical investigations of particular theories, disciplines, incidents, etc. General conclusions in the philosophy of science must rest on particular inquiries into particular sciences. Yet in order to investigate some limited area in science, like theories of capital and interest, one needs a great deal of philosophical apparatus. I had no choice except hesitantly and critically to rely on philosophical models of theories, explanations, laws, confirmation, objectivity, and the like. Once again the philosopher must anticipate the answers to his or her questions. If the conclusions of current philosophy of science were already well supported and already merited the esteem and confidence of philosophers and scientists, these anticipations would not be troubling. But a great deal of "established" philosophy of science is poorly confirmed and has been cast into doubt. In this last form the epistemological circle presents a pressing practical problem. I have made use of whatever philosophical wisdom I could; but the limitations in that wisdom have been palpable. Yet there is no way to contribute to the philosophy of economics or the philosophy of science in general except to rely on (while attempting to improve upon) conclusions of the past.

Empirical philosophers of science are caught in at least these four ways in the epistemological circle. Does this fact make dubious an empirical approach to the philosophy of science? Should the reader worry about whether the conclusions of this book are prejudiced by the philosophical presuppositions with which I began? Note that many of these presuppositions come from less self-conscious "investigations'' of precisely the same data (from the history of science and from experience of human learning) that the philosophy of science now examines more systematically. People already know a good deal about the world and they know how to get more knowledge about it. Without that knowledge, they could not inquire into the nature of our knowledge and the means of its acquisition—but then they would lack not only the means to carry out such an investigation, but also an object to investigate. If we really lacked even tacit knowledge about how to acquire knowledge, we would be unable to find out how to learn by investigating scientifically the knowledge we had. We would not know how to inquire, and we would have little or no knowledge to inquire about. The possibility of doing epistemology arises with the possibility of having serious epistemological questions. One may, of course, have good reasons to suspect bias in particular cases. However, general doubt about whether philosophers can achieve any knowledge through an empirical approach to the philosophy of science merely expresses skepticism about the possibility of human knowledge in general. It may turn out, of course, that one is unable in doing philosophy of science to come up with any interesting general results.

3. Philosophy of Science as a Social Science

Empirical philosophy of science, if itself a science at all, is a social science (where ''social science'' is understood to include history and psychology). Thus it may be that the structure, methods, etc. of philosophy of science will be unlike those of the natural sciences. As already mentioned, social scientific naturalists argue that, in crucial respects (goals, methods of justification, logical structure, fundamental ontology, or whatever), the social sciences are or should be identical to the natural sciences. Anti-naturalists argue for an essential difference in one or more of these respects. It seems to me that the empirical approach to the philosophy of science ought not *itself* to prejudge this debate. Both naturalists and anti-naturalists ought to be able to adopt empirical approaches to the philosophy of science. Otherwise it is hard to see how the philosophy of science can contribute to clarifying and resolving the many disputes between them. Individual empirical philosophers of science may prejudge the issue. I began by treating theories of capital and interest as if they were natural scientific theories.

The empirical approach to the philosophy of science does not presuppose that the structure, methods, etc. of the social sciences (and thus of the philosophy of science itself) are the same as those of the natural sciences. In fact, philosophers of science rarely study the sciences the way physicists study motion or matter. The actual practice of empirical philosophy of science is diverse. Much of it will remain for the foreseeable future more like intellectual history than like physics. While the object of the philosophy of science is all of science, its structures, methodologies, and the like should be those of some of the social sciences. The worst social scientific naturalists can say of this methodological clarification is that it is empty.

Notice that the question of social scientific naturalism is only a special form of the question of whether the methods, structure, goals, and so forth are, at a suitable level of generality, one and the same for all sciences in all historical periods. Although philosophers may sometimes have to beg this general question, they should not forget that it is there. It should not be a condition of doing the philosophy of science empirically that this question have only one answer. Otherwise one could not learn its answer in doing philosophy.

4. Method and Presuppositions

If the above view is correct, one cannot make philosophical pronouncements about economics or any other science without studying the relevant theories, debates, experiments, communities, etc. in detail. Without such careful study one will lack evidence for one's philosophical conclusions. The comments above should make clear why I undertook a "philosophical inquiry" into capital theory. Only through such an inquiry was I able to establish my views of the definition, subject matter, structure, and methodology of economic theory. Let me add a few words about how I proceeded in making this inquiry.

Actually, I began with questions. I had general questions, as outlined in my introduction, as well as such specific questions as: What is the Cambridge Controversy all about? Why do the participants rely on fictions about oversimplified states of affairs? What can one learn about economics from one-or two-commodity stationary equilibrium models? Do general equilibrium theories resolve the difficulties the Cambridge critics point to? Are general equilibrium theories adequate theories? Do they explain anything? What is Sraffa doing in his *Production of Commodities by Means of Commodities?* Does his work represent an alternative to general equilibrium theories? What, if any, role does ideology have in capital theory and controversies concerning capital theory? There were many other questions besides, and, of course, many more arose in attempting to answer these. How were such questions answered?

The general *technique*—to study the works of economists and philosophers which develop, apply, and discuss the issues—is certain not novel. In the actual course of my study, I had to rely heavily on the tentative results of contemporary philosophy of science and on initial judgments concerning the nature and worth of economic theory and of economics as a discipline. Merely to classify and to order what one finds when reading economics books demands that one have some idea of what a science is, what a theory is, what counts as a law, and so forth. The richness of philosophical work on the natural sciences and the extent of its influence made it tempting to suppose that a moderate naturalism is correct. Economists talk about their own work in many ways. As we have seen, they write about "models," "theories," "assumptions," and "predictions" and make use of previous work by epistemologists and philosophers of science. To interpret their comments and to describe accurately what they have done, one needs to know a great deal of philosophy of science. How else is one to decide, for example, whether the Austrian theory is even a theory?

Some of those most critical of traditional philosophy of science and most insistent on the need for a new empirical philosophy of science might object that no one knows enough philosophy now to understand the structure or methods of economics. There is some merit in this objection, but it is overstated. It would have helped, if I could have begun with solid and well-confirmed philosophical theses, but they are unavailable. A philosopher of economics studying economic theory is in the same philosophical position as any empirical philosopher of science seeking knowledge about the sciences. The only important difference is that philosophers of physics, for example, can begin with *fewer* doubts about the worth of the physics they study. Philosophers of physics are unlikely ever to conclude that Newton was a mediocre physicist. They can safely begin by regarding a large body of physics as "good physics." Revisions may be needed later. Philosophers of physics have, however, comparatively few practical problems deciding what to do when conventional philosophical wisdom does not fit the "good physics" studied. The difficulties facing a philosopher of economics are much greater.

Yet this contrast with philosophy of physics does not show that one should postpone philosophical examination of sciences like economics. What one learns about acquiring knowledge in physics may not apply to economics. Even if it does, philosophers of economics will probably have to find this out through their investigations of economics. Furthermore, although the practical differences between the tasks of philosophers of economics and philosophers of physics are considerable, they are differences in degree, not in kind. Philosophers of physics cannot assume that Newton or Einstein never blundered.

How then was I to proceed, if I could not simply import categories and theses concerning theories, laws, and so forth upon which philosophers agree? When abstract general equilibrium theories failed to fit current philosophical conceptions, I could not automatically conclude that something was wrong with the economics. I had to trim, revise, and even invent philosophical categories and theses in trying to make sense of economic theory. Philosophy of economics can neither start from scratch nor rely on authoritative philosophical dicta. Cautiously and critically, the philosopher of economics must begin with the most plausible among current philosophical views of the sciences, as ill-founded and wrong-headed as they may be. There is no alternative.

Consider the long argument of chapter 7. In assessing the explanatory worth of general equilibrium accounts of the phenomena of capital and interest, I began with Hempel's models of scientific explanation. Since these have been questioned by philosophers and do not fit scientific practice easily, I could not take their validity for granted. In examining the various ways in which general equilibrium accounts of capital and interest apparently fail to fit the model, I had to ask whether the discrepancies were due to inadequacies or misapplications of the philosophical models or to inadequacies in the economics. Although I wound up defending Hempel's model of nonstatistical explanatory arguments, I argued that it must be applied loosely and that simplifications and inexact laws are legitimate in explanations. I had no choice except in this way to begin with and rely on previous work in philosophy of science.

To make sense of theories of capital and interest, one needs both philosophical apparatus to systematize what one finds, and an idea of the sort of sense to make of the theory. Histories full of rational decision-making and debate certainly ''make sense'' (fit many of the facts). So do histories full of stupidity, stubbornness, dishonesty, and ideological distortion. When the economist's practice conflicts with the philosopher's dicta, which should be criticized? This question often arose. The Cambridge Controversy differs considerably from philosophical models of how scientists assess competing theories. Should one ''make sense'' of this controversy as a different sort of rational debate? Should one ''make sense'' of it by concluding that it is shot full of confusion, misunderstanding, and ideological distortion? Obvious answers may be deceptive. Yet one must make such assessments. In this particular case I found plenty of misunderstanding and confusion. Locating the source of the controversy in a deep-seated disagreement about the strategy of economic theorizing, I was, however, able to find rational grounds for the convictions of both parties. From the perspective of the neoclassical theorist, the Cambridge criticisms only reveal that the problems concerning capital and interest remain unsolved. Since the models of the critics can be interpreted as equilibrium models, the neoclassical theorist sees nothing in the critic's claim to have exposed some great inadequacy in neoclassical theory. The Cambridge critics, on the other hand, are not engaged in equilibrium theorizing. They look to a piecemeal alternative. Emphasizing how little help neoclassical theory is with questions of capital accumulation, income distribution, and economic growth and development, and espousing an alternative vision of economics, the critics are prepared to reject the whole neoclassical program. The decision is not simple. There is little empirical evidence that bears on it. No wonder that the controversy has its own peculiarities.

To aggravate the difficulties of assessing the work of economists, discussions of economic issues are sometimes biased and distorted because of their importance to interests of individuals and of various social groups. As Marx luridly put it, "In the domain of Political Economy, free scientific inquiry meets not merely the same enemies as in all other domains. The peculiar nature of the material it deals with summons as foes into the field of battle the most violent, mean and malignant passions of the human breast, the Furies of private interest" (1967, 1:10). Although I doubt that it is possible to find a completely neutral starting point and to avoid commitments, the philosopher of economics can address a broader audience and a wider spectrum of issues if he or she does not start by taking any one school of economics as the paradigm for what economics should be. The philosophy of economics must struggle to avoid becoming apologetics.

My inquiry into theories of capital and interest leads me to believe that the task of the philosopher of economics should be to show that the state and development of economics manifest imperfect rationality. The standard of scientific rationality comes from or develops out of existing philosophy of science, as inadequate as it may be. One should expect to find deviations in economics because of the Furies' influence, but on the basis of what I found, I believe that these will be important exceptions and complications, not the center of the story. If one succeeds in providing a compelling account that is in accordance with these expectations, one thereby provides evidence that these expectations are correct.

Seeking to find imperfect rationality in economics comes down to looking for good reasons for whatever one finds unless there are specific grounds to expect or to substantiate bias. Given the dubiousness of many of the conclusions of economics, it is crucial to distinguish carefully between judging the enterprise to be rational and judging its results to be correct. When, according to the standards of accepted philosophy of science, some feature of, for example, equilibrium theories appears irrational, one should look both for ways of improving the philosophical model and for evidence of the influence of ideology or of simple error. I know of no precise rules to decide such cases.

The methodology of the philosophy of economics is thus vague and imprecise. It hardly evidences a dramatic new approach to the philosophy of science, such as the empirical approach might initially appear to be. What the empirical approach implies in practice are the following: (1) Philosophers should demand historical and psychological evidence for their conclusions and, insofar as that evidence is scanty (which it has been) should be hesitant about philosophical "wisdom" concerning the sciences. (2) Philosophers of science should be more willing to study and to learn from particular sciences than they sometimes have been. I hope I have shown that much can be learned by employing this modest advice.

Bibliography

Albin, P. 1975. "Reswitching: An Empirical Observation." *Kyklos* 28:149–54.

Archibald, G. 1961–62. "Chamberlin versus Chicago." *Review of Economic Studies* 29:2–28.

—— 1979. "Method and Appraisal in Economics." *Philosophy of the Social Sciences* 9:304–15.

Arrow, K. 1968. "Economic Equilibrium." *International Encyclopedia of the Social Sciences*, pp. 376–89. New York: Macmillan.

—— 1974a. "General Economic Equilibrium: Purpose, Analytic Techniques, Collective Choice." *American Economic Review* 64:253–72.

—— 1974b. "Limited Knowledge and Economic Analysis." *American Economic Review* 64:1–10.

Arrow, K. and F. Hahn. 1971. *General Competitive Analysis*. San Francisco: Holden-Day.

Asimakopulos, A. and G. Harcourt. 1974. "Proportionality and the Neoclassical Parables." *Southern Economic Journal* 40.481–83.

Asquith, P. and R. Giere, eds. 1980. *PSA 1980*, vol. 1. East Lansing, Mich.: Philosophy of Science Association.

Asquith, P. and H. Kyburg, eds. 1979. *Current Research in the Philosophy of Science*. East Lansing, Mich.: Philosophy of Science Association.

Barr, W. 1971. "A Syntactic and Semantic Analysis of Idealizations in Science." *Philosophy of Science* 38:258–72.

Bear, D., and Orr, D. 1967. "Logic and Expediency in Economic Theorizing." *Journal of Political Economy* 75:188–96.

Becker, A. 1948. "Some Philosophical Aspects of Economics." *Philosophy of Science* 15:242–46.

Beth, E. 1949 "Towards an Up-to-date Philosophy of the Natural Sciences." *Methodos* 1:178–84.

Bhaduri, A. 1966 "The Concept of the Marginal Productivity of Capital and the Wicksell Effect." *Oxford Economic Papers* 18:284–88.

—— 1969. "On the Significance of Recent Controversies in Capital Theory: A Marxian View." *Economic Journal* 79:532–39.

—— 1970. "A Physical Analogue of the Reswitching Problem." *Oxford Economic Papers* 22:148–55.

Bharadway, K. 1963. "Value Through Exogenous Distribution." *Economic Weekly* 15:1450–54.

Blackburn, R. ed. 1973. *Ideology in Social Sciences*. New York: Random House.

Blakeley, G., and W. Gossling, 1967. "The Existence, Uniqueness and Stability of the Standard System." *Review of Economic Studies* 34:426–31.

Blalock, H. 1964. *Causal Inference in Non-experimental Research*. Chapel Hill: University of North Carolina Press.

Blaug, M. 1975. *The Cambridge Revolution: Success or Failure?* London: Institute of Economic Affairs.

Bliss, C. 1970. "Comment on Garegnani." *Review of Economic Studies* 37:437–38.

—— 1975. *Capital Theory and the Distribution of Income*. Amsterdam: North Holland.

Böhm-Bawerk. E. 1888. *The Positive Theory of Capital*. tr. William Smart, rpt. New York: G. E. Stechert & Co., 1923.

Bonar, J. 1893. *Philosophy and Political Economy*. rpt. London: Allen & Unwin, 1967.

Bose, A. 1975. *Marxian and Post-Marxian Political Economy*. Harmondsworth, Middlesex: Penguin.

Brahmananda, P. 1967. *The New-Classical vs. the Neo-Classical Economics: Standpoints at the Glow of a Circular Revolution*. Prasaranga, India: University of Mysore.

Braithwaite, R. 1953. *Scientific Explanation: A Study of the Function of Theory, Probability and Law in Science*. rpt. Cambridge: Cambridge University Press, 1968.

—— 1960. "Models in the Empirical Sciences." In E. Nagel, P. Suppes, and A. Tarski, *Proceedings of the Congress of the International Union for the Logic, Methodology and Philosophy of Science*, pp. 224–31. Stanford: Stanford University Press.

Bray, J. 1977 "The Logic of Scientific Method in Economics." *Journal of Economic Studies* 4:1–28.

Breit, W. and H. Hochman, eds. 1971. *Readings in Micro-Economics*, 2nd ed. Hinsdale, Illinois: Dryden Press.

Brodbeck, M., ed. 1968. *Readings in the Philosophy of the Social Sciences*. New York: Macmillan.

Brody, B., ed. 1970. *Readings in the Philosophy of Science*. Englewood Cliffs, New Jersey: Prentice-Hall.

Bromberger, S. 1965. "An Approach to Explanation," in R. J. Butler, ed. *Studies in Analytical Philosophy*, pp. 72–105. Oxford: Blackwells.

—— 1966. "Why Questions," in R. G. Colodny, ed. *Mind and Cosmos*. Pittsburgh: Pittsburgh University Press, rpt. in Brody (1970) pp. 66–87.

Bronfenbrenner, M. 1966. "A 'Middlebrow' Introduction to Economic Methodology," pp. 5–24. in Krupp (1966).

—— 1971. "The 'Structure of Revolutions' in Economic Thought." *History of Political Economy* 3:136–51.

Brunner, K. 1969. "'Assumptions' and the Cognitive Quality of Theories." *Synthese* 20:501–25.

Bruno, M., E. Burmeister, and E. Sheshinski, 1966. "Nature and Implications of the Reswitching of Techniques." *Quarterly Journal of Economics* 80:526–54.

Buechner, M. 1976. "Frank Knight on Capital as the Only Factor of Production." *Journal of Economic Issues* 10:598–617.

Burmeister, E. 1968. "On a Theorem by Sraffa." *Economica* 35:83–87.

—— 1974. "Synthesizing the Neo-Austrian and Alternative Approaches to Capital Theory: A Survey Article." *Journal of Economic Literature* 12:413–56.

Cairnes, J. 1888. *The Character and Logical Method of Political Economy*. 2nd ed. rpt. New York: A. M. Kelley, 1965.

Campbell, N. 1957. *Foundations of Science, the Philosophy of Theory and Experiment*. Formerly titled *Physics, the Elements*. New York: Dover.

Cartwright, N. 1980. "The Truth Doesn't Explain Much." *American Philosophical Quarterly*, 17:159–63.

Champernowne, D. 1945–46. "A Note on J. von Neumann's Article on 'A Model of Economic Equilibrium.'" *Review of Economic Studies* 13:10–19.

—— 1953–54. "The Production Function and the Theory of Capital: A Comment." *Review of Economic Studies* 21:112–35.

Chisholm, R. 1957. *Perceiving*. Ithaca: Cornell University Press.

Clark, J. 1902. *The Distribution of Wealth: A Theory of Wages, Interest and Profits*. New York: Macmillan.

Clark, R. 1973. "Prima Facie Generalizations," in Pearce and Maynard, eds. *Conceptual Change*, pp. 42–54. Dordrecht, Holland: Reidel.

Coats, A. 1969. "Is There a 'Structure of Scientific Revolutions' in Economics?" *Kyklos* 22:289–94.

Coddington, A. 1972. "Positive Economics." *Canadian Journal of Economics* 5:1–15.

Cohen, G. 1979. "The Labor Theory of Value and the Concept of Exploitation." *Philosophy and Public Affairs* 8:338–60.

Collard, D. 1973. "Leon Walras and the Cambridge Caricature." *Economic Journal* 83:465–76.

Cyert, R. and G. Pottinger 1979. "Towards a Better Micro-economic Theory." *Philosophy of Science* 46:204–22.

Davidson, D. 1963. "Actions, Reasons and Causes." *Journal of Philosophy* 60:685–700.

—— 1976. "Psychology as Philosophy." In J. Glover, ed. *The Philosophy of Mind*, pp. 101–10. Oxford: Oxford University Press.

Debreu, G. 1959. *Theory of Value: An Axiomatic Analysis of Economic Equilibrium*. New Haven: Yale University Press.

De Vroej, M. 1975. "The Transition from Classical to Neoclassical Economics: A Scientific Revolution." *Journal of Economic Issues* 9:415–39.

Dewey, D. 1965. *Modern Capital Theory*. New York: Columbia University Press.

Dixit, A. 1977. "The Accumulation of Capital Theory." *Oxford Economic Papers* 29:1–29.

Dobb, M. 1970. "The Sraffa System and the Critique of the Neo-Classical Theory of Distribution." *De Economist* 118:347–61.

—— 1973. *Theories of Value and Distribution Since Adam Smith*. Cambridge: Cambridge University Press.

Dorfman, R. 1959. "Waiting and the Period of Production." *Quarterly Journal of Economics* 73:351–72.

—— 1959–60. "A Graphical Exposition of Böhm-Bawerk's Interest Theory." *Review of Economic Studies* 26:153–58.

Dougherty, C. 1972. "On the Rate of Return and the Rate of Profit." *Economic Journal* 83:1324–49.

Dray, W. 1957. *Laws and Explanation in History*. Oxford: Oxford University Press.

Duhem, P. 1906. *The Aim and Structure of Physical Theory*. tr. Philip P. Wiener. Princeton: Princeton University Press, 1954.

Durkheim, E. 1895. *The Rules of Sociological Method*. tr. S. Solovay and J. Mueller, ed. G. Catlin. New York: Free Press, 1966.

Eatwell, J. 1974. "Controversies in the Theory of Surplus Value: Old and New." *Science and Society* 38:281–303.

—— 1975a. "The Interpretation of Ricardo's *Essay on Profits*." *Economica* 42:182–87.

—— 1957b. "Mr. Sraffa's Standard Commodity." *Quarterly Journal of Economics* 89:543–55.

—— 1975c. "Scarce and Produced Commodities: An Examination of Some Fundamentals in the Theory of Value, with Particular Reference to the Works of Ricardo and Walras." Dissertation, Harvard University.

Emmett, D., and A. MacIntyre, eds. 1970. *Sociological Theory and Philosophical Analysis*. New York: Macmillan.

Feinstein, C., ed. 1967. *Socialism, Capitalism and Economic Growth*. New York: Cambridge University Press.

Ferguson, C. 1972–73. "The Current State of Capital Theory. A Tale of Two Paradigms." *Southern Economic Journal* 39:160–76.

Ferguson, C. and R. Allen, 1970. "Factor Prices, Commodity Prices and Switches of Technique." *Western Economic Journal* 8:95–109.

Ferguson, C. and E. Nell, 1972. "Two Books on the Theory of Income Distribution: A Review Article." *Journal of Economic Literature* 10:437–53.

Feyerabend, P. 1977. "Changing Patterns of Reconstruction." *British Journal for the Philosophy of Science* 28:351–69.

Findlay, R. 1974. "Relative Prices, Growth and Trade in a Simple Ricardian System." *Economica* 41:1–13.

—— 1978. "An Austrian Model of International Trade and Interest Rate Equalization." *Journal of Political Economy* 86:989–1008.

Fisher, F. 1971. "Aggregate Production Functions and the Explanation of Wages: A Simulation Experiment." *Review of Economics and Statistics* 53:305–25.

Fisher, I. 1930. *The Theory of Interest as Determined by Impatience To Spend Income and Opportunity to Invest It.* rpt. New York: A. M. Kelley, 1965.

Fodor, J. 1968. *Psychological Explanation: An Introduction to the Philosophy of Psychology.* New York: Random House.

Friedman, M. 1948. "The Utility Analysis of Choices Involving Risk." *Journal of Political Economy* 56:279–304.

—— 1953. *Essays in Positive Economics.* Chicago: University of Chicago Press.

—— 1962. *Capitalism and Freedom.* Chicago: University of Chicago Press.

—— 1970. "Leon Walras and His Economic System." In I. Rima, ed. *Readings in the History of Economic Theory,* pp. 145–53. New York: Holt, Rinehart & Winston, Inc.

Friedman, M. and L. Savage, 1952. "The Expected-Utility Hypothesis and the Measurability of Utility." *Journal of Political Economy* 60:463–74.

Gantmacher, F. 1959. *Applications of the Theory of Matrices.* New York: Interscience.

Garb, G. 1964. "The Problem of Causality in Economics." *Kyklos* 17:594–611.

—— 1965. "Professor Samuelson on Theory and Realism: Comment." *American Economic Review* 55:1151–53.

Garegnani, P. 1966. "Switching of Techniques." *Quarterly Journal of Economics* 80:554–67.

—— 1970. "Heterogeneous Capital, the Production Function and the Theory of Distribution." *Review of Economic Studies* 37:407–36.

Geertz, C. 1964. "Ideology as a Cultural System." In D. Apter, ed. *Ideology and Discontent,* New York: Free Press.

Gellner, E. 1964. "Model." In J. Gould and W. Kolb, eds. *A Dictionary of the Social Sciences.* New York: Free Press.

Gibbard, A. and H. Varian, 1978. "Economic Models." *Journal of Philosophy* 75:664–77.

Giere, R. 1979. *Understanding Scientific Reasoning.* New York: Holt, Rinehart & Winston.

Godelier, M. 1972. *Rationality and Irrationality in Economics.* London: New Left Books.

Goldman, A. 1970. *A Theory of Human Action*. Princeton: Princeton University Press.

Gordon, D. 1955. "Professor Samuelson on Operationalism in Economic Theory." *Quarterly Journal of Economics* 69:305–10.

Gordon, H. S. 1973. "Alfred Marshall and the Development of Economics as a Science." In R. Giere and R. Westfall, eds. *Foundations of Scientific Method: The Nineteenth Century* pp. 234–58. Bloomington: Indiana University Press.

—— 1978. "Should Economists Pay Attention to Philosophers?" *Journal of Political Economy* 86:717–28.

Grandmont, J. 1977. "Temporary General Equilibrium Theory." *Econometrica* 45:535–72.

Green, E. "On the Role of Pure Theory in Positive Economics." In Pitt (1981).

Grundberg, E. 1978. "'Complexity' and 'Open Systems' in Economic Discourse." *Journal of Economic Issues* 12:541–60.

Hahn, F. 1973. "The Winter of our Discontent." *Economica* 40:322–30.

—— 1975. "Revival of Political Economy: The Wrong Issues and the Wrong Argument." *Economic Record* 51:360–64.

Hahn, F. and M., Hollis, eds. 1979. *Philosophy and Economic Theory*. Oxford: Oxford University Press.

Händler, E. 1980. "The Logical Structure of Modern Neoclassical Static Microeconomic Equilibrium Theory." *Erkenntnis* 15:33–53.

Hands, D. 1979. "The Methodology of Economic Research Programs." *Philosophy of the Social Sciences* 9:293–303.

Hansen, B. 1970. *A Survey of General Equilibrium Systems*. New York: McGraw-Hill.

Harcourt, G. 1964. "A Note on Mr. Sraffa's Sub-Systems." *Economic Journal* 74:715–22.

—— 1969. "Some Cambridge Controversies in the Theory of Capital." *Journal of Economic Literature* 7:369–404.

—— 1975a. *Some Cambridge Controversies in the Theory of Capital*. London: Cambridge University Press.

—— 1975b. "The Cambridge Controversies: The Afterglow." In M. Parkin and A. Nobay, eds. *Contemporary Issues in Economics*, pp. 305–33. New York: Barnes & Noble.

—— 1975c. "Decline and Rise. The Revival of (Classical) Political Economy." *Economic Record* 51:339–56.

—— 1976. "The Cambridge Controversies: Old Ways and New Horizons—or Dead End." *Oxford Economic Papers* 28:25–65.

—— 1977. "The Theoretical and Social Significance of the Cambridge Controversies in the Theory of Capital: An Evaluation." In Schwartz (1977), pp. 285–303.

Harcourt, G. and V. Massaro 1964. "Mr. Sraffa's Production of Commodities." *Economic Record* 40:442–54.

Harcourt, G. and N. Laing, eds. 1971. *Capital and Growth*. Harmondsworth, Middlesex: Penguin.

Hausman, D. 1978. "Economic Models: A Philosophical Inquiry into Capital Theory." Dissertation Columbia University.

—— 1979a. "Defending Microeconomic Theory." Unpublished address at the Conference on Philosophy and Economics, Michigan State University.

—— 1979b. "Review of Alexander Rosenberg, *Microeconomic Laws: A Philosophical Analysis*." *Nous* 13:118–22.

—— 1979c. "Review of *Models of Man: Philosophical Thoughts on Social Action*, by Martin Hollis." *Journal of Philosophy* 76:386–91.

—— 1980. "How To Do Philosophy of Economics." In Asquith and Giere (1980), pp. 352–62.

—— 1981. "Are General Equilibrium Theories Explanatory?" in Pitt (1981), pp. 17–32.

Hayek, F. 1941. *The Pure Theory of Capital*. Chicago: University of Chicago Press.

—— 1952. *The Counter-Revolution of Science*. Glencoe, Ill.: Free Press.

Hegel, G. 1830. *Enzyklopädie der philosophischen Wissenschaften in Grundrisse*, Erster Teil, 3rd. ed., tr. W. Wallace as *Hegel's Logic* Oxford: Clarendon Press, 1975.

Hempel, C. 1965. *Aspects of Scientific Explanation and Other Essays in the Philosophy of Science*. New York: Free Press.

Henderson, J. and R. Quandt, 1971. *Microeconomic Theory: A Mathematical Approach*. 2nd. ed. New York: McGraw-Hill.

Hesse, M. 1966. *Models and Analogies in Science*. Notre Dame, Indiana: University of Notre Dame Press.

Hicks, J. 1946. *Value and Capital*. 2nd ed. Oxford: Oxford University Press.

—— 1965. *Capital and Growth*. New York: Oxford University Press.

—— 1973. *Capital and Time: A Neo-Austrian Theory*. Oxford: Clarendon Press.

—— 1975. "Revival of Political Economy. The Old and the New." *Economic Record* 51:365–67.

—— 1979. *Causality in Economics*. New York: Basic Books.

Hirschleifer, J. 1966–67. "A Note on the Böhm-Bawerk/Wicksell Theory of Interest." *Review of Economic Studies* 34:191–99.

Hodgson, G. 1974. "The Falling Rate of Profit." *New Left Review* 84 (March–April):55–84.

Hollis, M. and E. Nell, 1975. *Rational Economic Man: A Philosophical Critique of Neo-Classical Economics*. London–New York: Cambridge University Press.

Hooker, C. 1979. "Discussion Review: Hollis and Nell's *Rational Economic Man: A Philosophical Critique of Neo-Classical Economics*." *Philosophy of Science* 46:470–90.

Hunt, E. and J. Schwartz, eds. 1972. *A Critique of Economic Theory*. Baltimore: Penguin.

Hutchison, T. 1938. *The Significance and Basic Postulates of Economics* rpt. with a new preface; New York: A. M. Kelley, 1960.

—— 1956. "Professor Machlup on Verification in Economics." *Southern Economic Journal* 22:476–83.

—— 1960. "Methodological Prescriptions in Economics: A Reply." *Economica* 27:158–60.

—— 1977. *Knowledge and Ignorance in Economics*. Chicago: University of Chicago Press.

Jaffe, W. 1942. "Leon Walras' Theory of Capital Accumulation." In O. Lange, F. McIntyre, and T. Yntema, eds. *Studies in Mathematical Economics and Econometrics*, pp. 37–48. Chicago: University of Chicago Press.

Jalladeau, J. 1978. "Research Program versus Paradigm in the Development of Economics." *Journal of Economic Issues* 2:583–608.

Jevons, W. 1871. *The Theory of Political Economy*, ed. R. D. Collison Black. Baltimore: Penguin, 1970.

Kaldor, N. 1937. "The Recent Controversy on the Theory of Capital." *Econometrica* 5:201–33.

—— 1938. "On the Theory of Capital: A Rejoinder to Professor Knight." *Econometrica* 6:163–76.

—— 1972. "The Irrelevance of Equilibrium Economics." *Economic Journal* 82:1237–55.

Keynes, J. M. 1936. *The General Theory of Employment, Interest and Money*. rpt. London: Macmillan, 1954.

Keynes, J. N. 1890. *Scope and Method of Political Economy*. 4th ed. rpt. New York: Kelley and Millman, Inc., 1955.

Klappholz, K. and J. Agassi, 1959. "Methodological Prescriptions in Economics." *Economica* 26:60–74.

—— 1960. "Methodological Prescriptions in Economics: A Rejoinder." *Economica* 27:160–61.

Knight, F. 1921. *Risk, Uncertainty and Profit*. rpt. Chicago: University of Chicago Press, 1971.

—— 1936a. "The Quantity of Capital and the Rate of Interest." *Journal of Political Economy* 44:433–63; 612–42.

—— 1936b. "The Theory of Investment Once More." *Quarterly Journal of Economics* 50:36–67.

—— 1936–37. "Note on Dr. Lange's Interest Theory." *Review of Economic Studies* 4:223–30.

—— 1938. "On the Theory of Capital: In Reply to Mr. Kaldor." *Econometrica* 6:63–82.

—— 1944. "Diminishing Returns from Investment." *Journal of Political Economy* 52:26–47.

—— 1956. *On the History and Method of Economics*, eds. W. Letwin and A. Morin. Chicago: University of Chicago Press.

Koopmans, T. 1949. "Identification Problems in Economic Model Construction." *Econometrica* 17:125–44.
—— 1957. *Three Essays on the State of Economic Science*. New York: McGraw-Hill.
—— 1979. "Economics Among the Sciences." *American Economic Review* 69:1–13.
Kornai, J. 1971. *Anti-Equilibrium: On Economic Systems Theory and the Tasks of Research*. Amsterdam: North Holland.
Kregel, J. 1971. *Rate of Profit, Distribution and Growth: Two Views*. London: Macmillan.
—— 1976. "Economic Methodology in the Face of Uncertainty." *Economic Journal* 86:209–25.
Krupp, S., ed. 1966. *The Structure of Economic Science*. New York: Prentice-Hall.
Kuenne, R. 1971. *Eugen von Böhm-Bawerk*. New York: Columbia University Press.
Kuhn, T. 1970. *The Structure of Scientific Revolutions*. 2nd ed. Chicago: University of Chicago Press.
Kunin, L. and F. Weaver, 1971. "On the Structure of Scientific Revolutions in Economics." *History of Political Economy* 3:391–97.
Laibman, D. and E. Nell, 1977. "Reswitching, Wicksell Effects, and the Neo-Classical Production Function." *American Economic Review* 67:878–88.
Lakatos, I. 1970. "Falsification and the Methodology of Scientific Research Programmes." In Lakatos and Musgrave, (1970), pp. 91–196.
Lakatos, I. and A. Musgrave, eds. 1970. *Criticism and the Growth of Knowledge*. Cambridge: Cambridge University Press.
Lange, O. 1935–36. "The Place of Interest in the Theory of Production." *Review of Economic Studies* 3:159–92.
—— 1936–37. "Professor Knight's Note on Interest Theory." *Review of Economic Studies* 4:231–35.
—— 1945–46. "The Scope and Method of Economics. *Review of Economic Studies* 13:19–32.
Latsis, S. 1976a. "The Limitations of Single-Exist Models: Reply to Machlup." *British Journal for the Philosophy of Science* 27:51–60.
—— ed. 1976b. *Method and Appraisal in Economics*. New York: Cambridge University Press.
Laudan, L. 1977. *Progress and Its Problems*. Berkeley: University of California Press.
Leontief, W. 1971. "Theoretical Assumptions and Nonobserved Facts." *American Economic Review* 61:1–7.
Lerner, A. 1953. "On the Marginal Product of Capital and the Marginal Efficiency of Investment." *Journal of Political Economy* 61:1–14.
—— 1965. "Professor Samuelson on Theory and Realism: Comment." *American Economic Review* 55:1153–55.

Lerner, M. ed. 1948. *The Portable Veblen*. New York: Viking Press.
Levi, I. and S. Morgenbesser, 1964. "Beliefs and Dispositions." *American Philosophical Quarterly* 1:221–32.
Lindahl, E. 1939. *Studies in the Theory of Money and Capital*. London: George Allen and Unwin.
Lipsey, R. and K. Lancaster, 1956–57. "The General Theory of the Second Best." *Review of Economic Studies* 24:11–32.
Loasby, B. 1971. "Hypothesis and Paradigm in the Theory of the Firm." *The Economic Journal* 81:863–85.
Lowe, A. 1965. *On Economic Knowledge: Toward a Science of Political Economics*. New York: Harper & Row.
McClelland, P. 1975. *Causal Explanation and Model Building in History, Economics and the New Economic History*. Ithaca: Cornell University Press.
Machlup, F. 1955. "The Problem of Verification in Economics." *Southern Economic Journal* 22:1–21.
—— 1956. "Rejoinder to a Reluctant Ultra-Empiricist." *Southern Economic Journal* 22:483–93.
—— 1960. "Operational Concepts and Mental Constructs in Model and Theory Formation." *Giornale Degli Economisti* 19:553–82.
—— 1960–61. "Are the Social Sciences Really Inferior?" *Southern Economic Journal* 27:173–84.
—— 1963. *Essays on Economic Semantics*. ed. M. Miller. Englewood Cliffs, N.J.: Prentice-Hall.
—— 1964. "Professor Samuelson on Theory and Realism." *American Economic Review* 54:733–36.
—— 1978. *Methodology of Economics and Other Social Sciences*. New York: Academic Press.
Malinvaud, E. 1972. *Lectures on Microeconomic Theory*. tr. A. Silvey. Amsterdam: North Holland.
Marshall, A. 1930. *Principles of Economics*. 8th ed. London: Macmillan.
Martin, A. 1964. "Empirical and A Priori in Economics." *British Journal for the Philosophy of Science* 15:123–36.
Marx, K. 1963. *Theories of Surplus Value*. Vol. 1 tr. E. Burns, ed. S. Ryazanskaya. Moscow: Progress Publishers.
—— 1967. *Capital*. ed. F. Engels, Vol. 1, tr. S. Moore and E. Aveling; vol. 2, 3 tr. anon. New York: International Publishers.
—— 1968. *Theories of Surplus Value*. Vol. 2, tr. and ed. S. Ryazanskaya. Moscow: Progress Publishers.
—— 1971. *Theories of Surplus Value*. Vol. 3, tr. J. Cohen and S. Ryazanskaya, ed. S. Ryazanskaya and R. Dixon. Moscow: Progress Publishers.
—— 1973. *Grundrisse*. Tr. M. Nicolaus, New York: Random House.
Massey, G. 1965. "Professor Samuelson on Theory and Realism: Comment." *American Economic Review* 55:1153–63.

Medio, A. 1972. "Profits and Surplus Value." In Hunt and Schwartz (1972), pp. 312–46.

—— 1977. "Neo-classicals, Neo-Ricardians, and Marx." In Schwartz (1977), pp. 381–411.

Melitz, J. 1965. "Friedman and Machlup on the Significance of Testing Economic Assumptions." *Journal of Political Economy* 73:37–60.

Menger, C. 1871. *Principles of Economics: First, General Part.* tr. and ed. J. Dingwall and B. Hoselitz. Glencoe, Ill.: Free Press, 1950.

—— 1883. *Problems of Economics and Sociology*, ed. L. Schneider, tr. F. Nock. Urbana: University of Illinois Press, 1963.

Metzler, L. 1950. "The Rate of Interest and the Marginal Product of Capital." *Journal of Political Economy* 58:289–306.

Milgate, M. 1979. "On the Origin of the Notion of "Inter-temporal Equilibrium." *Economica* 46:1–10.

Mill, J. S. 1836. "On the Definition of Political Economy and the Method of Investigation Proper to It." rpt. in Mill 1844.

—— 1843. *A System of Logic.* London: Longmans, Green & Co., 1949.

—— 1844. *Essays on Some Unsettled Questions of Political Economy.* rpt. in *Collected Works of John Stuart Mill*, vol. 4. Toronto: University of Toronto Press, 1967.

—— 1848. *Principles of Political Economy.* ed. W. Ashley; rpt. New York: A. M. Kelley, 1961.

—— 1873. *Autobiography.* rpt. New York: New American Library, 1964.

Morgenbesser, S. 1956. "Theories and Schemata in the Social Sciences." Dissertation, University of Pennsylvania.

—— 1958. "Role and Status of Anthropological Theories." *Science* 128:285–88.

—— ed. 1967a. *Philosophy of Science Today.* New York: Basic Books.

—— 1967b. "Psychologism and Methodological Individualism." In Morgenbesser (1967a), pp. 160–74.

—— 1969. "The Realist-Instrumentalist Controversy." In S. Morgenbesser, P. Suppes, and M. White, eds. *Philosophy, Science, and Method*, pp. 200–218. New York: St. Martin's Press.

—— 1970. "Is It a Science?" In Emmett and Macintyre (1970), pp. 20–35.

Morishima, M. 1966. "Refutation of the Non-Switching Theorem." *Quarterly Journal of Economics* 80:520–25.

Myers, M. 1976. "Adam Smith's Concept of Equilibrium." Journal of *Economic Issues* 10:560–75.

Nagel, E. 1961. *The Structure of Science.* New York: Harcourt, Brace and World.

—— 1971. "Assumptions in Economic Theory." In Breit and Hochman (1971), pp. 48–51.

Natanson, M. ed. 1963. *Philosophy of the Social Sciences: A Reader.* New York: Random House.

Nell, E. 1967. "Theories of Growth and Theories of Value." *Economic Development and Cultural Change* 16:15–26.

—— 1973. "Economics: The Revival of Political Economy." In Blackburn (1973), pp. 76–95.

Newman, P. 1962. "Production of Commodities by Means of Commodities." *Schweizerische Zeitschrift für Volkswirtschaft und Statistik* 98:58–75.

Ng, Y. 1974. "Harcourt's Survey of Capital Theory." *Economic Record* 50:119–29.

Nozick, R. 1974. *Anarchy, State and Utopia*. New York: Basic Books.

—— 1977. "On Austrian Methodology." *Synthese* 36:353–92.

Nuti, D. 1970a. "Capitalism, Socialism and Steady Growth." *Economic Journal* 80:32–57.

—— 1970b. "'Vulgar Economy' in the Theory of Income Distribution." *De Economist* 118:363–69.

O'Neill, J., ed. 1973. *Modes of Individualism and Collectivism*. London: Heinemann.

Papandreou, A. 1958. *Economics as a Science*. New York: J. B. Lippincott.

—— 1963. "Theory Construction and Empirical Meaning in Economics." *American Economic Review* 53:205–11.

Papineau, D. 1976. "Ideal Types and Empirical Theories." *British Journal for the Philosophy of Science* 27:137–46.

Pasinetti, L. 1966. "Changes in the Rate of Profit and the Reswitching of Techniques." *Quarterly Journal of Economics* 80:503–17.

—— 1969. "Switches of Techniques and the Rate of Return in Capital Theory." *Economic Journal* 79:508–31.

—— 1970. "Again on Capital Theory and Solow's 'Rate of Return.'" *Economic Journal* 79:508–31.

—— 1972. "Reply to Mr. Dougherty." *Economic Journal* 82:1351–53.

—— 1977. "On 'Non-Substitution in Production Models." *Cambridge Journal of Economics* 1:389–94.

—— 1978. "Wicksell Effects and Reswitching of Techniques in Capital Theory." *Scandinavian Journal of Economics* 80:181–89.

Pitt, J. ed. 1981. *Philosophy in Economics*. Dordrecht, Holland: Reidel.

Piron, R. 1962. "On 'The Methodology of Positive Economics': Comment." *Quarterly Journal of Economics* 76:664–66.

Plamenatz, J. 1970. *Ideology*. New York: Praeger.

Plato. 1974. *The Republic*, tr. G. Grube. Indianapolis: Hackett Publishing Co.

Polanyi, K. 1957. *Trade and Market in the Early Empires*. Glencoe, Illinois: Free Press.

Popper, K. 1968. *The Logic of Scientific Discovery*. 2nd ed. London: Hutchinson.

Quine, W. 1960. *Word and Object*. Cambridge: MIT Press.

Rawls, J. 1971. *A Theory of Justice*. Cambridge: Harvard University Press.

Rescher, N. 1970. *Scientific Explanation*. New York: Macmillan.

Ricardo, D. 1815. "An Essay on the Influence of a Low Price of Corn on the Profits of Stocks Showing the Inexpediency of Restriction on Importation." In Sraffa and Dobb (1951), 4:9–42.

—— 1817. *On the Principles of Political Economy and Taxation*. In Sraffa and Dobb (1951), 1.

—— 1823. "Absolute and Exchangeable Value." In Sraffa and Dobb (1951), 4:357–412.

Robbins, L. 1932. *An Essay on the Nature and Significance of Economic Science*. London: Macmillan.

—— 1979. "On Latsis' *Method and Appraisal in Economics:* A Review Essay." *Journal of Economic Literature* 17:996–1004.

Roberts, M. 1970. "Models and Theories in Economics: An Exploration of the Logical Status of Economic Theory with an Application to Welfare Economics." Dissertation, Harvard University.

Robinson, J. 1942. *An Essay in Marxian Economics*. New York: St. Martin's.

—— 1953–54. "The Production Function and the Theory of Capital." *Review of Economic Studies* 21:81–106.

—— 1961. "Prelude to a Critique of Economic Theory." *Oxford Economic Papers* 13:53–58.

—— 1962. *Economic Philosophy*. Chicago: Aldine.

—— 1964. "Solow on the Rate of Return." *Economic Journal* 74:410–17.

—— 1965. "Piero Sraffa and the Rate of Exploitation." *New Left Review* 31 (May–June):28–34.

—— 1966. *The Accumulation of Capital*. 2nd. ed. New York: St. Martin's Press.

—— 1970. "Review of Ferguson, *The Neo-Classical Theory*." *Economic Journal* 80:336–39.

—— 1973. *Economic Heresies: Some Old-Fashioned Questions in Economic Theory*. 2nd ed. New York: Basic Books.

—— 1977. "The Labor Theory of Value," *Monthly Review* 29 (December):50–59.

Roncaglia, A. 1978. *Sraffa and the Theory of Prices*. New York: John Wiley & Sons.

Roosevelt, F. 1975. "Cambridge Economics as Commodity Fetishism." *Review of Radical Political Economy* 7 (Winter):1–27.

Rosenberg, A. 1976a. "On the Interanimation of Micro and Macro Economics." *Philosophy of Social Science* 6:35–54.

—— 1976b. *Microeconomic Laws: A Philosophical Analysis*. Pittsburgh: Pittsburgh University Press.

—— 1978. "Hollis and Nell: Rational Economic Men." *Philosophy of the Social Sciences* 8:87–98.

—— 1979. "Can Economic Theory Explain Everything?" *Philosophy of the Social Sciences* 9:509–30.

Rotwein, E. 1959. "On 'The Methodology of Positive Economics.'" *Quarterly Journal of Economics* 73:554–75.

—— 1962. "On 'The Methodology of Positive Economics'" Reply." *Quarterly Journal of Economics* 76:666–68.

Rowthorn, B. 1974. "Neo-Classicism, Neo-Ricardianism and Marxism." *New Left Review* 86 (July–August):63–87.

Rudner, R. 1966. *Philosophy of Social Science.* Englewood Cliffs, N.J.: Prentice-Hall.

Ryan, A., ed. 1973. *The Philosophy of Social Explanation.* Oxford University Press.

Sahlins, M. 1974. *Stone Age Economics.* Chicago: Aldine.

Salmon, W. 1971. *Statistical Explanation and Statistical Relevance.* Pittsburgh: University of Pittsburgh Press.

—— 1978. "Why Ask, 'Why?'? An Inquiry Concerning Scientific Explanation." *Proceedings & Addresses of the American Philosophical Association* 51:683–705.

Samuelson, P. 1947. *Foundations of Economic Analysis.* rpt. New York: Atheneum, 1976.

—— 1955. "Operationalism in Economic Theory: Comment." *Quarterly Journal of Economics* 69:232–36.

—— 1959. "A Modern Treatment of the Ricardian Economy." *Quarterly Journal of Economics* 73:1–35; 217–31.

—— 1961–62. "Parable and Realism in Capital Theory: The Surrogate Production Function." *Review of Economic Studies* 28:193–207.

—— 1963. "Problems of Methodology—Discussion." *American Economic Review* 53:232–36.

—— 1964. "Theory and Realism: A Reply." *American Economic Review* 54:736–40.

—— 1965. "Professor Samuelson on Theory and Realism: Reply," *American Economic Review* 55:1163–72.

—— 1966. "A Summing Up." *Quarterly Journal of Economics* 80:568–83.

—— 1971. "Understanding the Marxian Notion of Exploitation: A Summary of the So-Called Transformation Problem Between Marxian Values and Competitive Prices." *Journal of Economic Literature* 9:399–431.

—— 1975. "Maximum Principles in Analytical Economics." *Synthese* 31:323–44.

Schoeffler, S. 1955. *The Failures of Economics: A Diagnostic Study.* Cambridge: Harvard University Press.

Schumpeter, J. 1954. *History of Economic Analysis.* ed. E. Schumpeter. New York: Oxford University Press.

Schwartz, Jacob T. 1961. *Lectures on the Mathematical Method in Analytical Economics.* New York: Gordon and Breach.

Schwartz, Jesse, ed. 1977. *The Subtle Anatomy of Capitalism*. Santa Monica, Ca.: Goodyear Publishing Company.

Scriven, M. 1959. "Truisms as the Grounds for Historical Explanations." In P. Gardiner, ed. *Theories of History*, pp. 443–75. Glencoe, Illinois: The Free Press.

—— 1962. "Explanations, Predictions and Laws." In H. Feigl and G. Maxwell, eds. *Minnesota Studies in the Philosophy of Science* 3:170–230. Minneapolis: University of Minnesota Press.

Seligman, B. 1967. "On the Question of Operationalism: A Review Article." *American Economic Review* 57:146–61.

Sen, A. 1970. *Growth Economics*. Harmondsworth, Middlesex: Penguin.

—— 1974. "On Some Debates in Capital Theory." *Economica* 41:328–35.

—— 1978. "On the Labor Theory of Value: Some Methodological Issues." *Cambridge Journal of Economics* 2:175–90.

Senior, N. 1836. *An Outline of the Science of Political Economy*. rpt. New York: A. M. Kelley, 1965.

Sensat, J. n.d. "Sraffa and Ricardo on Value and Distribution," Unpublished.

Shapere, D. 1969. "Towards a Post-postivistic Interpretation of Science." In P. Achinstein and S. Barker, eds. *The Legacy of Logical Postivism*, pp. 115–60. Baltimore: The Johns-Hopkins University.

—— 1977. "Scientific Theories and their Domains." In Suppe (1977), pp. 518–77.

Sidgwick, H. 1885. *The Scope and Method of Economic Science*. rpt. New York: Kraus Reprint Co., 1968.

Simon, H. 1957. Models of Man: *Social and Rational*. New York: John Wiley & Sons.

—— 1959. "Theories of Decision-Making in Economics and Behavioral Science." *American Economic Review* 49:253–83.

—— 1963. "Problems of Methodology—Discussion." *American Economic* Review 53:229–31.

—— 1964. "Rationality." In J. Gould and W. Kolb, eds. *A Dictionary of the Social Sciences*, pp. 573–74. Glencoe, Illinois: The Free Press.

—— 1965. "The Logic of Rational Decision." *British Journal for the Philosophy of Science* 16:169–86.

Smith, A. 1776. *An Inquiry into the Nature and Causes of the Wealth of Nations*. rpt. London: J. M. Dent, 1910.

Sneed, J. 1971. *The Logical Structure of Mathematical Physics*. Dordrecht, Holland: Reidel.

—— 1976. "Philosophical Problems in the Empirical Science of Science: A Formal Approach." *Erkenntnis* 10:115–46.

Solow, R. 1955–56. "The Production Function and the Theory of Capital." *Review of Economic Studies* 23:101–8.

—— 1956. "A Contribution to the Theory of Economic Growth." *Quarterly Journal of Economics* 70:65–94.

—— 1957. "Technical Change and the Aggregate Production Function." *Review of Economics and Statistics* 39:312–20.

—— 1961. "Notes Toward A Wickellian Model of Distributive Shares." In F. Lutz and D. Hague, eds. *The Theory of Capital*, pp. 245–65. London: Macmillan.

—— 1961–62. "Substitution and Fixed Proportions in the Theory of Capital." *Review of Economic Studies* 29:207–18.

—— 1963. *Capital Theory and the Rate of Return.* Amsterdam: North Holland.

—— 1967. "The Interest Rate and Transition Between Techniques." In Feinstein (1967), pp. 30–39.

—— 1970. "On the Rate of Return: Reply to Pasinetti." *Economic Journal* 80:423–28.

Sowell, T. 1974. *Classical Economics Reconsidered.* Princeton: Princeton University Press.

Sraffa, P. 1951. "Introduction." In Sraffa and Dobb (1951), 1:xiii–lxii.

—— 1960. *Production of Commodities by Means of Commodities.* Cambridge: Cambridge University Press.

—— 1962. "Production of Commodities: A Comment." *Economic Journal* 72:477–79.

Sraffa, P. and M. Dobb 1951. *The Works and Correspondence of David Ricardo.* Cambridge: Cambridge University Press.

Stalnaker, R. 1972. "Pragmatics." In D. Davidson and G. Harman, eds. *Semantics of Natural Language*, pp. 380–97 Dordrecht, Holland: Reidel.

Stanfield, R. 1974. "Kuhnian Scientific Revolutions and the Keynesian Revolution." *Journal of Economic Issues* 8:97–109.

Steedman, I. 1972. "Jevons's Theory of Capital and Interest." *Manchester School* 40:31–52.

—— 1975. "Value, Price and Profit." *New Left Review* 90 (March–April):71–80.

—— 1977. *Marx After Sraffa.* London: New Left Books.

Stegmueller, W. 1976. *The Structure and Dynamics of Theories*, tr. William Wohlhueter. New York: Springer-Verlag.

—— 1978. "A Combined Approach to the Dynamics of Theories." *Theory and Decision* 9:39–75.

—— 1979. *The Structuralist View of Theories.* New York: Springer-Verlag.

Stigler, G. 1941. *Production and Distribution Theories.* New York: Macmillan.

—— 1969. "Does Economics Have a Useful Past?" *History of Political Economy* 1:217–30.

Stiglitz, J. 1973. "The Badly Behaved Economy with the Well-Behaved Production Function." In J. Mirrlees and N. Stern, eds. *Models of Economic Growth*, pp. 117–37. London: Macmillan.

—— 1974. "The Cambridge Controversy: A View from the New Haven: A Review Article." *Journal of Political Economy* 82:893–903.

Stone, R. 1964. "The A Priori and the Empirical in Economics." *British Journal for the Philosophy of Science* 15:115–22.

Suppe, F. 1972. "Theories, Their Formulations, and the Operational Imperative." *Synthese* 25:129–64.

—— 1974. "Theories and Phenomena." In W. Leinfellner and W. Kohler, eds. *Development in the Methodology of Social Science*, pp. 45–92. Dordrecht, Holland: Reidel.

—— 1976. "Theoretical Laws." In M. Przłccki, K. Szaniawski and R. Wójcicki, eds. *Formal Methods in the Methodology of Empirical Sciences*, pp. 247–67. Wrocław: Ossolineum.

—— ed. 1977. *The Structure of Scientific Theories*. 2nd ed. Champaign: University of Illinois Press.

Suppes, P. 1957. *Introduction to Logic*. New York: Van Nostrand-Reinhold Company.

—— 1967. "What is a Scientific Theory?" In Morgenbesser (1967a), pp. 55–67.

—— 1969. *Studies in the Methodology and Foundations of Science*. Dordrecht, Holland: Reidel.

Sweezy, P. 1968. *The Theory of Capitalist Development*. New York: Monthly Review Press.

Thurow, L. 1977. "Economics 1977." *Daedalus* 11:79–94.

Tisdale, C. 1975. "Concepts of Rationality in Economics." *Philosophy of Social Science* 5:259–72.

Uhr, C. 1962. *Economic Doctrines of Knut Wicksell*. Berkeley: University of California Press.

Van Fraassen, B. 1970. "On the Extension of Beth's Semantics of Physical Theories." *Philosophy of Science* 37:325–39.

—— 1972. "A Formal Approach to the Philosophy of Science." In R. Colodny, ed. *Paradigms and Paradoxes*, pp. 303–66. Pittsburgh: University of Pittsburgh Press.

—— 1977. "The Pragmatics of Explanation." *American Philosophical Quarterly* 14:143–50.

Veblen, T. 1908. "Professor Clark's Economics." *Quarterly Journal of Economics* 22:147–95. rpt. in Hunt and Schwartz (1972).

—— 1948. "Why Economics is not an Evolutionary Science." In Lerner (1948), pp. 215–40.

Von Bortkievicz, L. 1906-7. "Value and Price in the Marxian System." *Archiv für Sozialwissenschaft und Sozialpolitik*. Tr., In *International Economic Papers*, No. 2 (1952):5–60.

Von Mises, L. 1960. *Epistemological Problems of Economics*, tr. G. Riesman. Princeton, N.J.: D. Van Nostrand Company.

Von Neumann, J. 1945–46. "A Model of General Economic Equilibrium." *Review of Economic Studies* 13:1–9.

Walras, L. 1926. *Elements of Pure Economics*, tr. William Jaffé. Homewood, Ill.: Irwin, 1954.

Weber, M. 1949. *The Methodology of the Social Sciences*, tr. and ed. E. Shils and H. Finch. New York: Macmillan.

Weintraub, E. 1979. *Microfoundations: The Compatibility of Microeconomics and Macroeconomics*. Cambridge: Cambridge University Press.

Weyl, H. 1963. *Philosophy of Mathematics and Natural Science*. New York: Atheneum.

Wicksell, K. 1893. *Value, Capital and Rent*. tr. S. Frowein. London: Allen & Unwin, 1954.

—— 1911. *Lectures on Political Economy*. Vol. 1, tr. W. Classen, ed. L. Robbins, 1934; rpt. New York: A. M. Kelley, 1967.

—— 1958. "Böhm-Bawerk's Theory of Capital." In E. Lindahl, ed. *Selected Papers on Economic Theory*, pp. 176–83. London: Allen & Unwin.

Wisman, J. 1978. "The Naturalistic Turn of Orthodox Economics: A Study of Methodological Misunderstanding." *Review of Social Economy* 36:263–84.

Wold, H. 1954. "Causality and Econometrics." *Econometrica* 22:162–77.

Wong, S. 1973. "The 'F-Twist' and the Methodology of Paul Samuelson." *American Economic Review* 63:312–26.

Woodbury, S. 1979. "Methodological Controversy in Labor Economics. *Journal of Economic Issues* 13:933–55.

Worswick, G. 1972. "Is Progress in Economic Science Possible?" *Economic Journal* 82:73–87.

Yeager, L. 1976. "Toward Understanding Some Paradoxes in Capital Theory Theory." *Economic Inquiry* 14:313–46.

Index